A Practical Guide to Recovery-Oriented Practice

A Practical Guide to

Recovery-Oriented Practice

Tools for Transforming
Mental Health Care

Larry Davidson
Janis Tondora
Martha Staeheli Lawless
Maria J. O'Connell
Michael Rowe

OXFORD
UNIVERSITY PRESS
2009

OXFORD
UNIVERSITY PRESS

Oxford University Press, Inc., publishes works that further
Oxford University's objective of excellence
in research, scholarship, and education.

Oxford New York
Auckland   Cape Town   Dar es Salaam   Hong Kong   Karachi
Kuala Lumpur   Madrid   Melbourne   Mexico City   Nairobi
New Delhi   Shanghai   Taipei   Toronto

With offices in
Argentina   Austria   Brazil   Chile   Czech Republic   France   Greece
Guatemala   Hungary   Italy   Japan   Poland   Portugal   Singapore
South Korea   Switzerland   Thailand   Turkey   Ukraine   Vietnam

Copyright © 2009 by Oxford University Press, Inc.

Published by Oxford University Press, Inc.
198 Madison Avenue, New York, New York 10016
www.oup.com

Oxford is a registered trademark of Oxford University Press

Library of Congress Cataloging-in-Publication Data

A practical guide to recovery-oriented practice : tools for transforming mental health care / by Larry
Davidson ... [et al.].
p. ; cm.
Includes bibliographical references and index.
ISBN 978-0-19-530477-0
1. Community mental health services. 2. Mentally ill—Rehabilitation. 3. Mentally ill—Services for.
4. Mental health policy. I. Davidson, Larry.
[DNLM: 1. Mental Disorders—rehabilitation. 2. Social Support. 3. Civil Rights. 4. Community Mental
Health Services. 5. Health Care Reform. 6. Mentally Ill Persons—psychology. WM 140 P8936 2008]
RA790.P66 2008
362.2'2—dc22   2008016589

Printed in the United States of America
on acid-free paper

This book is dedicated to individuals living with serious mental illness, their loved ones, and the practitioners who devote their careers to assisting them as they enter into and pursue recovery.

Contents

Acknowledgments

Most importantly, we would like to acknowledge and thank Thomas Kirk, Jr., Commissioner of the Connecticut Department of Mental Health and Addiction Services (DMHAS), and his senior staff for making the work described in this volume possible. As we describe in the Introduction, this book was based largely on the work we have done in collaboration with Connecticut DMHAS over the previous seven years, since Tom was first appointed Commissioner. His vision and courage in pursuing that vision, and his willingness to cultivate a close public–academic partnership despite the challenges often involved in such collaborations, have been crucial in providing us with the opportunity to begin to operationalize recovery in practice. This book would not exist without his steadfast and confident support and the talents and dedication of his senior leadership.

We also would like to thank Oxford University Press and our editors for having the foresight to agree to publish such a book before the idea of operationalizing recovery had come into vogue. This book has been seven years in the making, and Oxford's willingness to support its publication has been instrumental to our commitment to put these ideas on paper. While most of the material in this volume is new, we have had occasion to publish earlier versions of some selected pieces in a series of journal articles which we have published over the past few years. We cite these articles in appropriate places throughout the volume. It is our strong belief, however, that each chapter takes on additional salience and value when brought together with the others, producing a whole that is significantly greater than the sum of its parts.

Next, we would like to acknowledge our colleagues, both at Yale and beyond, who have been intimately involved in different aspects of this work over time. First, the staff and faculty of the Yale Program for Recovery and Community Health, past and present, including most prominently Kimberly Antunes, Luz Ocasio, Luis Bedregal, Joan Bushey, Miriam Delphin, Jennifer Frey, Dietra Hawkins, Stephanie Lanteri, Lesley Schwab, Mary Snyder, and David Stayner. We thank also the long-standing spiritual godfather, and cheerleader, of our program, John Strauss. The qualitative research upon which some of this material is based was conducted in collaboration with Marit Borg, Isabel Marin, Roberto Mezzina, Jaak Rakfeldt, Dave Sells, and Alain Topor. Among naturally intuitive "recovery coaches" from whom we have learned much, we would include Patty Benedict, Debbie Fisk, Ann Joy, Heather McDonald, Dorian Grey Parker, and Kyle Pedersen.

Finally, one of the hallmarks of Connecticut's initial transformation efforts was the leadership provided by the recovery community. As a testament to the tireless advocacy efforts of Karen Kangas, first outside of and then eventually inside of DMHAS itself, this culminated in the late 1990s with Tom Kirk—then acting as Deputy Commissioner under the leadership of the late Albert Solnit—inviting the recovery community to present its vision for a transformed system. Key leadership was provided in this effort by Yvette Sangster, then Director of Advocacy Unlimited, Inc., and Bob Savage, then Director of the Connecticut Community for Addiction Recovery. In addition to Karen, Yvette, and Bob, we thank the hundreds of people in recovery who have shown us the way, either by role modeling recovery in their lives or by being willing to share with us their stories. We hope that what we offer in this book represents some compensation to them for all of their hard work and generosity. They, obviously, are the true heroes in this story, as it should be.

Introduction

The first part of the twenty-first century promises to offer unprecedented opportunities for substantive reforms of mental health policy and practice aimed at improving the lives of people with serious
mental illnesses, their loved ones, and their communities. Beginning
with the adoption of "recovery" as the overarching aim of care in
the 1999 landmark *Report on Mental Health* of the Surgeon General
(DHHS, 1999), the U.S. government has moved steadily over the
intervening years to articulate an increasingly radical vision of the
nature of the changes required to make mental health services both
accessible and effective.

When held up against the expectations put forth by the Surgeon
General, the President's New Freedom Commission on Mental
Health, which issued its final report in 2003, found the mental
health system to be "fragmented and in disarray," leading to "unnecessary and costly disability, homelessness . . . and incarceration." In
particular, the Commission emphasized that our current approach
to care "simply manages symptoms and accepts long-term disability"
(DHHS, 2003, p. 1). It wasn't until the release of the *Federal Action
Agenda* (DHHS, 2005), which followed on the Commission's recommendations, that the degree of "transformation" required was made
fully apparent and explicit. In that document we read:

> Mere reforms to the existing mental health system are insuffi-
> cient . . . transformation is not accomplished through change
> on the margins but, instead, through profound changes in
> kind and in degree. Applied to the task at hand, transforma-
> tion represents a bold vision to change the very form and func-
> tion of the mental health service delivery system to better
> meet the needs of the individuals and families it is designed to
> serve. . . . Transformation . . . is nothing short of revolutionary.

It implies profound change—not at the margins of a system, but
at its very core. In transformation, new sources of power emerge
and new competencies develop. (DHHS, 2005, pp. 1, 5, 18)

Students of the history of mental health policy will not be unfa-
miliar with this kind of sweeping rhetoric, of course. Both the legislation launching the wide-scale construction of state hospitals in the
mid-1800s and the legislation responsible for the depopulation of
those same hospitals in the mid-1900s used similarly dramatic language. While both of these legislative initiatives did lead to major
shifts in the location and nature of the delivery of mental health
care, it is questionable whether either resulted in significant improvements in the lives of people with serious mental illnesses and
those of their loved ones. It remains the case at this juncture in the
history of mental health policy that the Los Angeles County, Cook
County, and Riker's Island jails are the largest institutions housing
people with serious mental illnesses in the United States—a situation not unlike that faced by Dorothea Dix when she began to offer
religious education to female inmates in the 1840s. While skepticism in the face of such "revolutionary" rhetoric is therefore certainly justified by history, it would be a tragic mistake to allow the
current window of opportunity to close without taking full advantage of this rare invitation to rethink the nature and delivery of
mental health care from the ground up.

In this book, we offer a beginning attempt to do just that. Our
foundation for doing so is twofold. First, we have been conducting
empirical research on processes of recovery from and in serious
mental illnesses (a distinction we clarify in the first chapter) for the
past 15 years, extending the body of research that began to accumu-
late in the 1970s demonstrating that many, if not most, people diagnosed with serious mental illnesses experience significant improvement over time (see, e.g., Bleuler, 1978; Ciompi, 1980; Harding,
Brooks, Ashikaga, Strauss, & Breier, 1987a, 1987b; Strauss &
Carpenter, 1972, 1974, 1977). Within the context of these long-term
longitudinal studies, we have held up a magnifying glass to the details of the everyday lives of people with serious mental illnesses to
see what helps them, and what hinders them, in their daily efforts to
live with, manage, and overcome effects of their illness. In addition
to in several journal articles, much of this work has been published
in a previous volume (Davidson, 2003) and will be assumed, and only

cursorily reviewed, as a basis for what follows. Readers who feel the need for more grounding in this literature are referred to our earlier publications (e.g., Borg & Davidson, 2007; Davidson, 1997, 2003; Davidson, Haglund, et al., 2001; Davidson, O'Connell, Tondora, Staeheli, & Evans, 2005; Davidson, Staeheli, Stayner, & Sells, 2004; Davidson, Stayner, & Haglund, 1998; Davidson, Stayner, Lambert, Smith, & Sledge, 1997; Davidson, Stayner, et al., 2001; Davidson & Strauss, 1992, 1995; Mezzina et al., 2006; Rowe, 1999).

Informed by these same findings, our second foundation for the principles, practices, and tools that we present below is provided by work we have carried out over the last seven years in collaboration with the State of Connecticut's public sector behavioral health authority, the Connecticut Department of Mental Health and Addiction Services (CT DMHAS). Under the bold and visionary leadership of Thomas J. Kirk, Jr., PhD, who has served as commissioner since 2000, and Arthur C. Evans, PhD, who was deputy commissioner from 2000 to 2004, we have had the opportunity and the privilege to contribute to taking the first few steps toward transforming a statewide system of behavioral health care for adults to promote resilience and recovery. We draw much of the material presented in this book from the work we have been able to conduct in collaboration with CT DMHAS and its senior leadership. As a result, the materials we offer have been field tested and bear marks of the trials by fire they have endured thus far. We readily acknowledge, though, that these efforts are preliminary and constitute only a beginning to what we envision to be a decades-long process of transformation.

Given the fact that the policy window that was opened by the Surgeon General and New Freedom Commission reports, and which currently is being propped open by the subsequent Federal Action Agenda, may close at any time, we felt it important to share these preliminary efforts with the field. As states across the country, and countries around the globe, begin to embrace the process of transformation, there is an urgent need for concrete ideas, guidance, and tools that can be used as alternatives to existing approaches to care. This is the focus of the present volume.

Prior to launching into the particulars of recovery-oriented practice, some background will be needed. In our first chapter, we begin with a much-abbreviated review of the current status of adults living with serious mental illnesses in the United States. Rather than duplicating the efforts of the New Freedom Commission, whose report provides an extensive review of this topic, we will focus only on the stark circumstances of the everyday lives of far too many people with serious mental illnesses, which serve as the backdrop for our transformation efforts. Next, we will discuss the various meanings of *recovery* currently at play in order to reduce confusions and ambiguities surrounding use of this term. This discussion will include, but will not be limited to, distinguishing between recovery *from* a serious mental illness and being *in* recovery *with* a serious mental illness, a distinction we have found increasingly useful as our work has evolved (see, e.g., Davidson & Roe, 2007). Returning to this task again in Chapter 2, our concern is that until consensus is achieved as to what precisely we are attempting to promote, and for whom and by what means we are promoting it, little progress will be made in doing so.

Based on this discussion of concepts of recovery, our first chapter then offers a conceptual framework for rethinking the nature of serious mental illnesses and their care accordingly. Convinced that enduring transformation will require dramatic changes in theory as well as in policy and practice, we make the case that mental health care has failed to appreciate fully that human beings are always already functioning as active agents, shaping their own lives and contexts at the same time as they are being shaped by their experiences and environments—a perspective that we refer to under the rubric of "action theory" (e.g., Davidson, Flanagan, Roe, & Styron, 2006; Davidson & Shahar, in press; Joas, 1999).

A slight digression on the tone of the following volume may be in order here, as several of the reviewers of an earlier draft of this manuscript took issue with our use of terms such as *failed*, as in "failed to appreciate fully that human beings are always already functioning as active agents, shaping their own lives and contexts at the same time as they are being shaped by their experiences and environments." Note that in the last sentence of the preceding paragraph we describe "mental health care" as failing to appreciate the fact that people with serious mental illness remain active agents in their own lives. We do not fault mental health practitioners, either individually or collectively, for this perceived failure, but rather the systems of care in which we all work. We pause to make this distinction, as we wish to be clear that the criticisms of existing services and models of care we offer in the following chapters should not be construed as directed toward practitioners per se. We are ourselves practitioners and appreciate that people who choose to work in this field do so out of compassion and a genuine desire to make positive differences in the lives of individuals who are struggling. Nothing that we write in this volume should be taken to imply otherwise.

You might wonder, why do we need to assure you of this? A major impediment to providing training in recovery-oriented care has been the concern among system leaders and managers that direct-care staff will be offended by the notion that what they are currently providing may not be the best care possible. If we are offering practitioners new skills and tools, one might think, this must imply that what they have been doing for the last couple of decades or so has been neither effective nor helpful. As one thoughtful leader in Connecticut pointed out, however, this is not ordinarily the assumption of medical staff attending continuing medical education seminars. They assume that medicine continues to evolve and that they should not be practicing today the way their successors (or they themselves) did a decade or two ago. Breakthroughs are being made in medicine every year. Why should the same not be true in mental health?

Our experience has not borne out the concerns of system leaders and managers who wish for us to tread lightly in our critiques of current approaches to care. When and where we have been given license to offer training in recovery-oriented care, these offerings have been oversubscribed and have generated waiting lists. Practitioners have typically been enthusiastic and eager in their desires to acquire new skills and tools that will enable them to be more helpful to their clients, precisely because they are in this field primarily *to be helpful to their clients* (i.e., not for the pay or prestige). They all too readily appreciate the limitations of current approaches, as they encounter them every day in their practice. In suggesting the need for revolution, we thus are not telling them anything they are not already made intimately familiar with on a daily basis, even though they may understand the source of these difficulties somewhat differently.

Most practitioners and system leaders would agree, in principle, that the individuals they attempt to serve could be served better. They may cite various obstacles and challenges as accounting for the current status of care, including long-standing inequities in political priorities leading to inadequate funding of mental health care, gaps in services and lack of integration and coordination in care, lack of training and difficulties in recruitment and retention of a competent and culturally diverse workforce, stigma and discrimination in society, and other issues. We take no issue with this list and agree that all of these challenges limit the quality (and quantity) of existing services and systems and are formidable difficulties. We hold no individual practitioner or collective professional body responsible for these issues, except for our society as a whole. It is just that to this list we add an additional set of obstacles that we also attribute to the history of, and societal attitudes toward, mental illness. We refer to these obstacles in our first chapter under the rubric of "mentalism."

Describing current structures within the mental health system and society as "mentalist" refers primarily to a cultural phenomenon; it is not to be construed as a criticism of direct-care staff or individual practitioners any more than critiques of institutional racism should be taken to refer to, or be the fault of, individual workers. What we are critical of in the following is the state of current mental health systems and the people they are meant to serve. We take the talk of the need for "revolution" seriously and suggest that current models of care and current services do not serve individuals with serious mental illnesses as well as they might—not due to poor motivation or performance of individual practitioners, managers, agencies, or organizations but due to a culture of mentalism that pervades systems as a whole. This is why we need a revolution and not just a quality-improvement initiative.

It is our long-term hope that it will be in the "overthrow" of mentalism that answers to the other legitimate and formidable obstacles and challenges described above will emerge. Perhaps it will be in the "new sources of power" that emerge through transformation that we, as a society, will find a way—finally—to redress the trauma, torture, and inequities that have befallen people with serious mental illnesses for centuries. Perhaps it will require 500 individuals in recovery and their families to rally outside the mayor's office, 5,000 individuals in recovery and their families to rally outside the state capital, or 500,000 individuals in recovery and their families to rally outside of the nation's capital for adequate political will to be mustered for mental health to ultimately be addressed "with the same urgency as physical health" (DHHS, 2003, p. 7). This is the way civil rights have traditionally been reclaimed in our society; why should it be different in mental health?

In our second chapter (the digression ends here) we begin to sketch out a map for our eventual journey to a post-mentalist mental health system. As we wish to base this map first and foremost on what people with serious mental illnesses need to do in order to manage their illness and reclaim their lives, we go to some lengths to describe what we think we know to date about the processes and components of recovery. Drawing from both our own empirical research and a review of first-person accounts and the research literature, we highlight concretely some of the ways in which people with serious mental illnesses play active roles in their own recovery, underscoring the importance of hope, self-determination, and community inclusion as cornerstones of recovery-oriented care. We integrate these findings into a model of recovery, which then serves as the foundation for development of recovery-oriented approaches to care. If, as we suggest, getting "into" and pursuing recovery is primarily the responsibility of the person living with the serious mental illness, then the focus of recovery-oriented care should be supporting the person's own efforts in doing so. Chapter 2 begins to lay out the various directions in which practitioners can go in their efforts to accomplish this.

In the chapters that follow, we delve in more depth and detail into the implications of what we know about recovery for designing, implementing, and evaluating recovery-oriented practice. In the third chapter, we examine the 10 most common concerns about recovery that we have encountered in our system-transformation efforts, sharing some of our struggles in making and keeping clear how recovery is a revolutionary concept for mental health care. In Chapter 4, we describe at length the practice guidelines that we have developed for recovery-oriented care, including sample standards for each of the eight domains of recovery-oriented practice here identified. The fifth and concluding chapter describes the key principles and elements of a "recovery guide" model that we offer as an alternative to current forms of case management. Finally, an appendix is included which offers two tools for assessing the recovery-oriented nature of care and the training and education needs of students, trainees, and mental health practitioners faced with the challenge of providing such care.

We hope that this volume will represent a first substantive step forward in successfully revolutionizing care to elicit and build on the agency and inherent resilience of people with serious mental illnesses—people who currently represent the most valuable, but also most untapped, resource available to our systems of care and to our society as a whole. While much work certainly remains to be done in implementing, evaluating, and refining the ideas presented here, we take comfort from the Taoist sentiment that a journey of a thousand miles still begins with a single step. In that respect, we thank you for joining us as we embark.

A Practical Guide to Recovery-Oriented Practice

1 The Recovery Movement and Its Implications for Transforming Clinical and Rehabilitative Practice

We begin with a snapshot of the world we hope to leave behind. While it may not be necessary to reiterate the reasons why transformation is needed for most readers—who, as we noted in the Introduction, may be only too familiar with the challenges presented by our current systems of care—we think it useful nonetheless to establish a point of departure. We also strive throughout this volume to make our ideas concrete through the use of stories derived from our own experiences, putting a human face on what might frequently appear to be abstract or idealistic concepts. In our experience, and in our previous publications (e.g., Davidson, Stayner, et al., 2001), there has been very little about mental health concepts of recovery that are either abstract or idealistic. In fact, we have consistently stressed the everyday nature of recovery (Borg & Davidson, 2007), finding it embodied and exemplified in such mundane activities as washing one's own dishes, playing with a child, or walking a dog.

We strive to continue this concrete focus in what follows, alternating our exposition of principles and practices with descriptions of real-life examples from our practice. This not only is our own preference in teaching and training but was strongly encouraged by the reviewers of an earlier draft of this book. We are happy to oblige.

A Day in the Life of (Far Too Many) People with Serious Mental Illness

Passage of legislation such as the Rehabilitation Act of 1973 and the Americans with Disabilities Act of 1990 held great promise for individuals with disabilities, especially in relation to their opportunity to participate fully in all aspects of community life. Unfortunately, it is now widely recognized that the implementation of these acts for persons with serious mental illness lags far behind parallel efforts in the broader disability community, with expectations for expanded access and opportunity largely still to be realized (Chirikos, 1999; Fabian, 1999; Hernandez, 2000; Wylonis, 1999).

In response to this national tragedy, several recent calls have been made for radical reforms to the mental health system. The Surgeon General's *Report on Mental Health*, for example, called for mental health services to be "consumer oriented and focused on promoting recovery" (DHHS, 1999, p. 455). The *Olmstead* Supreme Court decision, also of 1999, upheld the "integration mandate" of the Americans with Disabilities Act and demanded an expansion of opportunities for full community inclusion for people with psychiatric disabilities, while also requiring their active participation in the development of their community integration plans. It remains the case, though, that the full impact of the changes required to implement *Olmstead* has yet to be realized. There remains in particular a significant need to educate people with mental illnesses and ensure real choice, as well as a need to expand infrastructure and create a new set of resources, benefits, services, and supports that will enable these individuals to participate fully in community life. The following story illustrates these points.

> In his frequent efforts to promote the transformation agenda in Connecticut, Commissioner of Mental Health and Addiction Services Tom Kirk, PhD, tells the story of a 27-year-old man named Steve whom he met during a visit to a supported housing program. When he asked the staff how Steve was doing in his recovery, Commissioner Kirk reports that they responded favorably about how well Steve was doing in the program: following the rules, taking his medication as prescribed, and having his symptoms relatively under control. When asked if this was the kind of life they hoped this young man would live for the foreseeable future, the staff seemed puzzled, confident that they were doing

their best to serve him. His condition, after all, was stable, and he had not been admitted to the hospital for several years.

Commissioner Kirk, however, was not satisfied. He asked the staff to go one step further and consider whether or not this would be the kind of life that would make them content were they in Steve's place. Once it was phrased this way, the staff began to think that more could be done for, and expected from, this clever college graduate who was engaging, who loved cars and racing, and who had aspirations of becoming a mechanic. But how could they help him with that? They had little idea as to what they could do beyond treating his schizophrenia and encouraging him to participate in program activities as a way of luring him away from his television set. Becoming a mechanic seemed a long way off, if it was to be possible at all.

Steve's story, unfortunately, is living evidence of how our current mental health system, in the words of the New Freedom Commission Report, "simply manages symptoms and accepts long-term disability" (DHHS, 2003, p. 1). On any given day, there are more than 8 million Americans who, like Steve, are consigned to the long-term disability that historically has been associated with serious mental illnesses. Schizophrenia, bipolar disorder, and depression currently take a profound toll on the lives of people who experience them, as well as on their families and the community at large. This toll was powerfully documented in the Global Burden of Disease project, in which 5 of the 10 leading causes of disability worldwide were found to be mental illnesses (Murray & Lopez, 1996). In the United States, for example, mental illness is the number one cause of disability, accounting for more burden than that associated with all forms of cancer (McAlpine & Warner, 2002; WHO, 2001). Yet only 6% of all health care expenditures are devoted to the prevention and treatment of serious mental illnesses—a grossly inadequate investment in light of the overall burden these disorders impose (Mark et al., 2005).

Disproportionately low allocation of funding to address psychiatric disability follows on the disappointments of the deinstitutionalization era, in which state psychiatric hospitals were closed without redirecting commensurate resources to build community support systems. In fact, adjusted for inflation and population growth, states spent 30% *less* on mental health in 1997 than they did in 1955 (Bernstein, 2001; Manderscheid & Henderson, 2001). The original intention of community support systems was to provide persons with disabilities the opportunities they needed to experience a meaningful sense of community membership and enjoy all of the associated rights, freedoms, and responsibilities. Without adequate support, and despite the best intentions of deinstitutionalization, what has largely resulted has been only the physical co-location of persons with serious mental illnesses in community settings. Like the young man described above, people living outside of institutions far too often lack access to the supports they need in order to participate as fully integrated members and citizens of their communities.

As a result, research on community life for people with psychiatric disabilities is replete with poignant descriptions of loss; loneliness; and enduring, but unfulfilled, desires for love, friendship, and valued social roles (Davidson & Stayner, 1997). In addition to being shut out of the normal social and interpersonal rhythms of community life, people with serious mental illness continue to be denied equal employment opportunities. In fact, a person discharged from a psychiatric inpatient unit has a better chance of returning to the hospital than to work (Anthony, 1994). When compared to individuals with other types of disabilities, people with serious mental illness continue to have the lowest success rates of vocational rehabilitation, with fewer than 15% being competitively employed at any given time (Anthony, 1994; Kirsh, 1996; Marrone, Gandolfo, Gold, & Hoff, 1998). Even among those individuals who have access to supported employment, many find that their jobs do not last beyond an initial, brief period, with little if any opportunity for advancement.

Finally, despite the fact that the staggering costs of lost productivity and direct treatment expenditures associated with these disorders continue to rise (Connolly, Marrone, Kiernan, & Butterworth, 1996; Estroff, Zinuner, Lachiotte, Benoit, & Patrick, 1997; Mischoulon, 1999), most individuals with serious mental illness rarely receive care that is considered to be "evidence-based" (Drake et al., 2001; Hoagwood, Burns, Kiser, Ringeisen, & Schoenwald, 2001; McClellan, 2002; Torrey et al., 2001), with a significant proportion receiving no formal treatment at all (Lehman & Steinwachs, 1998; NCD, 2002). As is true in other forms of health care, this lack of access is greatest among people of color (DHHS, 2001). Far too many Americans with serious mental illness fall through the gaps of a poorly formed patchwork of ineffective safety nets that serve to trap people in dependency and despair—what Deegan has come to refer to as "handicaptivity" (Federal Task Force, 1992; Lamb & Weinberger, 1998; NCD, 2002). It is in the face of such stark realities that the New Freedom Commission on Mental Health framed its overarching goal for mental health care as being "a life in the community for everyone" (DHHS, 2003, p. 1).

Given this bleak portrait of the circumstances of many individuals living with serious mental illness in the United States at the beginning of the twenty-first century, it is certainly reasonable to ask how a civilized society would allow, and perpetuate, such neglect. When we took people out of state hospitals by the tens of thousands in the 1960s and 1970s, we promised them life "in the community in a normal manner" (Joint Commission on Mental Illness and Health, 1961, p. xvii). What happened? Why has deinstitutionalization been such an apparent failure? Part of the answer to this question lies in political and economic forces that lie outside of mental health and continue to confine individuals with serious mental illnesses to the margins of our communities, a sociological phenomenon that unfortunately did not disappear with the asylums. But part of this answer also lies in the history of contemporary psychiatry and its attitudes toward, and understandings of, serious mental illnesses.

Recovery *from* Serious Mental Illness

The Federal Action Agenda insists that "transformation is not accomplished through change on the margins." The "margins" this report refers to are the same margins the concept of recovery has largely hovered by for the past 30 years. Having emerged from two distinct sources in the mid-1970s, reforms of mental health policy and practice have come about as far as they can since that time as long as this concept remains confined to the margins of the field. These two sources—longitudinal clinical research stimulated by the World Health Organization and the Consumer/Survivor Movement founded by people with histories of institutionalization—came together in the mid-1970s in what has since been called the Community Support Movement (which we referred to above; Parrish, 1989; Turner & TenHoor, 1978). Despite the best efforts of thousands of earnest practitioners, people in recovery, and families strenuously advocating over the last 30 years the fundamental refashioning of the mental health system based on the community support model, this movement and its distinctive components (such as self-help and psychiatric rehabilitation) have remained peripheral to the field as a whole, regardless of how this is measured (e.g., by penetration rates, percentage of funding allocated, or numbers of providers).

While we describe these developments in more detail farther on, it is important for our present purposes to underscore the Action Agenda's insistence that further enhancing these marginal components of the field will not be sufficient to achieve transformation. No matter how well-intentioned or useful these programs may be, system leaders who propose to transform their systems simply by adding more peer support or psychiatric rehabilitation programs will merely be bringing their systems into line with expectations articulated almost 30 years ago, expectations that not only are outdated but also stop well short of the "revolution" required by transformation. As the revolution entailed in transformation is required in order to reorient services to promote recovery, a brief historical and conceptual digression into the various meanings of this concept in relation to serious mental illness will help to clarify how this is so.

Toward the end of the nineteenth century, Emil Kraepelin, the father of descriptive psychopathology, identified a disease entity he labeled *dementia praecox*, meaning "premature dementia." He chose this term to describe a disease he conceptualized as having a characteristic downward and deteriorating course beginning in adolescence, leading irreversibly to severe, persistent impairment, and ending in a premature state of incoherence and eventual death. Although his observations were based primarily on long-term residents of psychiatric institutions, his basic idea that dementia praecox—later referred to as schizophrenia—inevitably leads to progressive deterioration appears to reign in some sectors of the field to this day. This is not only true in the mental health field at large but continues to be true even in many professional training programs that are preparing future generations of mental health practitioners. It is for this reason that many people with serious mental illness still report being discouraged from taking steps forward in their recovery by a mental health practitioner whom they quote as having told them that they would "never be able to _____ again" (fill in the blank: "work," "attend school," "get married," "live independently," "have a family," etc.).

As early as the 1950s, however, the deterioration of overcrowded and hundred-year-old state hospitals and their budget-busting implications for state governments, along (secondarily) with the introduction of psychotropic medication, began to move policy makers to consider the possibility that people could live, and manage their illnesses, outside of hospital settings (Johnson, 1990). With the introduction of progressive social programs and entitlements in the 1960s and 1970s, hundreds of thousands of individuals with serious mental illness who in the past would have lived out the remainder of their lives in hospitals began to be discharged to fledgling and underfunded community-based services. Despite the fact, noted above, that even now—a half-century later—mental health services are funded at a level 30% *lower* than that provided for hospital care prior to 1960 (Bernstein, 2001; Manderscheid & Henderson, 2001), people with serious mental illness have experienced significant diversity in the courses and outcomes of these illnesses since being discharged from institutional settings. Even when discharged literally from the hospital to the streets, perhaps with a prescription for Thorazine and an appointment with a psychiatrist or case manager for weeks down the road, many people with serious mental illness did well outside of the hospital—better, in fact, than they would have done had they remained in the hospital.

Readers who consider such reports to be merely anecdotal will perhaps be surprised to learn that what has become accepted as the "heterogeneity" (Carpenter & Kirkpatrick, 1988) in outcome for serious mental illnesses has been confirmed repeatedly over the past 30 years of empirical research involving large samples and utilizing rigorous designs and standardized rating scales for assessing symptoms and functioning over time. As we noted above, the World Health Organization undertook the first such major study in the late 1960s in 11 countries, following people diagnosed with serious mental illness for over 11 years (WHO, 1973). This study was soon followed by others conducted all over the world, following people for as long as 32 years after onset or first contact with mental health services. A highly consistent picture has since emerged.

To combat the lingering legacy of Kraepelin's pessimism, we have recently published a collection of some of the most important of these studies (Davidson, Harding, & Spaniol, 2005). Taken together, these studies found that while some people diagnosed with serious mental illness did show a classic Kraepelinian deterioration in functioning over time, they accounted for only about 25% of each sample. Equally prominent were individuals who fell at the opposite end of the spectrum, showing no observable signs or symptoms and no residual impairments from the disorder between 2 and 32 years after onset. These individuals also accounted for approximately 25% of each sample. Given that signs, symptoms, and impairment are the classic—and really the only established—markers of illness, this 25% of each sample can be considered to have "recovered" in the traditional sense of the term. With publication of these studies, beginning in 1972, the possibility of any form of "recovery" in relation to serious mental illness was established (e.g., Strauss & Carpenter, 1972, 1974, 1977).

The reader may still wonder about the remaining 50% of the sample. If 25% of the sample resides at each end of the spectrum ranging from severe and persistent disability to full recovery, what is the fate of the remaining half? The term *heterogeneity* was selected, and has since been accepted, to refer to the fact that people have experienced illnesses that fall anywhere and everywhere along this continuum. Depending upon where the study was conducted, at least 45%, and up to 65%, of each sample was found to experience partial to full recovery, meaning that person's functioning and symptom levels improved over time. On the whole, then, this body of research has established not only that recovery is possible but that partial to full recovery is at least as common an outcome in serious mental illnesses, if not more common, than severe and persistent impairment.

With this reversal in expectations (i.e., from expecting the person's condition to deteriorate over time to expecting it to improve) we come to our first major definition of the term *recovery* in relation to serious mental illnesses: a sense we will refer to as "recovery from." Recovery from serious mental illness involves the person's returning to a healthy condition following onset of the illness. It is based on explicit criteria of levels of signs, symptoms, and deficits associated with the illness, and it identifies a point at which "remission" and/ or "recovery" may be said to have occurred (e.g., Andreasen et al., 2005; Liberman, Kopelowicz, Ventura, & Gutkind, 2002). This definition thus has many advantages from the point of view of research, such as being clear, reliable, and relatively easy to define, measure, and link to dysfunctions or well-being in other areas of life. Appearing as if they had never suffered from a serious mental illness, people who enjoy this sense of full recovery could be considered to have recovered from psychosis in the same way that other people may recover from an infection, a broken leg, or, in the case of recovery over a longer period, asthma.

This was not the only sense of "recovery" to emerge from the clinical research on course and outcome, however. Heterogeneity was discovered not only in the course and outcome of illnesses experienced by different people but also across various domains of functioning within any given individual and over time. Again beginning in the 1970s, researchers discovered that serious mental illnesses were complex and multidimensional disorders composed of several domains of functioning which were both conceptually and empirically distinct. Some people were able to recover functioning in one or more of these areas while continuing to experience impairments or symptoms in other areas. Not only did serious mental illnesses prove not to be permanent conditions for many people, but they also were found not to pervade the entirety of the person's life as was formerly thought.

Some people, for example, could live independently and work in challenging jobs while continuing to hear voices or entertain delusions. Others may no longer experience psychotic symptoms at all but still have moderate functional impairments in social relationships and/or employment. Taking into account the fact that these distinct domains are only "loosely linked" (Strauss & Carpenter, 1977), concepts of *partial recovery*, *social recovery*, and *symptomatic recovery* began to be used to describe various outcomes.

The 1970s also witnessed the early advocacy efforts of those individuals who have since come to refer to themselves as "ex-patients," "ex-inmates," "psychiatric survivors," or "consumers" or "users" of mental health services. As if these individuals were offering living proof both of full and of partial recovery from serious mental illness, these advocates—having left or been released from mental hospitals—demonstrated by example and argued that people with serious mental illness can, and should be entitled to, have a life beyond that of a "mental patient." As advocates intent on reforming mental health policy and practice, leaders of this movement had little interest in the conceptual or empirical distinctions employed in psychiatric research, drawing more from their own first-hand experiences of illness, incarceration, and reclamation of their lives.

In the life experiences of these advocates, the categories of *abnormal* and *normal*, *illness* and *health*, were not nearly as black-and-white as research and diagnostic practice suggested. In fact, the lines between these categories seemed fuzzy and permeable at best and arbitrary and political at worst (this was, for instance, during the Cold War, when many Soviet dissidents were placed in mental hospitals). As a result, the advocates' agenda was not so much recovering from or getting over a mental illness such as schizophrenia as it was figuring out how to live a safe, dignified, and autonomous life given whatever hand they had been dealt by fate. For guidance in this process, they had to look beyond the mental health system to examples of other populations who had faced adversity and overcome marginalization and discrimination. It is within the context of this agenda and from this appeal outside of mental health that a second major concept of recovery emerged.

Being *in* Recovery with a Serious Mental Illness

Our second major form of recovery in relation to serious mental illnesses, what we refer to as "being in recovery" as opposed to "recovery from," has its origin in the civil rights and independent living movements of the 1960s and 1970s. It also has been influenced by the notion of recovery that is integral to the self-help community in addiction recovery, as exemplified by such abstinence-based 12-step groups as Alcoholics Anonymous and its derivatives. As such, we might consider this form of recovery to be a kind of hybrid, sharing some characteristics of each of its parents but also being somewhat different from both.

In the 12-step community, for example, people consider themselves to be "in recovery" when they have managed to achieve some degree of abstinence from drugs or alcohol and are in the process of reclaiming or rebuilding their lives beyond the limits of the addiction per se. They do not consider themselves to be have recovered from addiction, as they view addiction as a lifelong disease that requires their ongoing vigilance and care in order to protect their sobriety, and their newly won life, from an underlying, continuing vulnerability to relapse. What mental health advocates appear to have found appealing in this sense of recovery is that people with long-term and potentially disabling conditions could reclaim control over their own lives and destinies while finding ways to minimize the destructive effects of the condition. Being "in recovery" in relation to serious mental illness likewise entails a process of minimizing the illness and its deleterious effects on the person's life over time, as the person figures out how to live with and manage an illness that may be with him or her for an extended period of time, if not for the remainder of his or her life. For the most part, however, it is here that the overlap with addiction recovery ends.

The civil rights and independent living movements have been equally crucial to the mental health consumer/survivor movement due to the fact that many of the more formidable barriers to recovery identified by mental health advocates have been social and political rather than stemming from the mental illnesses themselves. It is only recently that advocates for addiction recovery have begun to embrace a similar political and social agenda, and this, in part, follows the example set by their counterparts in mental health. To mental health advocates who often had been incarcerated in psychiatric hospitals against their will, it was evident from early on that their struggles were as much social and political struggles against prejudice, stigma, discrimination, and marginalization as they were personal struggles with particular psychiatric conditions.

As a result, this concept of recovery refers primarily to a person diagnosed with a serious mental illness reclaiming his or her right to a safe, dignified, and personally meaningful and gratifying life in the community despite his or her psychiatric condition. It emphasizes self-determination and such normal life pursuits as education, employment, sexuality, friendship, spirituality, and voluntary membership in faith and other kinds of communities beyond the limits both of the disorder and of the mental health system, and consistent with the person's own values, preferences, and goals. What is conspicuously absent in this concept of recovery is any notion of "cure." In fact, what has since come to be referred to as the "recovery movement" offers an alternative concept to that offered by clinical research, one that really only makes sense *in the absence* of clinical or symptomatic recovery. Whether this concept will be seen as contradictory or complementary to the clinical concept of recovery remains to be determined, but it is essential for our purposes to note that it is a very different concept with very different implications for practice (Davidson, Schmutte, Dinzeo, & Andres-Hyman, 2007).

So what has been meant by "being in recovery" for someone living with a serious mental illness, and what implications does this shift have for clinical practice and policy? Basically, we understand being "in" recovery to refer to a process of containing and minimizing the destructive impact of the illness while identifying and building on a person's strengths and interests in order for the person to have an identity and a life beyond that of a "mental patient." To the degree that this form of recovery involves managing symptoms, there is sympathetic overlap between this concept and current practice, and it is in this area that many people find existing mental health services most useful to them. However, to the degree that this form of recovery also involves establishing, reestablishing, or reclaiming a meaningful life in the community in the presence of enduring disability, this concept departs from much of current clinical and rehabilitative policy and practice. It is perhaps because this concept of rebuilding a life in the presence of a disability has not traditionally been within the purview of clinical psychiatry that these more positive elements of recovery are at times relegated to the category of "personal growth and development": something, in other words, that may be put off indefinitely until the "real" work of treatment and rehabilitation is completed. For many people with serious mental illness, however, existing treatments and rehabilitation may not be that effective for an extended period of time, if ever. For these people, being in recovery is not a matter of growth and development but of suffering and survival.

From our perspective, dismissing these positive elements of recovery by referring to them under the rubrics of "growth and development" or "quality of life" is a tragic mistake with far-reaching and disastrous consequences. More than the recovery skeptics and naysayers, it is this kind of fundamental misunderstanding of the nature of this form of recovery that we fear poses the major threat to real, substantial, and sustained change in mental health (i.e., transformation). By limiting the relevance of this form of recovery to considerations of growth, development, or quality of life, we have overlooked the crucial importance of civil rights, or the lack thereof, in determining the everyday lives, opportunities, and health of people with serious mental illness. We also make it possible for systems of care to claim a recovery-orientation by adding a few new components or programs that explicitly address such issues as education, employment, or sexuality without making any substantive changes to existing structures.

This view has led some influential policy makers to suggest, for example, that if you reallocate 5% of your state mental health budget to peer support services that address quality-of-life issues, you will achieve transformation. While offering the appeal of simplicity, we suggest that such directives will instead sound the death knell of the recovery movement.

It is perhaps easier to appreciate the central, as opposed to peripheral, importance of this issue in the lives of people with serious mental illnesses if we appeal to an analogy drawn from the broader disabilities field. As we noted above, the independent living movement led by people with physical disabilities was one source of inspiration for this form of recovery. Examples drawn from the broader disability field provide a clearer glimpse into what this concept of recovery adds to current approaches beyond a focus on "quality of life."

In the case of paraplegia, for instance, several things need to be in place for the person who has lost his or her mobility to resume the activities he or she enjoyed prior to his or her accident or illness. The most obvious, but also perhaps therefore the most often overlooked, requirement is that the person not wait to regain his or her mobility before pursuing these and other activities. This is occasionally referred to as "acceptance" of his or her trauma and disability, but for many people such a notion of acceptance connotes resignation and despair. The same has been true in mental illness, with many people refusing or being reluctant to "accept" the diagnosis of psychosis because of the helplessness and hopelessness—as well as the stereotypical pessimistic prognosis—associated with it. We prefer, then, to refer to the fact that the person will not have to wait to regain his or her mobility in order to resume his or her life. While not preferable, it is nonetheless possible to have a life without use of one's legs.

Once the person acknowledges that he or she cannot simply sit around and wait to regain his or her mobility, a next step would be to be fitted for, and learn to use, prostheses or other compensatory tools such as a wheelchair. No matter how well a person learns to maneuver his or her wheelchair, however, certain activities will remain extremely difficult, if not impossible, to resume unless other environmental accommodations are made. This is why the independent living movement put such effort into lobbying for passage of the Rehabilitation Act of 1973, which required public spaces to be accessible to people in wheelchairs. Without curb cuts in sidewalks and handrails installed in bathrooms, the world remained fairly restricted for people who used wheelchairs. Similarly, without Braille signs posted on doors and elevators, and without the mandate that service dogs be allowed in public spaces, people who had lost their vision would be very limited in their access to the opportunities and activities that make up the lives they want to lead in the community.

For people with these and other disabilities, issues of access and accommodation are not considered to be solely issues of growth and development or quality of life but are viewed rather as fundamental to the rights and responsibilities of citizenship. While they do not restore the person's mobility or vision, they can and do restore the person's status as a valuable and contributing member of society. It is for this reason that these issues are framed as issues of civil rights and social justice rather than as issues of health care. The same should be true, according to the recovery movement, for people with *psychiatric* "disabilities."

This approach is what is implicit in the notion of being *in recovery*. Advocates make this case explicitly in emphasizing that the recovery movement was first and foremost a civil rights movement (Davidson, 2006), but this emphasis is quickly lost or overlooked in clinical settings, where the focus typically remains on disorder, deficit, and disability. Practitioners have been trained primarily to focus on minimizing and/or containing pathology. On the surface, this would seem to have nothing to do with issues of civil rights or citizenship (except for the person's right to appropriate care). At best, perhaps these issues become relevant as the person's condition improves and he or she starts to reintegrate into community life. But from the perspective of the person with the psychiatric disability, focusing on deficit and pathology not only is overly narrow and limited in its utility; it misses the very point of the civil rights argument. It would be pointless for society to accord people with disabilities the rights of citizenship if those rights were made contingent on the person's overcoming his or her disability first. It is precisely in the presence of enduring disability that these rights become most pressing and most relevant.

Similarly, it is when people with serious mental illness are most disabled by their illness that their civil rights and responsibilities become most pressing and most relevant. In an analogous fashion to physical disability, being in recovery speaks primarily to the person's rights of social inclusion and self-determination irrespective of the nature or severity of his or her psychiatric condition. Recovery refers to the rights to access and join in with those elements of community life the person chooses, and to be in control of his or her own life and destiny, *even and especially while remaining disabled.*

A Revolution in Mental Health?

It is only if this last statement strikes the reader as preposterous, nonsensical, or naïve wishful thinking that we can be assured that we are providing an adequate introduction to this form of recovery. If, on the other hand, the point seems obvious, then we have failed our charge. For it is only through this argument for civil rights and membership in society for people with serious mental illness regardless of the severity of their disability—rather than through advances in psychiatric medications or an accumulating body of research on positive outcomes—that the concept of recovery has been pushed to the forefront of mental health policy in the United States and elsewhere. It is only on this basis that the New Freedom Commission was able to tout its vision of a day "when all adults with serious mental illnesses . . . will live, work, learn, and participate fully in their communities" (DHHS, 2005, p. 3).

Let us pause briefly to consider this important point. The Federal Action Agenda, like the New Freedom Commission report before it, places central emphasis on sending "the message that mental illnesses . . . are treatable and that recovery is possible" (DHHS, 2005, p. 6). If it is not additional research into the causes or cures for mental illness that is required, what, then, is needed in order to achieve the vision described above of all adults participating fully in community life? The federal government is not tackling serious mental illnesses in the way it might have tackled polio, for instance, or smallpox—that is, by accelerating research into the causes and cures of these diseases and by disseminating new treatments or preventive interventions. The federal agenda in relation to mental illness appears to be something different. According to the Action Agenda, we already know "how to enable people with mental illnesses to live, work, learn, and participate fully in the community" (DHHS, 2005, p. 1). If we already know how to do so, what stops us or gets in our way? What has to be different in order for us to achieve this vision?

Again according to the Action Agenda, "a keystone of the trans-formation process will be the protection and respect of the rights of adults with serious mental illnesses" (DHHS, 2005, p. 3). What we are dealing with is not so much an issue of science—not a break-through in understanding the nature of the disease or its cure—but an issue of civil and human rights. Perhaps it is for this reason that the Action Agenda frames the process of transformation as requir-ing "nothing short of a revolution" (DHHS, 2005, p. 18). Clearly, if all we were being asked to do was to hold out hope for clinical im-provement in the people we treat and to offer them the most effec-tive interventions available for reducing symptoms and enhancing functioning, there would be no need for this kind of rhetoric; there would be no "revolution." What may not yet be clear, though, is what such a revolution will entail and what a transformed system of care will look like once the revolution is over. What will be required of us to protect and respect the rights of adults with serious mental illness, or to enable them to be in control of their own lives and des-tiny, even and especially while remaining disabled? It is to these is-sues that we now turn.

If we take the civil rights and independent living movements as our guide, the nature of the revolution seems at first fairly straight-forward. The various civil rights movements established that people of color did not need to be white, women did not need to be men, and lesbian/gay/bisexual/transgendered individuals did not need to be confined to heterosexuality in order to be considered, treated as, and accorded all of the rights and responsibilities of full citizens. Similarly, as we noted above, the independent living movement made this case for people with physical disabilities, insisting that it is in the presence of enduring disability that people most need to be guaranteed their rights to self-determination and inclusion in com-munity life. Extrapolating to serious mental illnesses, the point would be that people living with these conditions do not need to be cured of their illness, do not need to become "normal," in order to pursue their lives in the community alongside everyone else.

It is important to note that this does not mean merely that peo-ple with serious mental illness can no longer be confined to hospi-tals against their will. It also means that they can make their own decisions, follow their own dreams, and pursue the activities they enjoy or find meaningful in the settings of their choice (within avail-able resources) *as they are.* Similar to the decision that a person with paraplegia need not wait to regain his or her mobility in order to resume his or her life, a person with a serious mental illness needs to be able to have a meaningful, gratifying, and self-determined life while continuing to have a psychiatric disability.

A story may help make this point concretely. The story of a woman we will call Celeste—who was 33 years old and enjoyed sewing, and who received different services from the same agency with different results—may be illustrative here.

Celeste's first clinician viewed her difficulties as due primarily to her mental illness. Although she voiced an interest in working, the clinician believed that Celeste could not yet work because she still experienced the hallucinations and paranoia associated with her psychiatric condition. The clinician thus focused on trying to get Celeste to take medication as prescribed and to attend a skills group for people who were interested in employment, hoping to address the sources of her difficulties before taking up seriously Celeste's stated desire to work.

If Celeste's disability were related to her mobility or vision, it would be obvious that this approach would result in her not acquiring a job until she no longer needed to use a wheelchair or had regained her vision. As it was, Celeste was soon discharged from treatment due to her failure to attend scheduled meetings and her refusal to be evaluated by the agency psychiatrist. From her perspective, she found the clinician indifferent to her needs and wants, saw no change in her condition, and began to feel that the agency was simply trying to drug her into a state of passivity and hopelessness, evidence for which she unfortunately found in the agency's waiting room among some of the older, more "chronic" clients. She did not want to become one of them.

After refusing these services but showing up repeatedly in hospital emergency rooms due to persistent, harassing voices, Celeste was approached by an outreach worker from the same agency who suggested that she could in fact work despite her disability. This clinician encouraged Celeste's desire to work and offered to help her find a job that interested her. With frequent personal contact and assistance with transportation, Celeste pursued and got a job working at a fabrics store. She then found, however, that hearing voices and feeling paranoid made it difficult for her to be comfortable at work, and she asked her clinician if she could do anything to help. The clinician described both pharmacological and psychosocial approaches to symptom management and suggested to Celeste that she discuss these concerns with her family and with a psychiatrist or nurse practitioner at the agency who might be able to suggest which medications in particular could help with these difficulties.

After some reluctance, Celeste eventually chose to describe her situation to a nurse, who, based on Celeste's concerns about being "drugged," initially suggested a low dose of an antipsychotic medication, explaining to Celeste that this would not make her too tired to work. Celeste found some relief from hearing voices with the medication, and, less harassed by the voices, began to feel more comfortable at the store. She began to bring in some of her sewing projects and made friends with a few of her co-workers, finding that her paranoia significantly decreased accordingly. In her case, working served several functions, including giving her a reason to use treatment and helping to offset her symptoms.

Some readers may consider Celeste's story to be simply an illustration of good, sound clinical work. Such readers should welcome the revolution of recovery-oriented transformation. It should be evident from this story, however, that neither the benefits of taking medication that reduced her voices nor the offsetting of her paranoia through social acceptance would have resulted from Celeste's waiting for her illness to abate. She might have found her own way around to these steps eventually, as people with serious mental illness have shown tremendous resilience in the absence of care, or her clinician may have practiced this way all along (i.e., prior to the recovery revolution), out of her empathy for and insight into Celeste's condition or her own intuitive sensitivity and resourcefulness.

However, the most important thing that Celeste's second clinician did, and something the first had failed to do, was listen. It certainly is not a revolutionary idea that practitioners need to listen, or that they should be trained in how to listen in a disciplined and respectful way. The practice of psychotherapy grew out of a conviction that listening is invaluable. But in psychoanalytic and psychodynamic psychotherapies, listening has the additional agenda of cultivating insight and understanding, which is expected eventually to lead to personal change.

But Celeste did not want, nor was she asked by her second clinician, to change. She was not seen as lacking in insight, nor was she offered any. In fact, the problem to be addressed was situated not within Celeste at all but rather in the poor fit between her disability and her environment. Celeste wanted to work, and her clinician helped her get a job that she thought she would like and which was consistent with her interests. Celeste was bothered by the voices brought on by her illness, and her clinician suggested a few options that she might try to make the voices less bothersome. Celeste was concerned that her co-workers and employer would not like her, and her clinician encouraged her to find out by actually trying to socialize and by sharing with them her interests and skills.

Against a historical backdrop of stigma and discrimination against people with serious mental illness, what appears to be revolutionary about this approach is that it assumes from the start that Celeste is a competent adult who is doing her best to manage a disabling condition which she neither asked for nor deserved as punishment for some earlier misdeeds. It assumes that Celeste will need to, and *will be able to*, figure out how best to live with this disability, and that she has many areas of health and competence alongside her mental illness. It assumes, most importantly, that Celeste will know best what is best for Celeste, and that the role of the clinician is to offer knowledge, expertise, and resources for Celeste's consideration and benefit.

From a theoretical point of view, then, this approach assumes that serious mental illnesses are like other illnesses for which we have a range of effective interventions to offer afflicted persons. It also recognizes that as an autonomous agent, it is ultimately the person's choice—in concert with his or her loved ones, if he or she so chooses—which interventions he or she will agree to try, including on what conditions, under what circumstances, and with what intended outcomes. People with serious mental illness have demanded this kind of care over the last decade, and this is a model of collaborative decision-making that is taking over other domains of medicine as well. What is revolutionary about it in mental health is that it requires treating psychiatry more broadly as a form of medicine or health care. This is the nature of the revolution that people with psychiatric disabilities have advocated and brought about, and one from which they vow not to turn back. The challenge they present is for the rest of the field to catch up.

For readers who are wondering how such a shift constitutes a revolution, we offer the following insight from John McKnight, a pioneer in the field of asset-based community development, an approach we will return to in Chapter 5. Subsequent to over 25 years of experience working with and advocating for people with developmental disabilities, McKnight suggested that "revolutions begin when people who are defined as problems achieve the power to redefine the problem" (1992, p. 3). For such a revolution to occur in mental health, we will need to shift from viewing people with serious mental illness as being themselves *the problem* we must address to according them the power to redefine the problem in their own terms. Rather than attempting to "fix" people with serious mental illness through treatment or rehabilitative interventions administered by caring others, the work of transformation entails accepting that these same people represent the greatest, if also least tapped, resource a mental health system possesses. Instead of being considered deficient, disordered, or dysfunctional, people with mental illness must come to be seen as *the experts* in defining their own needs, wants, and preferences. This is true not only in relation to life in general (e.g., where the person wants to live) but also more specifically in relation to the challenges posed by the illness and its other associated difficulties, such as stigma.

In the Introduction, we quoted the Federal Action Agenda as stating that "in transformation, new sources of power emerge and new competencies develop" (DHHS, 2005, p. 1). We are now in a position to clarify the first part of this enigmatic statement, suggesting that adults with serious mental illness themselves represent the "new sources of power" that emerge in the process of transformation. In a transformed system of care, it is primarily the power of the person with the serious mental illness that is identified and brought into the process, a process that currently affords the person an almost entirely passive and subordinate role. As a recent pamphlet from the National Alliance for Mental Illness (NAMI) suggests, we at times seem to think that the most a person can do to "help" his or her recovery along is to take his or her psychiatric medications as prescribed. In a transformed system of care, however, a person's recovery is not something that he or she might "help" along by being a compliant patient. As in addiction self-help, mental health recovery is the responsibility of the person with the serious mental illness. Recovery has to be pursued; it does not simply occur in response to medication or other treatments. Recovery, in this sense, refers primarily to what the person does to manage his or her illness and to reclaim his or her life in the presence of enduring disability. The major sources of power driving this process are thus the person's own efforts, energies, interests, and, most importantly, hope.

The question that remains, then, is what new competencies need to be developed to promote transformation. Consistent with this point, we suggest that it is in the second area of needed competencies that the expertise of people with serious mental illness is needed most urgently. This is not to place a limitation on their expertise, as they have already taught us much about factors that facilitate or impede recovery and ways in which mental health services could and should be delivered differently. But there is yet another area in which we still have much to learn: how the person comes to manage the illness and reclaim his or her life in the presence of an ongoing disability. It is in this area that we are currently most in the dark and therefore also most in need of the expertise and experience of people in recovery.

How can we say this? First, because we have spent the majority of the past two centuries attempting to figure out how, at worst, to get rid of "the mentally ill" (for instance, by sending them off to the countryside) or how, at best, to get rid of mental illness (through medications, insulin shock, etc.). As a result, we know very little about how people learn to live with, manage, and reclaim a life in the presence of the illness. The new competencies we need to develop are thus those involved in helping people to live meaningful, gratifying lives despite having a psychiatric disability—competencies which we suggest differ markedly from those involved in treating or containing a mental illness.

Second, who better to educate us about what is entailed in living with, managing, and reclaiming a life despite illness than people living with an illness themselves? Who knows better the issues and challenges people with psychiatric disabilities encounter *in their own efforts* "to live, work, learn, and participate fully in the community" (DHHS, 2005, p. 1) than these very people?

In this respect, the nature of the revolution at the core of the transformation agenda involves these same people who have been viewed as "the problem" in the past being accorded both the power and the opportunity to redefine the challenges they face in their own terms. The competencies that result are those required to facilitate a person's living a self-determined and productive life despite a continuing serious mental illness. Similar to what is required of the best midwives and orchestra conductors, doing so requires that recovery-oriented practitioners become competent in eliciting, encouraging, and supporting the person's own hopes, interests, assets, talents, energies, and efforts. Experienced midwives catalyze a mother's own natural processes and efforts to facilitate her baby's being birthed (as opposed to "delivered"). Skilled conductors bring out the unique contributions of each musician and instrument in order to create a whole that is greater than the sum of the orchestra's parts. Recovery-oriented care likewise focuses on identifying and maximizing a person's own interests and abilities in laying the foundation for "the work of recovery" (Davidson & Strauss, 1992).

Building on this foundation, what the person in recovery then needs most—just as in other health care arenas—is information about the nature of his or her difficulties, education about the range of effective interventions available to overcome or compensate for these difficulties, access to opportunities to exercise their strengths and use these interventions in regaining their functioning, and the supports required in order to be able to be successful in doing so. In the processes of evaluation, treatment, and rehabilitation, recovery-oriented practitioners therefore place as much, or possibly even more, emphasis on their clients' personal narratives and goals as they do on their clients' symptoms, deficits, and diagnosis.

What is to be gained by viewing people with serious mental illness as experts (rather than as problems) and listening to what they have to say about their own desires, needs, and goals (rather than telling them what to do)? In our earlier story of the young man whom we called Steve, who was compliant with treatment and had achieved relative symptom stability, this approach would suggest asking him what he would like to do, how he would like to spend his time on a daily basis, and/or what might make his life better. His responses, desires, or needs could then guide the efforts of the mental health practitioners working with him. In our experience, the goals most frequently identified by people when asked these questions are those of having their own place to live; being gainfully, meaningfully employed; belonging to a faith-based or other community of their peers; and being able to spend time with family, friends, and lovers.

In contrast to the kinds of goals we may expect (or fear) our clients to identify—such as being a rock star or the next president of the United States—these goals are both relatively modest and straightforward. Why, then, has it not been a simpler matter to address and meet these basic and everyday needs over the last 50 years of community mental health practice? If what people with psychiatric disabilities want is primarily "to live, work, learn, and participate fully in the community," what has made this so difficult to achieve? Another story suggests an answer.

A 57-year-old man in one of our previous studies, whom we will call Devon, complained to an interviewer about how empty and lonely his life had become since he was last released from the state psychiatric hospital nine months prior. When asked about his hopes for the future, Devon responded that he had no hopes to speak of, except for the hope that he would not have to suffer more than he had already. In his words, "I've been mentally ill for years, I'm mentally ill now, and I know I'll die mentally ill, I just hope I don't have to suffer too much more than I have already."

When asked more specifically about his mental illness, Devon explained that he had what the "doctors and nurses" told him was a "chemical imbalance" in his brain, for which he took several medications a day. None of the medications seemed to work properly, though, as Devon had yet to feel "balanced" enough to pursue any of things he acknowledged he most likely would have enjoyed, such as going out for pizza with other residents of the program, going to the movies, or getting a part-time job so he could better afford such activities. At this point in his life, he had become resigned to the thought that someone as "imbalanced" as he must be could do no more than smoke cigarettes and drink coffee while listening alone to the radio. At least, that is, until a medication comes along that "balances" him. (quoted in Davidson, Hoge, Merrill, Rakfeldt, & Griffith, 1995)

Action Theory and Creating the Possible from the Impossible

Transformation . . . is a way of creating something possible from the perceived impossible.

—DHHS, 2005, p. 1

Devon's situation represents a fundamental issue not only that he personally has to contend with but that transcends his particular circumstances and impedes the functioning of the mental health system as a whole. Consumer advocates have labeled this issue *mentalism* and perceive it to be a more basic and formidable barrier to recovery than the illness itself (Chamberlin, 1978, 1984; Deegan, 1992). As indicated by use of the suffix "-ism," mentalism is a form of prejudice directed against people who are perceived not to have all of their mental faculties intact—people considered, for example, to be mad, irrational, or insane. The unspoken, and largely unquestioned, assumption of mentalism is that people who are not diagnosed or labeled with a mental illness have all of their mental faculties intact (i.e., are rational, sane, etc.). In addition to there being a dearth of empirical evidence supporting this assumption, both the assumption itself and the prejudice derived from it are highly destructive influences in the lives of people with serious mental illness. But what could possibly be so destructive about such a simple assumption?

What is most destructive about this assumption is the demand it places upon people with serious mental illness—and, by extension, the practitioners who work with them—to be cured of their condition before they are allowed to resume or rejoin community life. It is for this reason that the path to community living has consistently been viewed as passing through compliance with treatments aimed at reducing symptoms and remediating deficits and/or through the acquisition of a variety of social, cognitive, or behavioral skills. Simply—yet importantly—stated, this assumption has led to a model of care in which *people with mental illness have to be rid of their illness first in order to participate fully in the lives of their communities.* Given that we do not yet have cures for serious mental illnesses, failing to meet this demand has led to a considerable amount of frustration, demoralization, and despair, not only on the part of individuals like Devon and others with serious mental illness but on the part of practitioners and systems of care as well.

But did we not already address this issue above when we suggested that people with serious mental illness, like people with paraplegia, need not wait to be cured of their illness in order to pursue their lives? Our focus then was on the person's decision and need to get on with his or her life while remaining disabled. Our point now—related to yet distinct from our earlier point—is that we have inherited a system of care that strenuously requires the opposite stance. It is not only Devon's personal decision to make, as if it were in a vacuum, as to whether or not he will resume his life in the face of mental illness. It is, even more importantly, an assumption of the system from which he receives care for this condition. It is as if the field of orthopedics had yet to accept the very idea of a wheelchair and instead insisted that people with paraplegia receive care and participate in rehabilitation programs until they regain their mobility, all the while lacking the technology or tools needed to be effective in restoring their mobility.

While this argument may sound absurd now, it was not that long ago that people with paraplegia were left largely up to their own devices to craft prostheses, and a life, outside of and with little help from the health care system. We suggest that this is analogous to where the current mental health system is in relation to the needs and desires of people with serious mental illness: offering little more than crutches or wooden carts to facilitate their inclusion in community activities. It is perhaps for this reason that so many people who initially do access mental health care choose not to follow through with prescribed treatments or actively refuse the services that are offered. Instead, they cobble together what supports they need and can find inside and outside of the mental health system in order to fashion as best a life they can, given the multitude of barriers to full participation that remain.

Readers who do not feel that the current situation warrants such a dire characterization are encouraged to consider the plight of the tens of thousands of people with serious mental illness who are still living out their lives confined to the locked wards and distant campuses of state mental hospitals around the country. How else are we to understand that caring professionals continue to insist that these people receive the same treatments and participate in the same rehabilitation programs they have already tried for upwards of 5, 10, 20, or 40 years, while nonetheless expecting different results?

If someone has sat through the same skills group twice a week for months, or years, without showing an appreciable improvement in skills acquisition, what reason do we have to think that the next several months, or years, will result in anything different? Our insistence on such an approach needs to be understood, we argue, as analogous to an orthopedic ward in a hospital focusing solely on the restoration of mobility through treatment, physical therapy, and exercise when none of these approaches is effective in enabling the patient to regain use of his or her legs. When a person with a prolonged, serious mental illness needs to be hospitalized at all, it is to assess his or her symptoms, functional deficits, and needs and to outfit him or her with a metaphorical wheelchair or other prosthesis to be used as a compensatory strategy or tool in his or her life. A hospital is no more a place for this person to live than it is for the person with paraplegia.

What we are suggesting is that our inherited approach to mental health care is based on the view that people need to be rid of their illness in order to have a life. Unfortunately, we do not yet possess such a cure for the most severe mental illnesses and are very limited in our ability to contain and/or minimize the effects of these illnesses. And if we do not yet have cures, why, then, do we insist on keeping people in hospitals until they "show sufficient improvement"? Maintaining "cure" as our singular goal dooms all of us, clients and practitioners alike, to inevitable failure—failures that are repeated over and over again, eventually leading to a sense of hopelessness such as that conveyed poignantly by Devon. As long as we continue to seek and fail to reach this unattainable goal, we will be destined to spin our wheels, placing Devon's life on hold indefinitely while consigning him to receiving ineffective yet endless doses of treatment and rehabilitation, with his time otherwise remaining empty. But why should Devon have to become what Deegan has referred to as "chemically balanced" in order to go out for pizza with friends, go to the movies, get a job, or, in general, have a life? We are, by law, no longer allowed to insist that a person wait to resume community life until he or she has overcome paraplegia or blindness. Why, then, do we continue to do so for people with mental illness?

Rather than offering speculations about the historical or political origins and functions of mentalism—a worthy topic, but one for a very different book—we will move on and offer what we hope will serve as a theoretical antidote to Devon's, and the mental health system's, demoralization and despair. This antidote is offered in the form of action theory, a perspective that we argue provides an especially useful conceptual framework for transformation to recovery-oriented care. To make this point concretely, we will examine alternative models of practice for the person with a serious mental illness: one model, based on mentalism, that is implicit in our current mental health system, and a second model, based on action theory, which we suggest for use in transformed systems of care.

Figure 1.1 depicts a model of practice in which prominent roles are occupied by the person's deficits and problems and the technical interventions offered by mental health practitioners in addressing these issues. Underlying assumptions of this model are that the

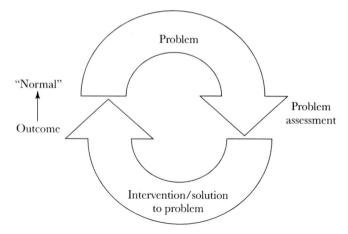

Figure 1.1 A deficit- and problem-oriented model. (*Source*: Davidson, Flanagan, Roe, & Styron, 2006.)

person was born more or less normal and then at some point in time developed a serious mental illness that robbed the person of his or her mental faculties. The illness and its associated impairments are then to be assessed and evaluated by mental health practitioners who are knowledgeable in the diagnosis of such issues and in the range of services and interventions available to address or reduce them, with the eventual, desired outcome being that the person is rid of the illness and restored to normality. Until such a time, however, the person is confined to the "sick role" of mental patient, and his or her activity is centered on receiving treatments or participating in rehabilitation programs aimed at restoring his or her functioning.

In practice, of course, the outcome of being rid of the illness or restored to normality is seldom achieved in the acute-care settings that dominate many systems of care, a fact that we typically blame on the illness itself (e.g., the traditionally poor prognosis associated with schizophrenia), the person's refusal to adhere to prescribed treatments, or other maladaptive behaviors (e.g., substance abuse). What is not questioned by this model is what sense it makes for us to view people as entities who can be normal or not to begin with, what can reasonably be expected from episodes of acute care within the context of prolonged conditions, and what roles a person can play in addressing, reducing, or overcoming his or her own problems. The person, as a flawed or fundamentally deficient object, is to be fixed from the outside, even if it is through the compassionate intervention of caring others (Davidson, 1997).

In the trainings on recovery-oriented practice we have been conducting over the previous five years, we have found it useful to refer to this model as the "couch potato" model of mental illness and treatment. Rather than launching into lengthy expositions of action theory, we have suggested that some prior approaches to treatment and rehabilitation have viewed and treated people in treatment as if they were immobile, inert things that needed to be stimulated and guided from the outside. The assumption has been that, left up to his or her own devices, the person, and the world in which he or she lives, would stay essentially the same, or perhaps deteriorate through atrophy.

Direct care staff readily identify with this challenge of prodding a withdrawn, isolative, and seemingly apathetic person off of his or her metaphorical (and possibly literal) couch, and have no difficulty sharing stories and examples of all of the efforts they have already made to do so, many of which they view as having failed. Even when their clients go along with staff suggestions, the effects of these excursions seldom appear to pay off in the way they had hoped. A staff-led outing to the grocery store or shopping mall, for example, seldom results in an individual client's taking the initiative to buy his or her own groceries or clothes. On the other hand, when their clients decide to get up off the couch on their own initiative—defying their couch potato sentence—they often show what staff view as poor judgment or engage in what staff consider high-risk or otherwise maladaptive behaviors such as abusing substances, squandering their limited income on cigarettes or other "unnecessary" expenses, hanging out with the wrong crowd, etc. Why work so hard trying to lead this horse to water, they ask in frustration, when he or she persistently refuses to drink?

In lighter moments, this situation reminds us of Harry Stack Sullivan's infamous remark that if you think people with paranoid schizophrenia are fragile, just try to change them. More to the point, however, is how unhelpful this approach is. *People with serious mental illness no more ask or want to be "changed" than people with other serious illnesses such as asthma, diabetes, or cancer. What they want is help in managing, living with, and/or recovering from their illness to the maximum degree possible.*

In doing so, no matter how much they may appear on the surface to resemble couch potatoes, they are more accurately, in light of action theory, conceptualized as trains churning down the tracks. They are always already in motion: making decisions, acting, and contributing to the ongoing generation of our shared world—even if they have come, through years of failed efforts, repeated losses, stigma, discrimination, and demoralization, to view themselves as having no real options.

We must be careful under such circumstances not to contribute to such a view or to ask, or insist, that people remain at the station and wait to be repaired before they resume their lives on the tracks. Action theory suggests that, unlike locomotives, it is not possible for people to stand entirely still; for them to attempt to do so is to mimic, and hasten, their own death. Insisting that people with mental illness be free from the signs or symptoms of an illness prior to their rejoining community life is to delay indefinitely the *beginning* of their recovery. And like justice, recovery delayed amounts in the end to recovery denied (Davidson, 2006).

It is useful to note in this respect that the definitions of recovery in serious mental illnesses that have surfaced in the field both prior to and following the New Freedom Commission report consistently emphasize the importance of having a life despite ongoing disability (Davidson, O'Connell, Tondora, Staeheli, & Evans, 2005). The definition of recovery that we have used in our own system transformation efforts, for example, describes recovery as "a process of restoring a meaningful sense of belonging to one's community and positive sense of identity apart from one's condition while rebuilding a life despite or within the limitations imposed by that condition" (Davidson et al., 2007).

In this case, recovery entails not so much cessation of symptoms or remediation of deficits as it does the person's efforts to live a meaningful and gratifying life in the presence of ongoing disorder—much as one might do in the face of asthma or diabetes. To the degree that this form of recovery refers to the "real life experience of persons as they accept and overcome the challenge of the disability" (Deegan, 1988, p. 150), it is his or her engagement in these experiences that matter more than the person's clinical or functional status (Davidson, Staeheli, Stayner, & Sells, 2004).

Figure 1.2 is meant to depict an action theory model of psychiatric practice as an alternative to the couch potato model in

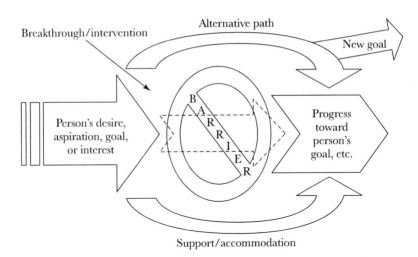

Figure 1.2 An action-oriented model. (*Source*: Davidson, Flanagan, Roe, & Styron, 2006.)

Figure 1.1. This so-called speeding locomotive model assumes that the person is always already in motion, directed toward his or her own interests and goals, and in pursuit of his or her own desires. Assistance may be requested or accepted when *the person* perceives that obstacles are in the way, or when he or she cannot continue this pursuit without the involvement of other people, but not necessarily when it is only other people who perceive a problem.

This, again, helps account for why so many people with serious mental illness do not seek care on their own early in the course of illness and may actively refuse the help others try to offer. This fact should not be used as justification, or as an excuse, for abandoning people to the ravages of the illness, however. It rather should encourage policy makers, family members, and practitioners to view educating this person about the nature of his or her difficulties as a first and very important task in supporting the person with a serious mental illness (Davidson, Tondora, et al., 2006)—preferably even before those difficulties take hold. Until we address stigma and provide education about mental illness as a matter of course, both in schools and in our communities, people will continue not to know what is happening to them when they begin to experience the early signs and symptoms of mental illness. In order to afford them the dignity and autonomy that is theirs as sovereign agents, we should offer education about these issues as our first approach. Despite its obviousness, this has yet to become common practice.

Returning to the model depicted in Figure 1.2, it follows from the priority we have given to the person's own goals and interests that any interventions or assistance mental health practitioners seek to provide should then be framed in terms of their utility in promoting the person's own agenda. Although some people will agree to take antipsychotic medication simply to make their symptoms go away, many others refuse to take it or take it only sporadically, as a result of the implicit cost–benefit analysis they conduct on their own (Lieberman et al., 2005). While taking the medication may quiet the voices, for example, it also may make the individual too fatigued to work. It is when medication or other interventions help them have the kind of life they want to have that people are most likely to choose to use or engage in them over time.

Within this context, mental health interventions are to be judged in terms of their efficacy not only in reducing the illness and its associated effects but also in promoting the person's ability to engage in the kind of activities that interest or appeal to him or her. Note that we did not suggest judging the efficacy of these interventions in terms of the person's success or "outcomes," as these may be influenced by a range of factors outside of the person's and the mental health system's control. In addition, the notion of "outcome" is problematic within the framework of action theory as long as an outcome is conceptualized, as it typically is, as a static or enduring end state. The only tangible outcome for human agents in this sense is their eventual death. Short of this, we are always already in motion, and our world is constantly evolving; our focus needs to remain on the activity itself rather than on its intended achievement of a fleeting state of being.

In promoting a person's activity, the mental health practitioner thus has several options, some of which are outlined in Figure 1.2. The first, and perhaps most obvious, possibility is to assist the person in removing or breaking through the perceived barrier. In the case of the more serious and disabling mental illnesses, however, the barriers are not so easily removed or broken through. Equally likely will be the necessity of the staff's exploration of the need for ongoing support or accommodation on the one hand and assisting their clients to explore alternative paths to their goals on the other.

As we have learned over the last decade through the practices of supported employment, education, and socialization (Becker & Drake, 1994; Davidson, Shahar, et al., 2004; Drake et al., 1994; Wehman, 1986), a woman who may at a given time be too disabled to raise children may begin instead by volunteering at a day care or community center or being employed at an animal shelter. A man with interests in aviation and aerospace may begin by working in a retail or fast food venue at an airport. For both client and staff, it will be important to hold out the possibility either that the first step will lead to a second and then a third step, moving the person incrementally toward his or her initial goal, or that the alternative path chosen may over time lead to the identification of a new and equally, if not more, compelling goal than the initial one.

One of the more important implications of action theory for practice is that the nature of the goal in and of itself is not as important as the person's engagement in meaningful and productive activity that moves him or her toward a goal. It is both pointless and the source of considerable frustration and demoralization for us to insist that clients drink the water to which they have been led. Clients, like horses, will drink when they are thirsty or when they find the water appealing. Efforts to persuade clients to drink when they are neither thirsty nor in the least enticed by the water will most often lead to failure.

In one of our earlier studies, a woman who was assigned to an assertive community treatment team responded to a research interviewer's query about her first impressions of the team with the comment, "Well, they seem to be running around and making a lot of plans for me, but they have no idea who I am" (Chinman, Allende, Bailey, Maust, & Davidson, 1999). Staff time and energy would appear to be better spent in getting to know the person and exploring and identifying his or her interests, desires, and goals, as well as the barriers he or she encounters in relation to them, before attempting to make such plans. Such efforts will make it more likely that the client will eventually drink the water he or she has been led to, but also, and more importantly, that he or she will take an active role in blazing his or her own trail to the river bank. The various ways practitioners can support people in their efforts to do so is a central focus of the remainder of this volume.

2   A Model of Being in Recovery as a Foundation for Recovery-Oriented Practice

We begin this second chapter where we left off in the preceding one, with the question of what is involved in the work of recovery and how practitioners can best support this work. On one hand, we understand the answer to this question to be very much a work in progress. There is much still to learn about recovery and recovery-oriented care, and we consider the field—including our own efforts in this regard—to be in the very early stages of its development. On the other hand, we have begun to learn some things about what processes of recovery entail and what the provision of recovery-oriented care looks like in practice, as well as about some of the structural conditions necessary for this kind of care to be implemented.

In this chapter, we share some of these lessons by describing components and processes of being in recovery that we have integrated into a model that can then serve as the foundation for developing recovery-oriented practices. The assumption of this approach, as we mentioned in the previous chapter, is that this form of recovery is primarily the responsibility of the person with a serious mental illness. What practitioners do should thus be oriented to supporting and facilitating the person's own efforts. We describe this perspective as a "bottom up" approach to service development, as it begins with the needs, preferences, and goals of the person in recovery—not only at the individual level of a person's "recovery plan" but also at the collective level of the system as a whole. What services and supports should a mental health system offer? Those, we suggest, that will enable persons with serious mental illness to lead safe, dignified, and gratifying lives beyond the illness—when possible—or, when that is not possible, within the boundaries imposed by the illness.

Before turning to the question of what services and supports we need to offer to promote and sustain recovery, we need to understand better what being in recovery entails. To frame the question in this way is not to ignore the other form of recovery (i.e., recovery from mental illness). Rather, we view "being in recovery" as the more inclusive of the two concepts. Processes involved in a person's entering into and being in recovery include the processes that appear to lead to a reduction in the illness as well. The opposite, however, would not necessarily be true. In other words, if we begin with describing the processes involved in minimizing deficit, disability, and dysfunction, we may never arrive at processes of maximizing the person's health and everyday life. Beginning with the person's everyday life and his or her efforts to live with the illness, on the other hand, naturally extends to efforts to minimize the illness as disrupting or posing barriers to that life. In brief, minimizing illness is not the same as maximizing health, and our model must incorporate both.

This chapter describes the nine components of recovery processes we have identified through a combination of qualitative research and a review of first-person accounts and the existing literature on recovery. These 9 components predate, but overlap and are similar to, the 10 components identified by the federal Substance Abuse and Mental Health Services Administration (SAMHSA) in its consensus definition of recovery (DHHS, 2005). We use each of these components as the basis for identifying and developing recovery-oriented practices and supports. As is evident in Tables 2.1 through 2.9, this bottom-up approach involved people with serious mental illnesses first describing what this component of recovery looked like for them (column 1), deriving from that what practices and supports needed to be provided to promote this aspect of recovery (column 2), and from that deriving the ways in which programs and systems needed to be structured and managed in order to provide such supports and practices (column 3).

At the levels of (1) practices and supports and (2) programs and systems, it becomes possible to develop instruments for measuring recovery-oriented practices associated with each component of recovery. The initial measures we have developed to assess both providers' understandings of and attitudes toward these components and the recovery orientation of a program or system of care linked to each domain are provided in the Appendix.

A Model of Being in Recovery

The data used for this section were derived from two primary sources, the first of which being hundreds of narrative, qualitative interviews conducted with people who were living effectively with (i.e., who were "in recovery," whether or not they used that phrase) or had recovered from a serious mental illness over the previous 15 years. These data were collected through a series of studies conducted in Italy, Norway, Sweden, and the United States in collaboration with several additional investigators, including, primarily, John Strauss, Jaak Rakfeldt, Dave Sells, Marit Borg, Isabel Marin, Roberto Mezzina, and Alain Topor. Detailed findings from these studies can be found in Davidson (2003) and in two special issues of the *American Journal of Psychiatric Rehabilitation* edited by Davidson, Sells, and Lawless (2005, 2006). The second source is first-person accounts of people in recovery and other investigators who have described processes and components of being in recovery.

For ease of comprehension, we begin with a narrative that sets the stage for the person to enter recovery. We then continue this narrative to describe each component as it has been experienced by people in recovery, alternating between this ongoing narrative and our efforts to conceptualize each component and link it with previous research. What follows results in an iterative process of moving back and forth between concepts and stories. With the exception of published first-person accounts, all names and other identifying features of the principals in these stories have been omitted or changed to protect the individuals' privacy.

> *"I didn't accept myself but I didn't know what I should do to get better."*
> *"I still see things around me, but I don't pay attention to them."*
> *"I tried above all to feel as if I were a 'normal' person."*

These three quotes reflect well the overall process people describe moving through in their recovery, and they provide a useful framework for this chapter. This process involves grappling with the onset of the illness, fighting or digging one's way out from under the ravages of the illness, and reestablishing a sense of routine everydayness: a sense of normacy not to be confused with usual meanings of the term *normal.* As Lilly, a Norwegian woman in one of our studies, described it, this sense of normalcy refers to having only the usual worries of everyday life to fret about. We will now explore each of these processes in a bit more detail.

> *I didn't accept myself but I didn't know what I should do to get better.*
> (Davidson, Borg, et al., 2005, p. 183)

This statement points to an early source of distress, and a major challenge, that is faced initially by many people experiencing the onset of a serious mental illness. Having a range of unprecedented and inexplicable experiences that appear to come out of nowhere, people find themselves unable to do things they used to do or in the ways in which they used to do them, and they gradually begin to lose hold of who they used to be. For the most part, people are unprepared for the onslaught of a serious mental illness and initially have no idea of what to do or how to survive, let alone manage, these new experiences. They are aware of no longer being "themselves" to some degree, but they have no idea of how to return from whence they came or where to turn for help. We might understand this situation as somewhat similar to Dorothy's in *The Wizard of Oz* when she recognizes that she is no longer in Kansas but has yet to encounter Glinda, the good witch.

In this situation, people are confronted continually with the new problems, sensations, and thoughts that are part of the mental illness—an experience that is more difficult to the degree that they find their customary ways of dealing with other stresses or difficult situations to fall well short of being adequate to the task at hand. As Tom reported:

> It's been an ongoing thing now . . . and it's something that I'm still struggling with. It's part of mental illness . . . I feel very isolated and alone and sort of go through this thing where I feel like nobody cares . . . and I kind of get out of it . . . It distracts me so much [that] even though I was with another person, I was still locked inside this misery . . . It's like being sick. It's like being nauseated or having a really bad headache and you're trying to

relate, but there's something bothering you. It's a distraction, you know . . . Like if you have a headache or something, you can relate, but there's always that pain, so you're going to be thinking of that pain. . . . (Davidson, Haglund, et al., 2001, p. 282)

This situation presents at least two primary challenges: (1) finding ways to manage the illness so that it is less disruptive, while (2) finding ways to connect to others despite the illness and its disruptive effects. We might frame the first task as "taming" the mental illness: finding ways to understand and minimize the intrusions and disruptions brought about by the illness in their everyday lives. Some individuals perhaps never come to identify their illness as an alien influence that needs to be tamed. For most individuals, however, this "taming" appears to require a prolonged process in which they gradually come to recognize or understand that there is now something new going on that they must figure out a way to manage if it is not to take over, and ruin, their lives as a whole. As noted above, most people are unprepared for this challenge, having never learned anything about, or having only common misperceptions of, mental illness. As Ulric described:

It took several years before I realized that this is something you have to work with, and really have a conscious relationship to, because in the beginning I guess I thought that this is sort of like breaking a leg. I thought it would take two or three years and then it would pass and it wasn't like that. It took some time for me to realize that. (Davidson, Borg, et al., 2005, p. 184)

For this realization to be channeled into constructive action on the person's part, a number of additional ingredients appear to be required. First and foremost among these is the role of *hope* in offering the person the possibility of a better life. In the words of Vivian, it is "hope of knowing that everything that is, that I go through, would not continue the rest of my life, that there would be an end of it and just knowing that I knew that I could keep going" (Davidson, Borg, et al., 2005, p. 184). In addition to hope, the person apparently needs to have the desire and *commitment* to contain the mental illness and its damage, what people have described as a determination to "get better." As Vivian continued, "My desire to get better, maybe the good fortune to finally realize that health is a precious thing . . . it's a matter of will power, of believing in myself, pushing myself" (Davidson, Borg, et al., 2005, p. 185).

This challenge of believing in oneself and pushing oneself, as it were, into the foreground to do battle with the mental illness is made more difficult by virtue of the fact that the illness and its associated effects will already have wreaked considerable havoc on the person's sense of self, confidence, and capacity. As Eric remarked, "The whole story of my health was a very difficult experience because I had to really reconstruct myself as a person" (Davidson, Borg, et al., 2005, p. 185). With the person's having taken a beating and suffered repeated losses and failures, this process of reconstruction often needs to begin in small steps with what may seem like trivial or insignificant accomplishments to outside observers. To the person himself or herself, however, these accomplishments may involve considerable effort, patience, and persistence over time and may embody his or her hope for a reconstructed self and a better future. As Candace described,

> Before I was in recovery I felt I couldn't do anything right. I constantly felt that I was stupid and dumb and everything my father told me. . . . But then I realized that . . . I'm not stupid and I'm not dumb, that I actually know quite a bit, and that I have a lot of knowledge and that if it wasn't for the knowledge that I have a lot of people wouldn't have gotten, you know, a lot of things . . . I've been able to make up recipes from scratch without, just thinking of put this together or that together and, you know, come up with a recipe, and have an idea of doing up a newsletter and dreaming up what to do and coming up with it and devising it and I've done that. (Davidson, Borg, et al., 2005, p. 185)

These accomplishments become possible and noticeable when the person begins to set and achieve realistic and short-term, if not immediate, personal goals such as getting out of bed, following a recipe, putting together a newsletter, or attending a class. In each case, these are activities the person must engage in himself or herself; they are not things that can be done for the person by caring and well-intended others. As Lilly emphasized, "I did this and no one told me to do it, I did it on my own and it works, for me" (Davidson, Borg, et al., 2005, p. 185). With these incremental steps the person is afforded an opportunity to see a gradual rebuilding of his or her abilities, competencies, and gifts, no longer feeling utterly bereft of value or worth.

As indicated in Table 2.1, we describe a first component of being in recovery involved in the narrative up to this point—that of *renewing hope and commitment* to one's life. Persons in recovery describe the importance of having hope and believing in the possibility of a renewed sense of self and purpose in the process of recovery (Davidson, Stayner, et al., 2001; Deegan, 1996b; Fisher, 1994; Jacobson & Curtis, 2000; Jacobson & Greenley, 2001; Mead & Copeland, 2000; Smith, 2000). This hope is based on a sense—no matter how vague or insignificant it may at first appear—that life can hold more for one than it currently does, and it inspires a desire and motivation to improve one's lot or to enter into and pursue recovery (Smith, 2000; Young & Ensing, 1999).

Among other sources to be described below, such a sense of hope might stem from seeing other people who have suffered in the same way and experienced the same challenges as the sick person and who are now living better or more fulfilling lives, thus suggesting a central role for peer mentoring or support in a recovery-oriented system. To support this component, a recovery-oriented system also will communicate a sense of hope by focusing on strengths and competencies, by using a language that reflects belief in potential and possibility, and by encouraging people to take risks (Deegan, 2001; Ridgway, 2001; Smith, 2000).

Peer role models are only one potential source of hope, of course. Many people describe hope as primarily coming from others, though, and who these others are varies considerably from person to person and culture to culture. This refers us to the second identified challenge: finding ways to connect to others despite the ongoing disruptiveness of the illness. The inescapably social nature of hope, and of the recovery process overall, implicated in this challenge is captured in part in Table 2.2, which describes a second important component of recovery as *being supported by others.*

What appears to be crucial to people in recovery in relation to this component is that they be *supported*, accepted, and, if possible, loved as a person of value and worth (i.e., not as a "mental patient"). This sense of being accepted and supported can stem from family and friends who knew and loved the person before he or she developed a serious mental illness and who continue to stand by the person

Table 2.1 Renewing Hope and Commitment

Person in Recovery	Service Provider	Manager/Administrator	Recovery Markers
To me, recovery means …	*I can support people in their recovery by …*	*I can lead an organization that supports recovery by …*	*We will know that we are working together toward recovery when …*
• having a reason to get out of bed. • having a sense that my life can get better. • being able to tackle every day. • realizing that there is more to life than mental illness. • feeling good about the future. • being determined to live well and take care of myself. • believing I can manage my life and reach my goals. • having dreams again. • having people I can count on.	• focusing on strengths. • complimenting people respectfully on their successes. • believing in the potential for growth and improvement Recovery is a possibility for everyone! • using a language of hope and possibility. • being hopeful even when clients cannot be. • understanding that recovery is an individualized process.	• reinforcing staff attitudes and activities that promote wellness and recovery. • providing education and training in recovery and recovery-oriented practices for people in recovery and for staff. • employing people in recovery to serve as role models and sources of hope for peers. • holding the agency accountable for implementation of "preferred practices," which have been shown to promote recovery from behavioral health disorders.	• staff pay as much attention to people who are doing well as to those who are struggling. • staff believe in the ability of people to recover.

Table 2.2 Being Supported by Others

Person in Recovery	Service Provider	Manager/Administrator	Recovery Markers
To me, recovery means …	*I can support people in their recovery by …*	*I can lead an organization that supports recovery by …*	*We will know that we are working together toward recovery when …*
• having people I can count on. • being loved and accepted as I am. • having people in my life who believe in me even when I don't believe in myself. • having something to give back. • feeling like a worthwhile human being. • being able to help others when they need me.	• helping people develop lasting connections to communities and natural supports. • being willing to include these natural supports in the recovery planning process. • being willing to help people get their basic needs met in the community (e.g., managing benefits and finding financial resources, food, shelter, and safety). • believing in people and sharing that belief with others. • being an "advocate" as well as a "provider." • valuing and exploring spirituality as a potentially critical source of support.	• educating staff and others about natural support networks and how to build them. • developing structured educational programs for families and members of natural support networks. • offering to host local, regional, statewide, and national consumer and family support services such as National Alliance on Mental Illness or other advocacy groups. • valuing and fostering use of peer-support and self-help throughout the agency.	• staff help build connections with neighborhoods and communities. • services are provided in natural environments. • peer support is facilitated and utilized. • natural supports are relied upon.

despite the ravages of the illness. One person who experienced such acceptance is Tyra, who described her grandmother's support in the following terms: "When I was going through my psychotic changes she was always there for me. She never turned her back on me."

For others it can be people whom they have met since they developed an illness but who are able to see beyond or behind the illness to the person who remains. This can be a mental health practitioner, but it more often appears to be someone with whom the person has developed a mutual, reciprocal relationship that extends beyond the boundaries of mental health settings. As Nate explained after describing the importance of having a girlfriend in his life after many years of isolation, "I'm nobody till somebody loves me. That's the way I look at it."

Some people appear to derive this basic sense of acceptance from God, or possibly through delusions (e.g., as mediated through hallucinated voices). The role of this form of acceptance in recovery is unclear. What is clear is that people who have become accustomed to passive roles of receiving help, assistance, and care from others often find a first step toward gaining a sense of value and worth through helping others—what they frequently describe as "giving back." As Timothy, who at the time was still struggling with a long history of disability and institutionalization, described:

> I could choose to be a nobody, a nothing, and just [say] "the hell with it, the hell with everything, I'm not going to deal with anything." And there are times when I feel like that. And yet, I'm part of the world, I'm a human being. And human beings usually kind of do things together to help each other out . . . And I want to be part of that . . . If you're not part of the world, it's pretty miserable, pretty lonely. So I think [a] degree of involvement is important . . . involvement in some kind of activity. Hopefully an activity which benefits somebody. [That gives me the sense that] I have something to offer . . . that's all I'm talking about. (Davidson, Stayner, et al., 2001)

Jorge described an added bonus to being in such a relationship with others: the feedback that may come along with it. As he described:

> It made me feel like I was being helpful and in situations like that I don't think so much about my illness. It kind of goes on

the back burner because sometimes I just think about my illness and it seems like when I'm helping somebody or somebody says something nice to me . . . as soon as people say that, oh, you look good, things like that, it makes me feel better about myself.

Finally, for others this sense of acceptance and belonging may come from animals, including both beloved pets and other animals they might associate with under different circumstances. Mira, for example, described the crucial role that volunteering at an animal shelter had played in her regaining a sense of self-worth. As another example, Eliot described the perhaps unexpected benefit that came from his participation in a riding program offered through his social club:

I think [riding the horse] helped me . . . It relaxed me. And, well, I guess it made me feel like the horse loved me. Spending time with the horse, it felt like unconditional love . . . you connect with the animal and with yourself and you're outdoors and it does something to you. It's hard to explain, but when you go home you think, "Wow, another lesson! Wow, I'm getting better!"

As we noted earlier, we have tried to capture this sense of recovery's being a social process (Jacobson & Greenley, 2001) in a second component labeled *being supported by others*. People in recovery often describe the importance of having someone believe in them, especially when they could not believe in themselves. Having supportive others, whether they are family members, professionals, community members, peers, or animals, to provide encouragement through the difficult times and to help celebrate the good has been noted as being critical to recovery (Ridgway, 2001; Smith, 2000; Sullivan, 1994). People in recovery also speak of the importance of having a person in recovery as a mentor or role model as they go through their journey. Role models help people know what recovery looks like and give them ideas about what to hope for (Baxter & Diehl, 1998; Fisher, 1994; Mead & Copeland, 2000; Ridgway, 2001; Young & Ensing, 1999). A recovery-oriented system will thus help people develop lasting connections to individuals in their communities, family, peers, and other people in recovery.

Table 2.3 Finding Your Niche in the Community

Person in Recovery	Service Provider	Manager/Administrator	Recovery Markers
To me, recovery means …	*I can support people in their recovery by …*	*I can lead an organization that supports recovery by …*	*We will know that we are working together toward recovery when …*
• getting involved in things I enjoy (e.g., attending church, volunteering, dating, taking classes, playing sports, visiting friends, attending support groups). • having nice places to hang out with my friends. • having a routine I enjoy. • making new friends. • catching up with old friends. • filling my day with things I like.	• supporting involvement in valued social roles. • highlighting employment as a path to recovery. • promoting leisure activities and hobbies based on each individual's interests. • being able to complete an assessment that focuses on a person's strengths as they relate to education, work, and leisure. • being knowledgeable of the full range of rehabilitation and community services that can help people achieve their goals and deliver services outside the boundaries of the treatment system in "in vivo" settings. • addressing medical or physical issues that might prevent people from pursuing social interests and hobbies.	• viewing reconnection to the community as a primary goal of services and reducing/fading services as people achieve that goal. • designating agency staff that are responsible for leading community integration initiatives. • assuring that these initiatives are valued and supported by all staff. • maintaining agency hours that do not conflict with normal life activities such as employment (e.g., adopt certain evening hours). • establishing outcome measures that evaluate services and providers based on their ability to help people achieve their individualized goals rather than arbitrary system indicators.	• staff play a primary role in helping people become involved in non-mental-health/ addiction-related activities. • services move beyond symptom management and focus on developing career and life goals, hobbies, and interests.

As Timothy mentioned in his quote, "human beings usually kind of do things together to help each other out," and the things they do usually entail "involvement in some kind of activity." This brings us to the third component of recovery, which we describe as *finding one's niche in the community*, as indicated in Table 2.3. This aspect of recovery involves the development of valued social roles in the community through involvement in meaningful activities (Anthony, 1993; Davidson, Stayner, et al., 2001; Ridgway, 2001; Young & Ensing, 1999). What is it that people have to offer as they regain the sense of being a worthwhile or valued person? The answer to this question provides the person with a sense of purpose and direction in his or her life. A recovery-oriented system will thus help people develop roles other than "mental patient" through employment or volunteering, developing hobbies and leisure activities, and connecting with organizations or groups of which they can be a part. Up to 70% of people in recovery express a desire to work, making employment a central way in which people can achieve more meaning and purpose in their lives and thus a key pathway to recovery (Fisher, n.d.; Rogers, 1995; Sullivan, 1994). Many people in recovery also discuss the importance of believing in something, of having faith in a higher or transcendent power (Sullivan, 1994). This suggests that spirituality and belonging to a faith community may be additional important activities or pursuits for people in recovery, offering additional foci for recovery-oriented systems of care.

As a natural extension of feeling accepted as a worthwhile person occupying a meaningful social niche, we describe a fourth component of recovery as *redefining self.* The redefinition of oneself as a person of whom mental illness is simply one part may be one of the most essential and overarching aspects of recovery. Mental illness has been described as a disease of the self (Estroff, 1989). Not only does a person experience psychological and emotional symptoms, social consequences, and stigma, but historically he or she may also have been socialized into assuming the role and identity of a mental patient. Such a role may have been reinforced by a system that has traditionally valued and rewarded compliance and passivity. As a result, for some people the process of recovery requires reconceptualizing their personal identity or definition of self to be expanded beyond the constricted role of "patient."

In our own consultation work, we unfortunately encounter the need for this component frequently when first meeting some people

Table 2.4 Recovery Dimension: Redefining Self

Person in Recovery	Service Provider	Manager/Administrator	Recovery Markers
To me, recovery means …	*I can support people in their recovery by …*	*I can lead an organization that supports recovery by …*	*We will know that we are working together toward recovery when …*
• seeing myself as a person with strengths and resources. • knowing my illness is only a small part of who I am. • not allowing "label" or a diagnosis to take control my life. • exploring life outside the mental health system. • learning what I have to offer. • proving wrong the people who said I'd never do anything with my life.	• helping people become more involved in valued social roles. • being responsive to their cultural preferences and values. • focusing on people as whole beings, not just on their illness. • using "person-first" language. • having the skills to allow people to share their personal experiences and how those experiences inform their worldview. • helping people plan for their life beyond the service system. • working "with" and not "for" people.	• promoting, using, and remaining faithful to a new language that reflects recovery-based and person-first principles. • supporting the concept that treatment involves helping people find their niche in the community, NOT merely symptom management. • conducting "asset mapping" of community places and resources (i.e., identify places that welcome and support people in recovery in positive roles). • establishing relationships with community organizations beyond the mental health service system (e.g., Adult Departments of Recreation, local civic and volunteer groups, faith communities, educational institutions, Chambers of Commerce).	• staff are knowledgeable about special interest groups and community activities. • staff are diverse in terms of culture, ethnicity, lifestyle, and interests. • opportunities are provided for people in recovery to discuss sexual and spiritual needs. • exit criteria are clearly defined.

with serious mental illness within the context of mixed staff-and-patient focus groups in hospital or community mental health settings. Such individuals will introduce themselves—in contrast to staff, who identify themselves by title or discipline—as being "just a patient." A typical response from one of us, acting as a consultant, of "Surely you're much more than 'just a patient,'" or something equivalent to that, is typically met with a blank stare or puzzled expression. It would appear that in these settings, few if any other positive roles or identities are available.

The need to redefine oneself may be due not solely to stigma, discrimination, and negative experiences of mental health services and settings, however, but also to aspects of the illness itself. In this case, component four overlaps with component five, which we describe as *incorporating illness.*

What we describe as *incorporating illness* is not to be confused with traditional notions of "accepting" one's illness, if by *acceptance* we denote a passive stance of resignation. What we describe as *incorporating illness,* both into one's identity and into one's everyday life, appears to be a highly active and determined process that overlaps also with the next component, *managing symptoms* (see later discussion). We distinguish this component from redefining self by focusing it more specifically on the person's role in "taming" or coming to understand and integrate the illness per se, while the focus of the fourth component is obviously more on the implications of this incorporation for the person's sense of self. We also distinguish this component from the following component (number six) of managing symptoms, because some symptoms may be incorporated without being managed and others may be managed without necessarily being incorporated into the person's sense of self (i.e., they may remain "other").

In this respect, the research literature and first-person accounts are consistent in suggesting that coming to some sense of understanding and incorporating the illness are essential steps in recovery (Hatfield, 1994; Munetz & Frese, 2001; Smith, 2000; Sullivan, 1994; Young & Ensing, 1999). This is not to say that a person must accept a particular framework or conceptual model of illness (e.g., a biological brain disease) in order to be in recovery any more than a person has to accept the identity of being a "mental patient." *Incorporating illness,* rather, refers to the person's active role in understanding his or her anomalous experiences and finding adaptive ways to assimilate

Table 2.5 Incorporating Illness

Person in Recovery	Service Provider	Manager/Administrator	Recovery Markers
To me, recovery means …	*I can support people in their recovery by …*	*I can lead an organization that supports recovery by …*	*We will know that we are working together toward recovery when …*
• knowing when I need to ask for help. • not feeling defeated. • dealing with setbacks. • avoiding the things that make me feel bad. • knowing how to take care of myself in good times and in bad. • accepting that there are some things that I can't do yet. • being proud of the things I can do. • taking one day at a time.	• following their lead and supporting them in their unique path toward recovery. • learning more about the recovery process by participating in educational activities led by persons in recovery. • referring to prominent role models who have experienced success and happiness despite mental illness.	• organizing staff training or conferences and inviting people in recovery to share their stories. • valuing the input of people in recovery by employing them or paying them for time spent on service planning, implementation, and evaluation activities.	• the agency provides formal opportunities for people in recovery, family members, service providers, and administrators to learn about recovery. • persons in recovery facilitate staff trainings.

this understanding into his or her everyday life and identity (Ridgway, 2001).

To promote this process, a recovery-oriented system will work toward creating a more welcoming and healing environment in which people can acknowledge their difficulties and be educated about the illness without losing their status, value, or identity. This education can be provided by people with first-hand experiences of illness and recovery, as well as by mental health professionals. Recovery-oriented systems also will invest in educating the public about mental illnesses and the need for timely access to effective care, so that the onset of a serious mental illness will not be quite as unexpected and inexplicable when it emerges in a person or in one's friends or loved ones as it tends to be today.

By describing the next component as *managing symptoms,* we *explicitly* acknowledge both that complete symptom remission is unnecessary for a person to be in recovery and that most people also find it necessary nonetheless to gain some degree of control over their symptoms (Fisher, 1994; Ridgway, 2001). The method by which people come to manage their symptoms does not seem to be as important as the fact that they do, and this can involve medication, education, peer support, psychotherapy, or alternative methods of healing and self-help. Throughout all of these options, being in recovery involves actively using treatment, services, supports, or other resources rather than being only a passive recipient of care provided by others (Deegan, 1996b; Ridgway, 2001).

A recovery-oriented system that appreciates that each person's recovery journey is unique will therefore offer access to and education about a variety of methods of help, from which people can choose those that will work best for them. As people in recovery and their loved ones in this way have the most intimate knowledge of what is effective in helping them manage the symptoms and other challenges associated with the illness, such a system will provide ample opportunities for, and actively seek input from, people in recovery and family members. The system will then use this input as a primary driver in all aspects of service planning, development, and implementation.

While conceptually it makes sense to distinguish components four, five, and six from one another, in real life, and therefore in qualitative research, these three components are most often interwoven. We see this if we return to the second quote with which we

Table 2.6 Managing Symptoms

Person in Recovery	Service Provider	Manager/Administrator	Recovery Markers
To me, recovery means ...	*I can support people in their recovery by ...*	*I can lead an organization that supports recovery by ...*	*We will know that we are working together toward recovery when ...*
• learning how my illness affects me. • asking questions when I don't understand something. • having ways to cope and be good to myself. • controlling my symptoms so that they don't get in the way of my life. • understanding what medication can and cannot do for me. • finding other tools to help me in my recovery. • knowing when to ask for help. • taking time to relax.	• providing access to/education about a variety of methods. • providing culturally responsive care that reflects appreciation of the cultural context of recovery. • understanding that medication is only one tool in the recovery toolbox and that not *all* people require medication to recover. • working with people to develop relapse prevention strategies, including advance directives. • teaching illness self-management so that people use their own experiences and knowledge to apply strategies that work best for them.	• cultivating an organization in which management of symptoms is not done in a "clinical vacuum" but crosses disciplines and aims to reduce the day-to-day impact of symptoms on work, school, home life, etc. • providing training in evidence-based practices such as illness self-management. • having minimal entry criteria for specialized rehabilitation (e.g., do not demand "work readiness" as a prerequisite for entry to vocational rehabilitation).	• the agency provides a variety of treatment options. • the agency offers specific services and programs for individuals with different cultures, life experiences, interests, and needs. • procedures are in place to facilitate referrals to more suitable programs.

- giving myself some slack.
- giving myself permission to be human.

- understanding that symptoms do not have to be eliminated before people can pursue recovery.
- letting people express their feelings, including anger and dissatisfaction, without attributing this to symptoms or relapse.
- encouraging the use of peer-support and recovery-based coping models (e.g., Wellness-Recovery Action Planning).

- assembling a full array of services that can address people's needs across levels of disability and over time, matching supports to needs at each level, in each phase, and in each area of disability.
- ensuring that a menu of culturally competent services, including access to nontraditional therapies, is available.

1. Renewing Hope + Commitment
2. Being supported by others
3. Finding your niche in the community
4. Redefining self
5. Incorporating illness
6. Managing Sx
7. Assuming Control
8. Overcoming stigma
9. Becoming an empowered citizen

opened this section of the chapter, in which Ulric said, "I still see things around me, but I don't pay attention to them" (Davidson, Borg, et al., 2005, p. 183), and to the narrative of the overall process that speaks to these components.

For some people, the interrelated processes of redefining self, incorporating illness, and managing symptoms begins with a need first to orient themselves to their present situation. Whether it was due to the mental illness or to the person's ruminating on a lost past or a wished-for but unlikely future, several participants in our studies came to recognize, in Vivian's words, that they "didn't live in the present." Orienting oneself to the present situation or moment, even though at times it requires considerable concerted effort, appears to have a liberating effect that opens up new possibilities for the person to consider or act upon. As Vivian explained, in Zen-like terms, "I live small moments more intensely. Now we're here, you and I, and my whole life is all here, only here, it doesn't matter what else happens" (Davidson, Borg, et al., 2005, p. 186). With this grounding in the present moment, people find a number of things they can do to offset the intrusions of the mental illness and/or to "recharge [their] batteries" so that they can reenter the battleground renewed and replenished.

A first thing a person can do is simply take the time to consider his or her options. As Clarisse described, "I feel that my life has changed quite a bit. I feel that I've been able to take time to think about the situation that comes up, different situations that come up for me and I decipher what has to be done next instead of making snap decisions like I used to" (Davidson, Borg, et al., 2005, p. 186).

In addition to trying to sort out possible next steps alone, the person also can consult with trusted others and benefit from their input and advice. As Clarisse continued, "I will also call people that are my supports to ask for assistance in making decisions where I feel I need some input, when I feel that I have got a little bit of a problem making the decision, as to what I should do" (Davidson, Borg, et al., 2005, p. 186).

Beyond sorting out potential next steps, being grounded in the present affords the person the latitude to begin to consider which aspects of his or her experience are due to the illness and its various effects (e.g., poor concentration, memory loss) and which are parts of normal, everyday life (e.g., being nervous before starting a new job). This is a beginning phase of incorporating the illness, as it and

its various effects first must be distinguished from the person's sense
of self in some way. The psycho-education or psychotherapy offered
by mental health practitioners is one of several potential sources of
information available to assist the person in this process, but it often
is described, at least initially, as one of the least trusted or credible
of these sources. The perspectives or experiences of family, friends,
and other trusted people in the person's life (e.g., clergy) and information gleaned from self-help materials or the Internet are some of
these other sources. For many people, however, their own "experimenting" proves to be a highly effective vehicle for sorting out which
parts of their lives need to be attributed to the mental illness and
which not.

In an earlier work (Davidson, 2003), we offered the example of
a young man with schizophrenia, whom we shall here call Sean, who
described the seven-year process he went through to determine
whether the voices he heard in his head were broadcast to him from
the CIA or were attributable to the serious mental illness 37 different psychiatrists had informed him that he had. Believing that the
voices were part of thought experiments conducted by the CIA led
Sean to stop taking his anti-psychotic medications, lose his friends
and jobs, and get evicted from his apartment. Believing that the
voices were hallucinations, on the other hand, led him to take the
medication and allowed him to work, socialize with friends, and live
independently. The cost of this choice, however, was to have to view
himself as a mental patient rather than as a CIA operative. It was
partly for this reason that Sean's experimenting went on for seven
years.

As suggested by Sean's story, it is in relation to this process of
experimentation and implicit cost–benefit analysis that many of the
aspects of current treatments are experienced as most useful, as tools
to be used by the person in his or her own recovery. As Jeannette
stressed when describing the importance of her anti-psychotic medication to her recovery, "What is crucial for my health is taking
Risperidal, it attacks the psychosis" (Davidson, Borg, et al., 2005, p.
187). Others describe using their increasing knowledge of the illness to identify hallucinations or delusions and to test their validity
against what they know about reality. This process, which psycho-
therapists refer to as "reality-testing," not only diminishes the po-
tency of these symptoms but also appears to reduce their frequency
and duration. As Jorge described, "I started to believe, to deliberate,

weighing for and against, whether what is in the psychosis is correct or it is not. And then I made a decision that it is not, increased the medication, and went home and went to bed. The next day it was gone" (Davidson, Borg, et al., 2005, p. 186).

As Jorge suggests, determining that a hallucination, delusion, or paranoid thought is part of a psychotic condition may at times be enough to make it go away (with or without medication). For others, this knowledge is enough to make the symptom recede to the background and no longer be distracting or disruptive, as described by Ulric when he noted that he no longer pays as much attention to his visual hallucinations.

The flip side of the person's attempts to bring the symptoms and other disruptions or impairments of the illness somewhat under his or her control is his or her concurrent efforts to gain some sense of control in everyday life. As the third quote with which we opened this section suggests, people try "above all to feel as if [they] were a 'normal' person" (Davidson, Borg, et al., 2005, p. 183). Apart from learning to manage the effects of the illness, people also describe the importance of regaining normalcy or resuming an ordinary life. Our final three components may be understood as referring primarily to the processes involved in this multifaceted aspect of recovery. These may include reengaging in ordinary activities of daily life, such as attending school, getting a job, developing friendships and romantic interests, and participating in natural social and recreational activities. These may also, however, be the less noticeable, but perhaps more important, "micro-processes" of everyday life (Davidson & Strauss, 1995) that make these other pursuits possible.

For individuals who have been seriously disabled by a mental illness, it is through these first, often imperceptible, steps that they are able to reestablish a simple sense of routine in their everyday lives. Without the sense that life is predictable and consistent, and that they are able to manage their everyday affairs and be effective in the world, it is extremely difficult, if not impossible, for them to consider more substantial steps forward, such as returning to school or taking a job. Natalia described this challenge of pursuing something active or creative in terms of such mundane activities as lighting a cigarette or taking a walk:

My way is to simply see to it that I have something to do, to take a walk, light a cigarette, drink a cup of coffee, eat an apple, watch TV and be on the go. Like, I can't just sit around or lie down and sleep all day, I can't do that. It's just not something I can do. First of all, I can't sleep even when I take a sleeping pill. I've tried but I'm wide awake anyway. I feel well enough now that I want to do something, I want to be active, creative, have some company around me. I want to make something positive of the day, meet people, I want to talk. I'm pretty keen on having company and I don't just lie in bed and sleep all day . . . I can't understand how you could waste your days when you only have one life. And so you have to make something of it.

She then described how these incremental steps can build on each other in a positive way to address other, more ambitious goals further down the line.

So I take it step by step. I have learned to hurry slowly and do it in stages and set partial goals when I have discovered that it makes sense . . . doing it by partial goals and making it manageable, then you get positive feedback that it's going okay and then you don't hit the wall. That's my strategy, the strategy for success: partial goals and sensible goals and attainable goals, and that's something I've learned to do in order to achieve things. When I have been able to deal with something that's been a struggle and feel secure, I move on. Step by step, put things behind me.

It was to just such a process of "hurrying slowly" that Eric referred above when he said that he had to "reconstruct" himself as a person.

Counterbalancing, in part, the enjoyment and meaning people derive from such activities when they are successful is an inevitable, if perhaps less acknowledged, element of this process—the person's acceptance that even so-called normal life has its own problems, its own ups and downs, and its own joys and disappointments, beyond the scope of the psychosis and its effects. In other words, being in recovery does not mean that one then can live, as in a fairy tale, "happily ever after." For people who may have experienced the onset of a serious mental illness in late adolescence or early adulthood and whose normal development may therefore have been disrupted or delayed, this may be a bitter pill they have not yet had to swallow. As Lilly explained, "There are problems but I think no matter what situation you get into there's going to be problems, no matter what. You've got to learn to work through problems because if you don't you aren't going to live . . . that's a human being. In order to get from one place to another you've got to learn to get through the problems or around the problems in order to get to the next step" (Davidson, Borg, et al., 2005, p. 188).

In addition to being somewhat of a bitter pill to swallow, people may experience relief with this dawning awareness as they come to understand that not every sign of stress or distress necessarily stems from mental illness but may instead be something that everyone experiences in life. In contrast to the devastating experiences of illness and despair, this kind of everyday upset, frustration, or disappointment can be a welcome sign of improvement. In fact, as we noted above, Lilly viewed being able to have "*ordinary* worries" as a sign of her recovery. As she concludes in describing another of the more important things she has learned in her recovery:

I have to make the best of what I have. If you don't make the best of what you have then you are just going to be more and more depressed. I can't see going back to where I was. It's not an option. I've come too far to go back . . . Where is back? Back is being miserable, hating myself, hating life, not wanting to live, wanting to just curl up and die but being too afraid to kill myself. (Davidson, Borg, et al., 2005, p. 188)

We propose the concepts of *assuming control, fighting stigma,* and *becoming an empowered citizen* as the ways of characterizing the final main components of these processes.

By *assuming control,* as indicated in Table 2.7, we mean to refer to the processes by which people assume primary responsibility for their transformation from a person with a mental illness or disability to a person in recovery (Baxter & Diehl, 1998; Fisher, n.d.; Frese, Stanley, Kress, & Vogel-Scibilia, 2001; Hatfield, 1994; Jacobson & Curtis, 2000; Jacobson & Greenley, 2001; Leete, 1994; Lehman, 2000; Lovejoy, 1982; Mead & Copeland, 2000; Ridgway, 2001; Smith, 2000). Taking responsibility for one's life and, by extension, one's treatment increases a person's sense of control over one's self and efficacy in the world (Fisher, 1994; Lovejoy, 1982; Ridgway, 2001; Walsh, 1996)

Table 2.7 Assuming Control

Person in Recovery . . .	Service Provider	Manager/Administrator	Recovery Markers
To me, recovery means . . .	*I can support people in their recovery by . . .*	*I can lead an organization that supports recovery by . . .*	*We will know that we are working together toward recovery when . . .*
• knowing when, and how, to voice my opinion.	• providing opportunities for choice and offering options to choose from.	• establishing policies that allow people in recovery maximum opportunity for choice and control.	• people in recovery can choose and change their service provider.
• having control over my life and treatment.	• allowing people the right to make mistakes and valuing this as an opportunity for people to learn.	• regularly collecting satisfaction surveys from people in recovery and using results to inform service development.	• staff do not use threats or coercion.
• taking risks and trying new things.			• achievement of goals is celebrated.
• accepting the consequences and learning from my mistakes when things don't work out as planned.	• avoiding controlling behaviors.	• collecting satisfaction data in a manner that allows people to freely express feedback and criticisms.	• risks are encouraged.
• being able to appreciate someone else's view and reach a compromise.	• understanding and delivering person-centered planning.	• establishing formal grievance procedures to address dissatisfaction with services and fully informing people about these procedures on a regular basis.	• the voices of people in recovery are listened to.
• telling people what I want and need from them.	• avoiding the "professional knows best" attitude and relating to people as equals.	• avoiding aversive and coercive strategies to promote engagement.	
• not taking no for an answer!		• enforcing ethical practice with human resource oversight that holds staff accountable for giving people maximum control over their treatment.	

and, when needed, can help a person "shed the role of the victim" (Young & Ensing, 1999). In order to take responsibility and make choices, however, people must be afforded opportunities to make their own decisions and must have options from which to choose. Otherwise, there is no way for them to exercise and gain a sense of their own agency. A recovery-oriented system thus can support the development of a sense of personal responsibility and control by providing options people can choose from and allowing people to take risks and experience the consequences of their own decisions, including their own failures (Bassmann, 1997; Deegan, 1996b; Deegan, 1988; Jacobson & Curtis, 2000; Munetz & Frese, 2001; Walsh, 1996).

Overcoming stigma, addressed in Table 2.8, refers to overcoming both internalized and external stigma. While stigma may first enter a person's experience through other people, it also unfortunately has a way of becoming internalized under certain less-than-ideal circumstances. Part of the process of "taming" the illness, of identifying and distinguishing the illness from one's sense of self, thus may also involve addressing and overcoming such internalized stigma, should it exist (Ridgway, 2001). Since societal stigma cannot be simply ignored or dismissed (Perlick, 2001), people in recovery are moved to find a way to deal with this historical legacy that is comfortable for them. Some people choose to fight against stigma actively, whether by becoming advocates, offering community education in schools or other venues, or simply addressing it whenever it occurs (e.g., by writing a letter to the editor of a paper that had "Mental Patient Goes Berserk" as its headline). Others find less visible, direct, or explicit ways of dealing with stigma, such as "passing for normal" (Davidson, 2003), only disclosing their history to intimates whom they select, or limiting their options to mental health or other safe settings in which they do not expect to encounter discrimination or rejection.

Stigma, for the foreseeable future, will remain a fact of life, and recovery-oriented systems will thus need to find ways to address it. This involves working with local communities to transform settings into environments that are accepting of disabilities and value differences, as well as ensuring that mental health services themselves do not perpetuate stigma and discrimination through their own practices (e.g., having separate bathrooms for patients and for staff).

Table 2.8 Overcoming Stigma

Person in Recovery	Service Provider	Manager/Administrator	Recovery Markers
To me, recovery means …	*I can support people in their recovery by …*	*I can lead an organization that supports recovery by …*	*We will know that we are working together toward recovery when …*
• feeling good about myself. • learning ways to overcome the negative attitudes of others. • finding places in the community where I feel at home. • not feeling ashamed about having a mental illness. • being proud of myself. • having role models. • not letting people put limits on me. • knowing when I am being discriminated against. • standing up for myself when I have been mistreated. • not buying into stereotypes of mental illness. • realizing that other people have problems too. • knowing when I deserve better and demanding it.	• avoiding stigmatizing language and labels. • helping transform communities into more accepting environments. • being able to confront personal prejudices. • teaching people how to manage stigma by advocating for themselves and others and getting involved in things like "stigma-busting," program evaluation, and state politics. • not wearing badges when working with someone in the community (i.e., staying behind the scenes).	• educating staff members, consumers, family members, and the community about the harm caused by stigma. • involving people in recovery who can share their stories as part of this education. • developing relationships with local media representatives to publicize success stories. • establishing structures to link services across professional disciplines (rehabilitation and clinical), service sectors (public and private), and contexts (community and treatment system).	• the agency provides structured educational activities to community and employers about mental illness and addictions.

Table 2.9 Becoming an Empowered Citizen

Person in Recovery	Service Provider	Manager/Administrator	Recovery Markers
To me, recovery means …	*I can support people in their recovery by …*	*I can lead an organization that supports recovery by …*	*We will know that we are working together toward recovery when …*
• feeling like I have choices. • choosing where I live and how I spend my time. • voicing my opinion. • giving back and sharing my experiences with other people working toward recovery. • being a responsible citizen (e.g., by voting, volunteering, working, paying taxes, managing my own money, keeping up with my bills). • having other people respect me. • being a responsible parent, a caring friend, or a good neighbor. • making a difference in my community. • taking responsibility for my recovery.	• listening to people and respecting their choices. • helping people find their voice and encouraging involvement in advocacy activities. • involving people in recovery in all aspects of service planning, development, and implementation. • understanding and teaching people about how they are protected by disability and mental health law. • referring people to appropriate oversight bodies (e.g., P&A, EEOC, CLRP) as warranted. • encouraging people to be responsible citizens (e.g., by voting, volunteering, organizing a neighborhood block-watch). • valuing assertiveness and independence as growth and reducing supports in response to this growth.	• creating advisory boards where people in recovery have genuine influence on service planning and implementation. • holding the organization accountable for responding to the recommendations of people in recovery. • providing training and requiring staff to be knowledgeable about mental health and disability law. • supporting the development of person-centered recovery planning.	• staff help people become involved with community services. • people in recovery are involved in the development, evaluation, and provision of programs and services. • people in recovery are regular members of advisory boards.

Lastly, although they do not use these exact terms, people in recovery stress the importance of what we describe in our ninth and final component as *becoming an empowered citizen.* Empowerment, or gaining a sense of mastery and control over one's environment and self, may have been implicit in component seven, assuming control, but in this context it takes on a more social or political connotation and is, in this way, the flip side of stigma and discrimination (Walsh, 1996; Young & Ensing, 1999). Taking back control of one's life need not happen only in private; it may begin there, but eventually it can extend to taking back control of one's life in public as well. To the degree that people are able to address, overcome, or bypass stigma effectively, they are able to reclaim the rights and responsibilities of citizenship that are their birthright.

A recovery-oriented system will aim to facilitate this sense of social or political empowerment by offering people accurate and accessible information they can use in their own decision-making and recovery, eliciting and valuing the input of people in recovery in all aspects and at all levels of the system, and validating the value of the experiences gained through the recovery process by hiring people in recovery as staff. While people have the right to be different, they also have the right to be the same. Systems acknowledge this right by treating people with serious mental illnesses the same, as much as possible, as people with other serious illnesses who may need and can benefit from health care. In addition, however, they also have to acknowledge the political realities of the current situation and offer education and assistance for people in how to advocate for themselves when needed (something that may not be required by someone with an illness such as asthma). Systems offer an array of options, from involvement in advocacy activities to speak out against injustices to helping people find ways to give back to their communities and put a positive face on recovery on an individual and informal basis (Fisher, n.d., 1994; Ridgway, 2001; Walsh, 1996).

As these data and concepts suggest, there are many things that the person in recovery can do—and some he or she may need to do—in order to take up "the work of recovery" (Davidson & Strauss, 1992). How practitioners can facilitate these processes is the chief focus of the remainder of this volume.

3   The Top 10 Concerns about Recovery

Encountered in System Transformation

The second chapter begins with descriptions of some of the many ways in which people with serious mental illness are key agents in their own recovery. In these descriptions, we find that the cornerstones of recovery are both the hope that a better life is possible and the desire the person has to pursue such a better life once this hope has taken root. For an individual, both hope and action appear to be required to make recovery a reality. As we begin to understand more fully the role of systems of care and of the practitioners within those systems in facilitating recovery, we suggest that achieving, in the words of the New Freedom Commission report, "profound change—not at the margins of a system, but at its very core" also will require both hopeful attitudes and concerted efforts.

While the remaining chapters in this volume will deal more explicitly with the kinds of concerted efforts required to achieve transformation, this chapter focuses primarily on attitudes toward recovery and the kinds of concerns systems and practitioners have raised (to date) as they have gone about the process of understanding and implementing recovery principles in practice. It has been our experience, however, that the federal mandate to transform systems of care to promote recovery has left many policy makers, program managers, practitioners, and even the recovery community itself under increasing pressure to move to a recovery orientation without first examining the concerns of stakeholders within those systems about this new notion of recovery and its implications. As a result, we are all at risk of overlaying recovery rhetoric on top of existing systems of care, failing to effect any real or substantial—not to mention revolutionary—changes due to our urgency to just "get it done."

In this chapter, we pause to consider some of the more common concerns we have encountered in attempting to introduce and implement care based on the vision of recovery that we have articulated thus far. Addressing these concerns, we believe, is a necessary first step in changing the attitudes that underlie current practices in the process of replacing these attitudes with the more hopeful, empowering, and respectful attitudes demanded, and deserved, by people in recovery. That said, we also feel it is important to note that the majority of people who share these concerns are motivated by compassion for the suffering endured by people with serious mental illnesses, and by a sense of responsibility for improving their lot. We therefore do not view those practitioners who have been willing to voice the concerns we describe below as uncaring or resistant but instead feel they are to be thanked and rewarded for their courage in bringing such issues explicitly into the public debate and putting them squarely on the table, so that we may all find our way to a more respectful and effective stance.

As discussions of such core attitudes and beliefs can at times elicit tensions, controversy, and conflict, we have chosen the title of "Top 10 Concerns"—derived from *Late Night with David Letterman*—to introduce some levity into the situation (Davidson, O'Connell, Tondora, Styron, & Kangas, 2006). These concerns, listed in Table 3.1, have been culled from a series of presentations, discussions, and trainings conducted over the last several years as the state of Connecticut has moved toward a recovery-oriented system of mental health care. With each concern identified, we provide a brief discussion of the basis for the concern and an alternative understanding of the issue from a recovery perspective, with possible strategies for addressing the concern in ways that remain consistent with the overarching vision of "being in recovery" as we currently understand it. After outlining these 10 concerns, we conclude this chapter by briefly addressing the issues of resources and culture change—two major issues that often underlie these more specific concerns—and thus provide system leaders with points of departure for their discussions with their own stakeholders.

Table 3.1 Top 10 Concerns about Recovery

10. Recovery is old news. "What's all the hype? We've been doing recovery for decades."

9. Recovery-oriented care adds to the burden of mental health practitioners who already are stretched thin by demands that exceed their resources. "You mean on top of everything else I'm already doing, I have to do recovery too?"

8. "Recovery" means the person is cured. "What do you mean, our clients are 'in recovery'? Don't you see how disabled they are? Isn't that a contradiction?"

7. Recovery in mental health is an irresponsible fad that sets people up for failure. "This is just the flavor of the month, and it's cruel to set people up for failure. Why raise false hopes?"

6. Recovery happens for very few people with serious mental illness. "You're not talking about the people I see. They're too disabled. Recovery is not possible for them."

5. Recovery only happens after, and as a result of, active treatment and the cultivation of insight. "My patients won't even acknowledge that they're sick. How can I talk to them about recovery when they have no insight into being ill?"

4. Recovery can only be implemented with additional resources, through the introduction of new services. "Sure, we'll be happy to do recovery: just give us the money it will take to start a new recovery program."

3. Recovery-oriented services are neither reimbursable nor evidence-based. "First it was managed care, then it was evidence-based practice. But recovery is neither of those."

2. Recovery approaches devalue the role of professional intervention. "Why did I just spend 10 years in training if someone else, with no training, is going to make all the decisions?"

1. Recovery increases provider exposure to risk and liability. "If recovery is the person's responsibility, then how come I get the blame when things go wrong?"

Concern #10. Recovery Is Old News. "What's All the Hype? We've Been Doing 'Recovery' for Decades."

BASIS FOR CONCERN   The idea of "recovery" has in fact been around for many years in several different forms. Addiction recovery, for example, is derived from the 12-step, self-help community, in which people who are achieving or maintaining abstinence have described themselves for over half a century as being "in recovery." Visions of recovery specific to serious mental illnesses have similarly been around for over 25 years, since the dawning of the contemporary mental health consumer movement and publication of the initial findings of the World Health Organization's *International Pilot Study of Schizophrenia,* which both took place in the 1970s. It is not clear to some providers what is new or different about the current vision of recovery or what was not already captured in this earlier generation of practice innovation, which included self-help/peer support, psychiatric rehabilitation, community support services, and assertive community treatment, among others.

RECOVERY-ORIENTED RESPONSE   The current body of work explicitly acknowledges the valuable contributions of pioneering individuals and groups who have championed the cause of recovery in these and other forms. Proponents of the current recovery movement are indebted to their efforts and hope to build on their experiences and successes to promote system change. Many of the changes in care that have been recommended as recovery-oriented in the past, however, have yet to be implemented broadly or fully (e.g., supported education, housing, and employment). In addition, new legislation and new strategies have emerged in recent years that have profound implications for care. These strategies shift care from an acute model of treatment and aftercare provided by practitioners to a *civil rights* model that views serious mental illnesses as disabilities that the ill person is responsible for learning how to manage. Based on the premise that full access to community and civic life is the fundamental right of all people with disabilities, this approach emphasizes both the person's right to pursue his or her own life and recovery goals—including *opportunities* for participation in the naturally occurring community activities of his or her choice—and the need for provision of *supports* over time for the person to use in taking advantage of these opportunities successfully.

In addition to implementing previously recommended changes that have yet to be adopted as broadly as proposed, it will be important also to incorporate more recent and emerging recovery-oriented approaches and supports that focus more directly, and are based more substantially, on the principles and values of self-determination, social access and inclusion, and the restoration of community life *regardless* of disability status. In this area—that is, in the area of offering community supports to people with psychiatric disabilities on a par with the supports provided to people with other disabilities (e.g., wheelchairs, sign language, Braille)—there remains much to discover, learn, and develop. In fact, some of it is so new that it is unclear what it will look like in practice. Person-centered planning technologies, menus of supports, and flexible funding that ties resources to individuals and their choices provide some initial clues, but much work remains to be done in order to live up to the promise of this form of recovery.

Concern #9. Recovery-Oriented Care Adds to the Burden of Mental Health Practitioners Who Already Are Stretched Thin by Demands That Exceed Their Resources. "You Mean on Top of Everything Else That I'm Already Doing I Have to Do Recovery, Too?"

BASIS FOR CONCERN   Several forces at the federal level, some of which were mentioned in the preceding section, as well as incentives coming from state and county systems have been encouraging providers to develop and further enhance recovery-oriented systems of care for their citizens. They have been encouraged to attend conferences, lectures, and training sessions about recovery and barraged by advocates demanding recovery-oriented care, and they have seen recovery language begin to creep into official documents that cross their desks. Some practitioners have been taking these messages to mean that they need to offer recovery to their patients, clients, consumers, or recipients of service *in addition* to everything else they already offer. A typical response has been on the order of, "What?! Now in addition to everything else you have us doing you want us to do recovery! We don't even have enough time/staff/resources to treat symptoms and contain risk—how can we possibly do more?" Given the many pressures on mental health systems over the past decade—including managed care, privatization, changes in Medicaid, increased costs of new medications, state budget deficits, and so on—this certainly poses a reasonable concern.

RECOVERY-ORIENTED RESPONSE   One of the major points that must be made in response to such concern is that recovery is not something practitioners can do *to* or *for* people with psychiatric disabilities. Being in recovery with a serious mental illness, as others and we have defined it, refers instead to the ways in which a person with a psychiatric disability manages his or her own condition in the context of his or her everyday life in the community. In this sense, recovery has been and continues to be the primary goal of all mental health services, with the possible exception of forensic services for offenders who also experience mental illness (whose primary goals may be containment and community safety). This concern can thus be turned on its head, leading one to ask practitioners, "But if what you are providing now is not oriented to promoting recovery, then what is it for? And, more importantly, why should the system pay for it?" Similarly, if there are ways in which what practitioners offer could be more recovery-oriented, and perhaps thereby more effective at achieving its aims, why would they not want to learn about it and do it? As one system leader in Connecticut has often declared, if he went to a health care professional who was practicing internal medicine the same way today that he or she had practiced it 30 years ago, he would not go back; instead he would search out someone whose practice was more in line with current knowledge. There is no reason why this should not be true of mental health practitioners as well.

Recovery-oriented care, as we reiterate further on, cannot be considered an add-on to existing services. There is a common misconception among practitioners that they must provide treatment first, and then perhaps they can focus on offering rehabilitation (if they have the time or resources), while promoting recovery is something that can be delayed until the day when mental health care is finally funded adequately. As this misconception is both common and, in our experience, enduring, we cannot state strongly or often enough that recovery-oriented care is neither a "boutique" form of care for the advantaged few nor an add-on to existing care that will be funded when new, discretionary dollars are made available for that purpose. (We return to this issue in Concern #4.)

In response to this concern, it also is important not only to distinguish between different meanings and uses of the term *recovery* but to distinguish between *processes of recovery*, which the person with a serious mental illness engages in, and *recovery-oriented care*, which is what mental health treatment and rehabilitation practitioners offer in support of the person's recovery efforts. As the advocacy community has reminded us consistently, recovery belongs to the person with the disability; it is what I, as a person with a psychiatric disorder, do on my own behalf. Practitioners can offer me information, materials, resources, and tools that I can use in the process, and they can enhance my access to opportunities and supports, but recovery is both my right and my responsibility. To make this shift in role clear, we have informally adopted the motto of the Home Depot to reframe the message we want practitioners to convey to their clients: "You can do it. We can help." (The Norwegian version is even stronger and translates as, "Of course you can!") Perhaps more than most of the policies, guidelines, and standards we have developed to articulate recovery-oriented practice, this simple slogan appears to help practitioners rethink the boundary between where their responsibilities end and where the (rights and) responsibilities of their clients begin.

Concern #8. "Recovery" Means the Person Is Cured. "What Do You Mean Our Clients Are 'In Recovery'? Don't You See How Disabled They Are? Isn't That a Contradiction?"

BASIS FOR CONCERN   As we noted in our first chapter, this is the customary meaning of "recovery" in primary care and in everyday life. It also is relevant to many people who have and recover from an episode of mental illness and who in fact do not have additional episodes of illness or residual impairments. If this is the only acceptable meaning of the term *recovery*, then most providers in public-sector settings are right to question its relevance to their work. Such people can be considered *cured* in the traditional sense of the term, but these are not the people who are typically seen within the context of a public mental health system. These individuals experience an episode of distress or dysfunction, get timely and appropriate care (or not), and may go back to their lives as usual, having no reason to disclose their history of mental illness or to talk about recovery at all. While it still is important to know that people can recover fully from these episodes, the lessons offered by such examples are limited when we generalize to people with more prolonged or severe illnesses.

RECOVERY-ORIENTED RESPONSE   The definition of recovery as "no longer having symptoms or deficits associated with a serious mental illness" is the least likely to apply to the people most often seen in the context of public mental health services. We agree, then, that this sense of recovery has limited relevance to our own work. While most people will agree that using a word that has multiple meanings in multiple contexts is not optimal for clear communication, it is a situation we have inherited, and we will need to make the most of it until a better alternative emerges. It is with recognition of these various meanings that we have offered several different definitions of recovery (e.g., Davidson, O'Connell, et al., 2005) and encourage others to try to be as clear and concrete as possible about which meaning is being used when, for whom, and under what circumstances. Within this context, we suggest that the form of recovery that does not require cure or remission of symptoms or deficits but that allows for—and really only makes sense within the context of—continued disability is the most relevant for the work of public-sector mental health systems. This is true for two fundamental reasons.

First, this is the form of recovery that speaks most directly and forcefully to the issues of civil rights and membership in society, issues that people with serious mental illnesses have identified as even more entrenched and difficult to address than those posed by the illnesses themselves. These are the issues of discrimination, second-class citizenship, inclusion, self-determination, and, most fundamentally, power. As suggested by its parallel in the independent living movement, this model of recovery insists that persons with serious mental illness remain in control of their own lives, including their own mental health care, until, unless, and only for as long as there are clear and convincing reasons, grounded in law, for their sovereignty to be handed over temporarily to others. This does not mean merely that they can no longer be confined to hospitals against their will for protracted periods of time; it also means that they can make their own decisions; pursue their own hopes, dreams, and aspirations; and select and participate in the activities they enjoy or find meaningful in the settings of their choice *even while disabled.*

Just as it is unreasonable and unethical to insist that a person with paraplegia regain his or her mobility in order to live independently, or that a person with visual impairment regain his or her vision in order to be gainfully employed or attend school, it is both unreasonable and unethical to insist that a person with a serious mental illness no longer experience symptoms or have functional impairments in order to have sex or attend church. The fact that this principle applies to anyone with a serious mental illness, regardless of the severity of the illness or the various types of recovery accessible to the person, suggests the second reason why we propose the civil rights sense of recovery as the most relevant and inclusive for public-sector mental health.

Focusing solely on promoting recovery from mental illness runs the risk of abandoning people with severe disabilities—people who in this sense are not recovering—to repeated failure and despair. Restoring to people their civil rights and focusing on their hopes and participation in the enjoyable and meaningful activities of their choice, on the other hand, would not seem to run the risk of leaving anyone behind. In fact, research suggests that identifying and pursuing activities consistent with the person's interests and individuals' learning ways to manage and minimize the destructive effects of the illness contribute to recovering from serious mental illness, whether it be over a period of weeks, months, or years (Becker & Drake, 1994; Davidson, Stayner, Lambert, Smith, & Sledge, 1997). As one example, focusing on how a person can learn to live with auditory hallucinations appears to result in a decrease in their severity and frequency (Chadwick, Birchwood, & Trower, 1996), while simply waiting for the symptoms to disappear leaves the person inactive, isolated, and alone.

Concern #7. Recovery in Mental Health Is an Irresponsible Fad That Sets People up for Failure. "This Is Just the Flavor of the Month, and It's Cruel to Set People up for Failure. Why Raise False Hopes?"

BASIS FOR CONCERN   Even among some practitioners who are familiar with the different meanings of "recovery," there still is a concern about how realistic the goal of recovery is, even when it does not entail cure, and whether this is a lasting vision or simply a fad introduced by a vocal, but unrepresentative, minority. It is not uncommon to hear comments about how the visible champions of the recovery movement (i.e., ex-patients/survivors and mental health advocates) often (a) do not appreciate the important differences between mental illness and addiction or physical disability, and/or (b) are exceptions to the rule, neither representing nor speaking for the larger population of people with serious mental illness. Based on the perception that the vision of recovery promoted by these advocates is unrealistic for at least a significant minority (if not the majority) of people with serious mental illness, some practitioners view both the advocates and other proponents of recovery-oriented system change as irresponsible at best, and unethical and destructive at worst, for imposing this additional burden on people who already are doing the best they can just to survive on a day-to-day basis. From this perspective, providing people with false hopes and unrealistic expectations of recovery is not only a waste of time but also a cruel hoax.

RECOVERY-ORIENTED RESPONSE   Whether or not the vision of recovery offered by the leaders of the recovery movement is shared by everyone who has a serious mental illness, we suggest that there are important elements of this vision that have universal appeal and pose meaningful opportunities for reform. We suggest that rather than representing the latest fad, these elements hold the potential for dramatically improving practice, perhaps even especially among the most disabled segment of the broader population. The promise that recovery holds even, and perhaps especially, for these individuals challenges the form of prejudice and discrimination we have referred to as "mentalism" (Chamberlin, 1974; Deegan, 1992), which suggests that mental illness deprives people of the capacity to take care of themselves because they are "not in their right minds." By challenging mentalism and offering hope, expectations for recovery, and opportunities to exert one's power, recovery can help a person shed the role of "mental patient." Everyone, even individuals most disabled by mental illness, is entitled to a life that extends beyond the identity of "mental patient."

How might this civil rights concept of recovery influence our policy and practice for persons with the severest disabilities? First, it can restore to them their fundamental human dignity and encourage us to view them as people, first and foremost, who are battling severe illnesses. Second, it can encourage us to identify and cultivate those aspects of the person's life least damaged by the illness and/ or over which he or she retains the most control. In both of these ways, this concept of recovery encourages us to view people with serious mental illness as we do people with any other serious, and potentially lethal, illness for which available treatments have limited efficacy.

When we have asked some of the people remaining in long-stay hospitals what would make their lives better, they have not said "more or better treatments," "the acquisition of more or better insight or skills," or even "being cured of the illness." What they have said are things like "going out to the movies and for pizza a couple of times a month," or "having a part-time job," or "seeing my family more often, or "having friends to go to church or shopping with," or "a lover to have sex with." One participant in a study examining processes of recovery reported that, for him, recovery would involve things like picking up his neighbor's trash can if it fell into the street or being in a position to give fatherly advice to kids on his block (Davidson, 2003). The wishes these people have had for how they would like to spend their time have not differed significantly from those of people who have other disabilities or chronic illnesses, with the possible exception that, given their history of institutionalization, they may more often focus on "giving back" to others (e.g., picking up the neighbor's trash can). Our practices, however, have been significantly different, but for what are perhaps not very good reasons, based as much in "mentalism" as in sound clinical evidence.

To determine which of the elements of current practice are helpful and needed as opposed to those that are lingering legacies of our institutional past, we suggest a strategy of engaging people with psychiatric disabilities in identifying ways in which they remain stigmatized or discriminated against in their day-to-day lives. This includes eliminating stigmatizing attitudes, policies, and practices both inside and outside the mental health system and working to cultivate welcoming environments in which the contributions of people with severe disabilities will be valued, also both inside and outside the mental health system. It also includes identifying and promoting practices aimed at improving quality of life despite continuing disability. A core tenet of these approaches is that the person himself or herself is the best source of information about what works and what does not, and to what ends. It is when this core tenet is lost, and practitioners stop asking these questions out of a belief that they already know what recovery-oriented care looks like, that recovery becomes most vulnerable to the accusation of being simply the latest fad in the unfortunate history of a field that has been slow to embrace the importance of evidence.

**Concern #6. Recovery Happens for Very Few People with
Serious Mental Illness. "You're Not Talking about the People
I See. They're Too Disabled. Recovery Is Not Possible
for Them."**

BASIS FOR CONCERN   A corollary to Concern #7, this concern stems
from over 100 years of psychiatric theory and practice in which serious mental illnesses have been viewed as pervasive (taking over the
entire person) and as causing permanent deficits and dysfunction.
While many people with such illnesses may have shown improvements over time, they were then considered not to have had very
"serious" forms of the illness or to have been misdiagnosed. Other
explanations for their apparent recovery included the notion that
they must have been extraordinary people with extraordinary resources (e.g., Nobel laureate mathematician John Nash) or that they
really remained ill but lived in communities that had a higher toler-
ance for deviance, and thereby overlooked their continued disability. The belief that very few, if any, people actually recover from serious mental illness continues to be a common and influential perception, despite being described over 20 years ago as a function of
the "clinician's illusion" (Cohen & Cohen, 1984).

RECOVERY-ORIENTED RESPONSE   The perception above lingers despite over 30 years of outcome research that has consistently documented a 45% to 65% recovery rate for schizophrenia, the severest
mental illness, even when *recovery* is defined in a narrow clinical
fashion as "remission in symptoms and other deficits" (e.g., Harding
et al., 1987a, 1987b). This same research has shown that symptoms
also vary in severity and duration in addition to in their impact on
the person's functioning over time. There is, in brief, tremendous
variability in the nature, severity, and impact of serious mental illnesses within the life-context of any given person. When combined
with an assessment of the person's remaining areas of health and
competence, the picture becomes even more dynamic, variable, and
complicated over time (Davidson & McGlashan, 1997; Strauss, Hafez,
Harding, & Lieberman, 1985).

   This research holds important implications for broadening the
notion of recovery in mental illness, and for adopting a more finely
tuned approach to assessment and rehabilitation in which we pay
more detailed attention to the ways the illness compromises some

domains of function and leaves other domains relatively intact. Full recovery, in which both symptoms and other deficits disappear completely, may in fact not be possible for a minority of individuals with mental illness. This does not mean, however, that other forms of recovery—such as being in recovery—do not remain possible for people with severer illnesses.

We would not suggest, for example, that by virtue of losing his or her sight, hearing, or mobility, a person necessarily becomes any less able to decide what he or she wants, needs, likes, or can aspire to. This line of research suggests that the same may be true for many people living with serious mental illness. Just because I hear voices when no one else is around does not mean that I am any less capable of deciding what I want to have for dinner than a person who does not hear voices. Similarly, just because I have difficulty concentrating and remembering things does not mean that I am any less capable of deciding where and with whom I want to live than someone who has no such difficulties. Finally, having to battle anergia, anhedonia, and withdrawal (i.e., negative symptoms of schizophrenia) does not make me any less capable of deciding what kind of job I would like to have; in fact, it may make it even more critical for me to be the one to make that decision (i.e., to ensure that the job provides me with a sufficient reason to get out of bed).

Concern #5. Recovery Only Happens After, and as a Result of, Active Treatment and the Cultivation of Insight. "My Patients Won't Even Acknowledge That They're Sick. How Can I Talk to Them About Recovery when They Have No Insight into Being Ill?"

BASIS FOR CONCERN   As the Surgeon General's report on mental health highlighted several years ago (DHHS, 1999), psychiatric treatments work, very effectively, for very many people. In fact, many psychiatric treatments are more effective than many commonly accepted interventions for other medical conditions such as cardiac disease or asthma. In addition, it is difficult to imagine how recovery can be relevant to someone who is experiencing an acute episode of psychosis or mania. It would seem that the person would need to get better before recovery could be discussed or even considered.

As a result, some practitioners question the ethical issues involved in focusing on strengths, hopes, and dreams when a person may be faced with such urgent needs as safety, shelter, and stabilization. It therefore seems reasonable to assume that recovery follows after, and as a result of, treatments delivered by knowledgeable practitioners.

RECOVERY-ORIENTED RESPONSE   While many treatments do work well, this same Surgeon General's report highlighted the fact that the majority of people with diagnosable mental illness neither seek nor receive specialty mental health care (DHHS, 1999). While some of these individuals will die or end up in jail, in the hospital, or homeless, many others apparently find recovery through other means. The fact that recovery rates for psychosis are significantly better in the developing world, where fewer resources are allocated for specialty mental health care, further reinforces this point (Lin & Kleinman, 1988).

The primary issue here, however, is not whether people should access or receive care for their mental illness. Most, if not all, mental health practitioners will agree with the Surgeon General's admonition to people in need of care and their loved ones that care is available, that care works, and that people should make use of it in as timely a manner as possible (DHHS, 1999). The issue, rather, has to do with what role recovery plays in treatment or, alternatively, what role treatment plays in recovery. While the first of these perspectives may seem more natural to care providers, the recovery movement suggests that the second perspective (i.e., what role treatment plays in recovery) is the more natural perspective of the person with the disorder. This shift has important implications for how we conceptualize and deliver care and the degree to which this care is acceptable to and effective for the people we serve.

In terms of acute care, "recovery" refers to a process, not a goal of treatment. Most people who may be described as "in recovery" with a serious mental illness neither think nor talk about the term *recovery* at all. They talk about getting a job, making friends, having faith, living on their own, and generally getting their lives back. Their engagement in this process is equally relevant to all phases and forms of treatment, though the goals of each phase or form may differ. In this vein, we suggest that a useful distinction for practitioners may be that while few people express a desire to "work on their recovery," many people express a desire to get their lives back.

Acute inpatient care, like outpatient or rehabilitative services, may play a crucial role in assisting the person in this process. The process itself both predates and extends well beyond each acute episode, however. The recovery process doesn't start after the acute episode resolves, nor can the recovery process be put on hold while the person is receiving treatment for an acute episode. From the person's perspective, it is rather that the acute episode has temporarily disrupted his or her ongoing process of recovery, and treatment received during this period can either promote or undermine that process. In this way, we suggest reframing the treatment enterprise from the perspective of the practitioner to that of the person with the illness.

There can be a similar reframing in terms of the aims and functions of ongoing care and support. Use of a disability or disease-management model suggests a reversal in priority and sequencing of different elements of care. Rather than so-called aftercare following acute care, approaches oriented more to the needs of individuals with prolonged conditions situate acute episodes within a longitudinal, life-context model (Davidson & Strauss, 1995; White, Boyle, & Loveland, 2003; White & Godley, 2003). This means that people need not delay the resumption of ordinary activities until their illness has been adequately treated. Rather, it is in pursuit of these activities that people can most effectively make use of treatment, rehabilitation, and supports. Within this model, care is to be viewed as a tool or resource to be used by the person in his or her own recovery rather than as a prerequisite *to* recovery (recall the Home Depot motto: "You can do it. We can help").

The issue of medication adherence provides a ready example. We ask practitioners to think about when people will be more likely to take their medications as prescribed: when they are told, "Take this medication because you have a psychotic illness. Once you do, and if your symptoms abate, we can talk about getting you some vocational training," or when they are told, "If you don't want to be so bothered by those voices when you're at work, why not try this medication? It's been known to help other people better control the voices they hear that are similar to yours." (For further discussion of recovery-oriented psychopharmacology, interested readers are referred to the excellent work of Noordsy and his colleagues [Noordsy et al., 2000]).

Such examples lead us inevitably back to the question of insight. In the first example above, the expectation is clearly that the person will accept having a serious mental illness, for which medication has been one prescribed treatment. In the second example, however, the person may only be expected to acknowledge hearing voices that are distressing. Is there a difference between the two? Is insight into having an illness a requirement for recovery? And if so, how does this impact the role of the practitioner?

If by *insight* we refer to the expectation that people will accept having a pervasively and permanently disabling condition that dooms them to a life of dependency and despair, then the obvious answer to the question about it being required for recovery is no. This kind of unwarranted pessimism masquerading as insight has been very destructive to hundreds of thousands of individuals with serious mental illness over the preceding century, and it is an expectation that we need to jettison from a recovery-oriented system of care. If, at the other end of the spectrum, by *insight* we mean the expectation that the person with a serious mental illness will be aware of the fact that something has gone terribly wrong in his or her life, then we have yet to meet a person with a serious mental illness who does not already possess this form of insight. What is at issue in the considerable middle ground between these two extremes is how the person perceives, manages, and reacts to what he or she thinks has gone so terribly wrong. This often ambiguous middle ground presents a fertile territory for exploration in recovery-oriented care, and commands much of the initial attention of the "recovery guide" we describe at some length in Chapter 5. For now, we will have to be satisfied with leaving this question somewhat open, while suggesting a couple of broad principles to guide a more extensive discussion at a later point.

In conventional models of psycho-education, practitioners view their role as providing information to clients and their families about the nature of serious mental illnesses, the need for adherence to treatment (typically medication), and possibly ways to manage some of the symptoms of the illness (e.g., self-care strategies for the person or ways for the family to reduce "expressed emotion"). While these approaches may be highly effective early in the course of illness for some youths and their families—particularly in the case of relatively mild forms of illness—they have often been very limited in their utility in public-sector settings that serve people either with severer forms of illness or further along in the course of their illness, when they have had several years of living with the illness prior to receiving such education. In these cases, there are at least two factors that limit the effectiveness of such straightforward psycho-educational efforts.

First, it is understandable that someone would reject the notion that he or she has a permanent, disabling brain disease for which there appears to be little or no "hard" evidence. We cannot show people lesions on X-rays or CAT scans, nor can we show them elevated or depressed blood levels of key organic compounds on laboratory reports. Given the state of the science at present, it unfortunately is also the case that medications are only partially effective, and even then for only some people, with many people refusing or disconti-nuing medications because they do not see tangible evidence of their utility. Add to these considerations the side effects of many treat-ments and the stigma and discrimination that continue to surround serious mental illnesses, and one can begin to appreciate how diffi-cult it may be for some individuals to come to accept that they have what we describe to them as a serious mental illness.

Second, the descriptions we currently provide to people of the illnesses we suggest they have are woefully inadequate and often fall well short of capturing those people's experiences. There seldom is a direct link drawn between what the person has experienced as having gone wrong in his or her life and what we describe as inher-ent to the illness itself. Perhaps due in part to how little we know about these conditions and in part to our almost exclusive focus, since the third edition of the *Diagnostic and Statistical Manual of Mental Disorders* (American Psychiatric Association, 1980), on objective and observable characteristics of various diagnostic categories, we have little ability as a field to tailor our psycho-educational efforts to the actual, subjective realities of our clients' everyday lives (Flanagan, Davidson, & Strauss, 2007). In the research literature, this is referred to as a lack of "ecological validity" (Green, 1999) or "clinical relevance" (Kazdin, 2005), and is decried as a major impediment to progress.

Through their intuitive sensitivity and accumulated experience—and despite the current limitations of the field—some practitioners are more much adept than others at making these links between the person's distress and his or her illness. What their practice suggests is that making such links in conjunction with the person is both more effective and more important than getting the person to accept having an illness per se. Thus in the second example above, the practitioner suggested to the client that certain medications have been found by other people who hear similar voices to help make the voices less disruptive. Such a suggestion does not require that the person acknowledge or accept any particular diagnostic label, nor does it entail making any long-term prognosis—a prognosis that, we point out, the practitioner often does not have scientific data to support.

As we noted earlier, we have neither the space nor the data to make a strong case for determining whether people with serious mental illness have to accept having such illness in order to be in recovery. What we can suggest at this point as an alternative to conventional psycho-education, however, is that people can be assisted both in managing their illnesses and in managing their lives without their expressing such insight. Such assistance can take many forms, ranging from recent advances in cognitive-behavioral psychotherapies, which do not require use of an illness model (Kingdon & Turkington, 1994), to the provision of community supports, such as supported housing, supported employment, supported education, and supported socialization (e.g., Becker & Drake, 1994; Carling, 1990; Drake et al., 1994; Wehman, 1986). In these approaches, accepting that one has a mental illness is no more required for, or relevant to, the person's benefiting from the support offered than insisting a person acknowledge the cause of his or her paraplegia is required for, or relevant to, that person's ability to use a wheelchair.

Concern #4. Recovery Can Only Be Implemented with Additional Resources, through the Introduction of New Services. "Sure, We'll Be Happy to Do Recovery: Just Give Us the Money It Will Take to Start a New Recovery Program."

BASIS FOR CONCERN   The provision of community supports is an excellent example of the kinds of new services that will be required by a recovery-oriented system of care. This poses a real problem, however, particularly in times of budget constriction. How can we possibly develop these new services and supports when we do not even have enough resources to fund adequately the care we already provide?

RECOVERY-ORIENTED RESPONSE   This concern is based on the assumption that recovery-oriented services and supports will have to be *added* to an existing system of care, which needs to continue to be funded as it currently is. As we asked in relation to Concern #9, if our current services do not promote and support recovery, then what

functions or purposes do they serve? While there are effective treatments available for most disorders, the growing literature on evidence-
based practices teaches us that much of the care currently being offered does not incorporate these advances and, in fact, lacks any
evidence supporting its utility or effectiveness (Drake et al., 2001;
Hoagwood, Burns, & Kiser, 2001; McClellan, 2002; Torrey et al., 2001).
Much of it has been inherited from previous generations of well-
meaning professionals, but little of it has been shown to actually be
helpful to people with serious mental illness.

Therefore, there is much work that can be done in reallocating
existing resources to better serve the aims of recovery and community integration before additional resources can be strenuously demanded. Moreover, recovery-oriented care involves a broader distri-
bution of responsibilities to natural supports, thus lessening the burden
on any individual practitioner, program, or agency. We therefore
suggest reviewing existing services and supports to identify those that
support recovery and those that undermine or pose additional barriers to recovery. Based both on available research and on the input
of people in recovery and their loved ones, progress can be made in
reallocating existing resources to fund local community-based systems of recovery-oriented care that afford people meaningful choices
from an array of effective and accessible services and supports that
go beyond the current one-size-fits-all paradigm.

Concern #3. Recovery-Oriented Services Are neither Reimbursable nor Evidence-Based. "First It Was Managed Care, Then It Was Evidence-Based Practice. But Recovery Is neither of Those."

BASIS OF CONCERN   Evidence-based practice initiatives are intended
to ensure that funds go to the services that have been shown to be effective. Many recovery-oriented practices have yet to amass an evidence
base demonstrating their efficacy. In a related vein, practitioners
often are limited to offering care they can be reimbursed for, either
by third-party payers or, in the case of much publicly funded care,
by Medicaid, Medicare, or other government entitlement programs.
But these payers insist on criteria of medical necessity and accentu-
ate acute and clinically driven models of care, and they deny or restrict access to and use of rehabilitative, supportive, peer-based, and

other presumably recovery-oriented practices. How can providers implement recovery-oriented practices when these practices directly contradict the directions they are required to take by the funding, regulatory, and professional bodies they rely on for their financial and practical survival?

RECOVERY-ORIENTED RESPONSE   The fact that few recovery-oriented practices have amassed evidence speaks to their relative newness on the scene, not to any intrinsic difference in their nature that would make them impossible to study. We need to study them in the same ways we study other practices to see if they do indeed bring about the desired outcomes they promise. We are not aware of anything sacred about recovery-oriented practices that would protect them from scientific scrutiny. To the contrary: those in favor of introducing these practices should welcome the opportunity to determine their utility and effectiveness in as rigorous and scientifically credible a way as possible. It is just that much of this work remains to be done.

In the interim, we suggest that the argument practitioners make about there not yet being adequate evidence to justify the introduction of recovery and recovery-oriented practice misses a fundamentally important point. Not only is there an over-30-year history of accumulating evidence that establishes improvement to be as common as, if not more common than, prolonged disability in serious mental illness, as we described above, but effectiveness in mental health should be assessed by the degree to which services or supports promote recovery as their primary outcome. In other words, the evidence that is being sought or established is evidence of the degree to which an intervention contributes to a person's recovery, not the degree to which recovery contributes to a given intervention's effectiveness. Waiting to see how the introduction of recovery improves the quality of care provided and the outcomes produced prior to adopting a recovery orientation is thus to come at this issue backwards. Rather than conflicting with a recovery orientation, we suggest to the contrary that an emphasis on "evidence-based practice" can be extremely useful in contributing to system change. Discontinuing costly services for which there is no evidence of effectiveness offers a ready source of funds for reallocation, for practices with evidence of effectiveness and/or for practices that people in recovery identify as useful and request (e.g., housing and employment supports) but which may have yet to be the object of empirical evaluation.

With respect to payer issues, it is interesting to note that more progress has been made in this arena than in the scientific arena of evidence-based practices. Relying on more pragmatic and less rigorous evaluations of their utility and cost-effectiveness, both third-party payers and Medicaid have begun to fund rehabilitative and recovery-oriented practices. Georgia, Rhode Island, and Minnesota in particular have taken several significant steps in using Medicaid waiver and rehabilitation options to fund some of these services; this constitutes a promising beginning at least.

We suggest that recovery-oriented practices need not be incompatible with an emphasis on evidence and that they can, in fact, be reimbursable, with some posing minimal cost. We also suggest reframing evidence-based practice initiatives within the context of recovery and client choice,emphasizing the fact that the notion of *choice*—a core value to recovery—is really only meaningful when people have a range of accessible and effective alternatives from which to choose (Anthony, 1993). Given the relative dearth of practices that have amassed an adequate evidence base, we consider it premature to limit systems of care to these few options. In the interim, and given the dramatic data on cultural disparities in health care (Manderscheid & Henderson, 2001), we suggest including in evidence-based practice initiatives both recovery-oriented and culturally responsive services and *at the same time* collecting information on their utility and effectiveness. In addition, while much work remains to be done on the issues of funding and reimbursement, many lessons have been learned from early-adopter states that can be transferred to others.

Concern #2. Recovery Approaches Devalue the Role of Professional Intervention. "Why Did I Just Spend 10 Years in Training if Someone Else, with No Training, Is Going to Make All the Decisions?"

BASIS OF CONCERN   As noted previously, recovery models acknowledge that some people do well in the absence of specialty mental health care and that treatment and rehabilitation are only one source among several that people may find useful in promoting and sustaining their recovery. In addition, recovery models recognize that some aspects of the mental health system have historically imposed barriers to recovery rather than promoted it, generating their own iatrogenic effects. As a result, some practitioners may be under the impression that recovery is opposed to, or devalues and diminishes the role of, professional care or intervention.

RECOVERY-ORIENTED RESPONSE   We suggest in response that a recovery-oriented approach moves mental health closer to other medical specialties in which it is the specialist's role to assess the person's functioning, diagnose his or her condition, educate the person about the costs and benefits of the effective interventions available to treat the condition, and then, with provision of informed consent/permission to treat, competently provide the appropriate interventions. About this much even the consumer and family advocacy groups agree: mental illness is an illness like any other and should be treated as such, both by medical staff and by the general public. If this basic tenet is accepted, it is difficult to understand how practitioners—particularly psychiatrists—could continue to object that their roles are being diminished when they are being viewed on a par with, as no less important than, and as requiring no less skill or training than those of other medical specialists such as cardiologists or oncologists.

When presented with this argument, discussions have turned quickly to the issue of whether or not informed consent or permission to treat needs to be conceptualized differently in mental health than in other medical specialties. Adopting a civil rights model of psychiatric disability, we suggest first that the notion of recovery does extend to established constructs of informed consent and permission to treat in mental health. As in other forms of medicine, this means that no matter how expert or experienced the provider, it is ideally left up to the client and his or her loved ones to make decisions about his or her care. It is not the practitioner's role or responsibility to make such health care decisions *for* the person. We understand the recovery vision as applying these same constructs of informed consent and permission to treat to the majority of individuals with serious mental illness most of the time. However, given that one of the obligations of public mental health is to protect the community, we understand, and insist, that—again just as in other forms of medicine (e.g., emergency medicine)—there are exceptions to this rule.

These exceptions, as clearly delineated in federal and state statutes, invariably involve a person who poses a serious risk, either to
himself or herself or to others. This includes people in states of
acute distress and/or disorganization who are vulnerable to doing
things in such a state that they would never choose to do otherwise.
In these cases, just as in emergency medicine, the issue of informed
consent/permission to treat is suspended temporarily in order to
perform life-saving measures. These cases do not contradict the recovery vision but pose important challenges to it, challenges that may
in the future be addressed through such mechanisms as psychiatric
advance directives or other creative means to enable people to retain
control over their own lives even in such extreme circumstances.

Concern #1. Recovery Increases the Provider's Exposure to Risk and Liability. "If Recovery Is the Person's Responsibility, Then How Come I Get the Blame When Things Go Wrong?"

BASIS FOR CONCERN   There is a fundamental role for choice in
recovery-oriented care, both in terms of health care decisions and
in terms of everyday life decisions. This focus on choice has raised
the specter of risk for practitioners, who feel that they are already
held accountable for actions and behaviors of their clients over which
they have little, if any, control. Encouraging client choice thus appears
to contradict the community safety function of mental health au-
thorities as well as recent emphases on assessing and managing risk.

RECOVERY-ORIENTED RESPONSE   There are several responses to this
concern. First, most people with psychiatric disabilities pose no significant risk to the community. In fact, surveys consistently have
shown that this population is much more likely to be victimized than
to victimize others (Sells, Rowe, Fisk, & Davidson, 2003; Monahan,
1992). They also are much more likely to be victimized than the
general population, while generally posing no greater threat of com-
mitting violent acts (Monahan & Arnold, 1996; Mulvey, 1994). In
combination with the civil rights model of recovery described above,
these data suggest that people with serious mental illness (like all other
U.S. citizens) should be presumed innocent until proven otherwise.
In the realm of choice, this means being allowed to make one's own

decisions unless and until there are clear and persuasive grounds for imposing restrictions on this most fundamental of our civil rights (NCD, 2000).

Rather than arguing about whether or not the recovery vision increases risk (an issue about which we do not yet have data), it is perhaps more important to point out the ways in which a recovery-oriented approach actually clarifies and reinforces the need that already exists for appropriate risk assessment and management. Within the context of a recovery-oriented system of care, the competent conduct of risk assessments will be needed precisely in order to identify the circumstances in which people cannot be allowed to put themselves or others at risk. It is in no one's best interest to allow tragic and destructive actions (such as murders, suicides, and accidental deaths due to psychosis) to take place, *including the best interests of persons with serious mental illness*. Secondary to the people affected directly by such actions, people with psychiatric disabilities suffer most from these rare but tragic events, as these events serve only to confirm or increase existing fear, stigma, and discrimination among the general public.

By defining those cases or periods of time in which people pose sufficient risk to have others step in and make decisions for them, competent risk assessment and management leads to the additional by-product of delimiting a domain of behavior and a population of people who do *not* need the same intervention. This is an important by-product, as the recovery vision emphasizes not only the rights of people with serious mental illness but also the *responsibilities* they carry associated with community membership. In the majority of circumstances in which people do not pose immediate risks to themselves or others, it is not only their right to make their own decisions but also their responsibility. As Deegan (1992) has suggested, people need to have "the dignity of risk" and "the right to fail" in order to learn from their own mistakes; this constitutes an important source of growth in the process of recovery, as it does in life in general. Given the social climate in which mental health care is currently offered, it will be primarily through the timely and appropriate use of risk assessment and management strategies that this latitude will become possible.

Similar to the issues we discussed in the case of evidence-based practices, recovery advocates are neither afraid of nor do they dismiss the scrutiny of risk assessment. They welcome it. But they welcome it on the condition that, in the majority of cases, when people are found not to pose serious or imminent risks to themselves or others, they then are allowed to make their own choices, and, by necessity, their own mistakes. So, while a recovery orientation might in fact increase risk, it is primarily the person's access to opportunities for taking risks that needs to be increased, not necessarily the provider's or the community's exposure to risk.

In the end, then, we agree that recovery-oriented care entails risk. It entails risk because everyday life entails risk, as does the responsibility for managing one's own civic roles and duties. For the most part, however, this should involve risk-taking by the person with the serious mental illness, not by the practitioner. As it is primarily the ill person who has to do battle with his or her illness, it also is primarily the ill person who has to take risks to pursue his or her own recovery.

Discussion

In closing this chapter, we consider briefly two of the more fundamental issues that underlie these specific concerns. The first major issue that concerns practitioners and systems is, understandably, that of resources. The second, which accompanies any large-scale transformative efforts, pertains to the risks and fears entailed in culture change.

Primarily due to stigma and discrimination—both against our clients and against our field as a whole—mental health care has never been funded adequately. Not only has this historically been the case, but the introduction of managed care in the 1990s also resulted in cost-shifting and further declines in the levels of funding, which were already insufficient for behavioral health. As we noted earlier (but consider worthy of repeating), recent estimates suggest that the amount of funding currently provided for mental health care is 30% *lower* than that expended prior to deinstitutionalization (Bernstein, 2001; Manderscheid & Henderson, 2001).

To acknowledge this does not justify, however, the response of practitioners and systems that they will be happy to open new "recovery programs" or to make care more recovery-oriented if and when they are offered the requisite resources. As we argued above, recovery-oriented care cannot be considered as an add-on to existing care.

If we do not have adequate resources to begin with, we certainly do not have the resources needed to create a recovery-oriented system parallel to yet distinct from existing systems of care and conceptualized as an adjunct or ancillary service. There is no question that resources will be needed to fund recovery-oriented services and supports and to carry out the staff training and consultation needed to retool the mental health workforce. But until funding for mental health care is increased proportionately to need and is valued by our society more on a par with funding of physical health care, these resources will have to be derived in large part from those currently allocated to fund existing services, supports, and training.

That said, recovery-oriented systems of care will not stop offering active treatment to reduce the signs and symptoms of mental illness, nor will they stop offering rehabilitative interventions to address functional impairments. What primarily will be different about recovery-oriented systems of care, as we envision them, is that these interventions and supports will be provided in ways much more similar to than different from other health care services for other health care conditions. The people receiving these services will likewise continue with their ordinary lives, either recovering from the illness when possible or, when not yet possible, accessing the technologies, tools, and environmental accommodations needed for them to incorporate the illness or disability into their lives as only one component of a multidimensional existence and multifaceted sense of personal identity. In doing so, they will have to face no more discrimination or externally imposed threats to their personal sovereignty (i.e., as distinct from those posed by the nature of the illness itself) than people with diabetes, asthma, or arthritis.

Some well-meaning practitioners believe that this form of recovery-oriented care is something that is already being provided, and perhaps in some exemplary communities it is. Systemic transformation, however, will take time, and we expect the paradigm shift involved to require at least a generation to materialize in any substantive way. In the interim, it is ironic, perhaps, that taking the risk of offering recovery-oriented care promises to be one of the few ways possible to increase available resources. The more that programs implement elements of choice, self-determination, and a focus on the person's life goals and aspirations, and the more that data are collected to demonstrate effectiveness, the better our chances of advocating successfully for parity in coverage for mental illness. The more responsive our care, the more likely people with mental illness and their loved ones will be to join us in these advocacy efforts and to support, rather than challenge, the legitimacy of the work we do. Finally, the more effective our efforts at promoting community integration, the less people will need from the mental health system, allowing us to reduce caseload sizes and spend more of our time pursuing the aims that brought us into the field to begin with.

As our colleague Joe Marrone has eloquently pointed out, "Change is difficult, no matter how long you put it off." The culture change required by transformation is no exception. Reaching the tipping point in this process involves realizing that our commitment to the Hippocratic dictum of *Primum non nocere* ("First, do no harm") can no longer be a rationale for avoiding the risks entailed in recovery-oriented care. It involves recognizing that harm is in fact already being done every day that a person with a serious mental illness spends marginalized and demoralized, losing increasing control over, and responsibility for, his or her own life. Harm is done directly every day that a person is deprived of the right to make his or her own decisions and indirectly by reinforcing the notion that he or she is, and will remain, disabled rather than a *person* who can and will learn how to manage a disability in order to get on with his or her life. Now that we know that managing disability and reclaiming one's life are possibilities for people with serious mental illness, we can no longer settle for services that stop short of turning these possibilities into reality.

Moving beyond our current limitations will require some of the same conditions that are entailed in pursuit of recovery. We will need to afford our system and practitioners the same "dignity of risk" and "right to fail" that we consider basic to the rights of people with serious mental illness. And once it is firmly established, the recovery vision will allow us to see, albeit in retrospect, that the costs incurred by not taking such risks—the costs of institutionalization, chronic illness, despair, and homelessness—far outweigh the costs of doing so.

4   Practice Standards for

Recovery-Oriented Care

What does a recovery-oriented system of care look like in practice? As we suggested in the preceding chapters, the primary aim of recovery-oriented care is to offer people with serious mental illness a range of effective and culturally responsive interventions from which they may choose those services and supports they find useful in promoting or protecting their own recovery. In addition to diagnosing and reducing symptoms and deficits, a recovery-oriented system of care also identifies and builds on each individual's assets and areas of health and competence to support that person in achieving a sense of mastery over his or her condition while regaining a meaningful, constructive sense of membership in the broader community (Davidson et al., 2007).

While the goal of recovery-oriented care may appear, in this way, to be relatively clear and straightforward, the ways in which care can be used to promote recovery are neither so clear nor so straightforward—neither, unfortunately, are the ways in which care, as currently configured, may impede or undermine recovery. The following practice standards are offered as a beginning roadmap of this territory, bringing together what we think we know at this point about how care can best promote and sustain recovery, and how care may need to be transformed to no longer impede it. These standards are drawn from over two years of conversations with practitioners, people in recovery, families, and program managers and are informed by the current professional literature on recovery and recovery-oriented practice.

These standards focus primarily on the concrete work of practitioners and provider agencies so as to provide practical and useful direction to individuals and collectives that are committed to implementing recovery-oriented care. We recognize, however, that many of the practices described will require a broader commitment of agency leadership to significant and ongoing administrative restructuring. In the future, we also anticipate that systems will want to add domains to the ones we propose here, in such areas as prevention, early intervention, cultural competence, and the assessment and monitoring of outcomes. At present, however, our perception is that the field has only achieved consensus in the following domains:

A. Primacy of Participation
B. Promoting Access and Engagement
C. Ensuring Continuity of Care
D. Employing Strengths-Based Assessment
E. Offering Individualized Recovery Planning
F. Functioning as a Recovery Guide
G. Community Mapping, Development, and Inclusion
H. Identifying and Addressing Barriers to Recovery

A. The Primacy of Participation

An essential characteristic of recovery-oriented mental health care is the primacy it gives to the participation of people in recovery and their loved ones in all aspects and phases of the care delivery process. Beginning with the Federal Rehabilitation Act of 1973 and reaffirmed in 1990 in Public Law 99–660, federal and state governments have mandated the involvement of people with psychiatric disorders in all components of designing and implementing systems of community-based mental health care. This mandate has been confirmed consistently in numerous federal and state statutes and regulations issued since, and it forms the foundation of any effort to transform a system of care to a recovery-oriented model.

For the involvement of people in recovery and their families to be meaningful and substantive, it must go well beyond asking them to sign off on provider-driven treatment plans or endorse the adoption or replication of practitioner-driven models of care. Recovery-oriented care requires that people in recovery be involved in all aspects and phases of the care delivery process, from the initial framing of questions or problems to be addressed and the design of the capacity and needs assessments to be conducted, to the delivery, evaluation, and ongoing monitoring of care, and finally to the design and development of new services, interventions, and supports.

As recovery is what the person with the mental illness *does*, rather than something that can be done *to* or *for* the person by a care provider, people in recovery, by definition, are understood to be the foremost experts on their own needs and preferences for assistance in managing their condition and reconstructing their lives. As a result, recovery-oriented care consistently elicits and is substantially informed by the input and involvement of people in recovery across all levels, from recovery planning led by individual clients (see "E. Individualized Recovery Planning"), to program development and evaluation, to policy formulation.

You will know that you are placing primacy on the participation of people in recovery when:

1. People in recovery are routinely invited to share their stories with current service recipients and/or to provide training to staff.
2. People in recovery compose a significant proportion of representatives to an agency's board of directors, advisory board, or other steering committees and work groups; persons in recovery are provided orientation to their committee role by the chair and actively contribute to the group process; and their involvement in these groups is reflected in meeting minutes and in decision-making processes.
3. The input of people in recovery is valued, as reflected in the fact that the agency reimburses people for the time they spend participating in service planning, implementation, or evaluation activities; providing peer support and mentoring; and/or providing educational and training sessions for clients or staff. Where system involvement is a mutually negotiated volunteer activity, people in recovery are reimbursed for out-of-pocket expenses that may be associated with their participation.
4. Each person served is provided with an initial orientation to agency practices regarding client rights, complaint procedures, treatment options, advance directives, access to their records, advocacy organizations (e.g., protection and advocacy, human rights commissions), rehabilitation and community resources, and spiritual/chaplaincy services. Contact information on

program staff and agency leaders is made available. Provision of orientation is documented in the person's record.

5. Initial orientation is supplemented by the routine availability of information and agency updates to people in recovery and their loved ones. This information is provided in a variety of formats (e.g., information tables, service directories, educational programs, newsletters, Web postings) to enable people in recovery and their loved ones to make informed choices about treatments, rehabilitation, and supports and to provide meaningful input about program and agency performance. Feedback is regularly solicited from people in recovery and their loved ones regarding their informational needs.

6. Policies are established and maintained that allow people in recovery maximum opportunity for choice in and control over their own care. For example, people in recovery are able to (a) access their records with minimal barriers, (b) incorporate psychiatric advance directives in their recovery and crisis plans, (c) secure the services of local or state advocacy services as necessary, (d) request transfer to an alternative practitioner within agency guidelines, and (e) participate actively in agency planning activities. These policies and procedures are highlighted on admission to the agency and are routinely publicized throughout the agency via newsletters, educational postings, consumer empowerment councils, and so forth. This process is particularly crucial in relation to such services as "money management," within which the line between providing a service and infringing on people's rights can easily be blurred in the absence of clear programmatic guidelines and safeguards.

7. Measures of satisfaction with services and supports are collected routinely and in a timely fashion from people in recovery and their loved ones. These data are used in strategic planning and quality improvement initiatives to evaluate and make meaningful changes in programs, policies, procedures, and interventions. Feedback mechanisms are in place to inform people in recovery and their loved ones of changes and actions taken based on their input.

8. Formal grievance procedures are established and made readily available to people in recovery and their loved ones to address their dissatisfaction with services. People in recovery and their loved ones are fully informed about these procedures on a

regular basis, and the frequency and focus of grievances are tracked to inform agency or program quality-improvement processes.

9. Administration enforces ethical practice through active human-resource oversight. This oversight prohibits the use of coercive practices and holds all staff accountable for affording people in recovery maximum control over their own treatment and rehabilitation.

10. Assertive efforts are made to recruit people in recovery for a variety of staff positions they are qualified for. These include positions that their personal experience of disability and recovery make them uniquely qualified for (e.g., peer support), as well as positions for which they are qualified by virtue of licensure (e.g., nursing, psychiatry) or other training or work experience (clerical, administrative, medical records, etc.). Assertive efforts include establishing mentoring programs for employees in recovery so they can advance in their skills and attain the necessary credentialing that will allow them to occupy a more diverse range of agency positions.

11. Active recruitment of people in recovery for existing staff positions is coupled with ongoing support for the development of a range of peer-operated services that function independently of, but in collaboration with, the professional agency. This will help ensure that the recovery community's role is supported, while avoiding co-opting by transforming the community into an adjunct service provider. As one example, recovery community centers operated by people in recovery should be available in all areas. Such recovery centers are neither treatment centers nor social clubs; they are places where people who are interested in learning about recovery can meet with other nonprofessionals to get support, learn about recovery and treatment resources, and simply find people to talk with.

    Agencies can demonstrate their support for peer-operated services by offering material and supervisory support to emerging programs. For example, technical assistance or mentoring regarding business management, attainment of 501(c)3 status, human resource practices, and so on, can greatly facilitate the establishment and long-term viability of emerging peer-operated services. Care should be taken to ensure capacity-building and enhanced independence in the peer-operated program over time. As with all community support programs, peer-operated services should be well integrated with the agency at large in terms of committee membership, and recovery planning should take place at the individual level.

12. Self-disclosure by employed persons in recovery is respected as a personal decision and is not prohibited by agency policy or practice. Supervision is available to discuss the complex issues that can arise with self-disclosure.

13. Staff appreciate that many people in recovery may not, at first, understand that they are the foremost experts on the management of their own condition. Persons who have come to depend upon services and professionals to alleviate their distress may neither believe themselves capable of being the experts nor recognize that they are entitled to occupy this role. Therefore, staff members must encourage individuals to claim their rights and to make meaningful contributions to their own care and to the system as a whole. Success occurs when, for example, individuals are encouraged to become involved in local and state advocacy as a means of developing their confidence and skills in self-determination and collective action, agency efforts to enhance the participation of service users are widely publicized to the recovery community, and general education is offered regarding the necessity of active service-user involvement to achieve recovery outcomes. While people are to be encouraged to become involved at all levels of the system, not everyone will want to participate beyond the primary level of involvement (i.e., their personal recovery plan). As in other areas of self-determination, this too is respected as a valid choice.

14. The agency offers to host local, regional, and/or state events and advocacy activities for people in recovery and their loved ones (e.g., meetings of 12-step fellowships; local chapters of the National Alliance on Mental Illness [NAMI], Schizophrenics Anonymous, and GROW).

What you will hear from people in recovery when you are placing primacy on participation:

- *You know, at first I thought, "What do I know or what could I possibly say at this meeting?" But then I could tell that what I had to say made a difference. People were really listening to me. I finally got a place at the table!*

- *I knew I was in recovery when I could help somebody else who was in the same awful place I used to be. But I think about where I am today: healthy and drug-free, and being a real Grandma. And getting back in the work field as a peer provider makes me feel good, makes me understand that I can do this. I can really do this. And if I could do this, anybody can do this. Folks get hope when they look at me.*

- *I don't have to hide who I am—even the part of me that isn't well. Because it's that part of me and all the things I've experienced as a client here—good and bad—that gives me ideas for how things could change.*

- *I just didn't think my program was a good fit for me. I was sticking it out, but lots of other folks stopped showing up. But then somebody came in and we had a great talk about what was working and what wasn't in the program, and some changes actually got made. Things are a lot better now. The group is packed every week!*

B. Promoting Access and Engagement

A core principle of the deinstitutionalization movement of the 1950s and beyond was that people with serious mental illness should receive mental health services in the least restrictive setting possible within their home communities. Community mental health centers and clinics were developed in large part in response to this principle. Unfortunately, many people with serious mental illness did not receive care due to a variety of factors, such as inadequate funding for community-based services, administrative and bureaucratic barriers that discouraged people from seeking care, expectations of motivation for treatment that did not take into account internal (to the person) or external (in the person's environment) barriers to care, a lack of knowledge of ways to engage people living in the community in psychiatric treatment, clients' avoidance of the mental health system because of previous negative experiences, and clients' inability to meet the requirements of treatment (e.g., appointment times) due to the exigencies of their lives of poverty and/or homelessness or due to their psychiatric symptoms. Thus, many people who were eligible for services did not receive them and suffered impoverished lives without adequate treatment, social support, or material resources in the community.

For these, and additional, reasons, the Surgeon General's Report on Mental Health (DHHS, 1999) suggested that for each person who seeks and receives specialty mental health care for a diagnosable psychiatric disorder, there remain two individuals with similar conditions who will neither seek access to nor receive such care. This report was followed by a supplement on culture, race, and ethnicity, which further identified lack of access to care as an even more formidable obstacle to recovery among people of color (DHHS, 2001). These facts clearly warrant the attention of the mental health system, including a greater focus on efforts to enhance access and engage people in care.

For our purposes, *access to care* involves facilitating swift and uncomplicated entry into care, and it can be increased through a variety of means. These include conducting outreach to persons who may not otherwise receive information about services or who may avoid institutional settings where services are provided and establishing numerous points of entry into a wide range of treatment, rehabilitative, social, and other support services. The following is an example of a successful sequence: a public health nurse working with a homeless outreach team facilitates a person's entry into mental health care, a clinician helps the person gain access to vocational services and entitlement income support, and, with the client's permission, all of these service practitioners meet with or talk to each other regularly to coordinate their work with the person. Lastly, facilitating access includes ensuring that information about services is made readily available and understandable to people through public education and information, liaison with other agencies, and links to self-help groups and other venues.

Access to care also involves removing barriers to receiving care— including bureaucratic red tape, intimidating or unwelcoming physical environments and program procedures, schedule conflicts, and modes of service provision that conflict with the life situations and demands of persons with serious mental illness. It also means that access to care goes far beyond mere eligibility to receive services. Finally, access to care involves moving away from traditional philosophies of treatment—including the need to "hit bottom" first (e.g., "People can't be helped until they hit bottom and have lost everything") and incrementalism (e.g., "People can't work until they are

stable on medication and their symptoms have been reduced")—
and toward *stages of change* approaches, recognizing that addressing
basic needs, employment, and housing can enhance motivation for
treatment and recovery.

Engagement in services is closely tied to access to care. Engagement
involves making contact with the person rather than with the diagnosis or disability, building trust over time, attending to the person's
stated needs, and, directly or indirectly, providing a range of services in addition to clinical care. The process of engagement benefits
from new understandings of motivational enhancement, which sees
people at various points on a continuum from pre-readiness for treatment to being in recovery, rather than as being either "motivated"
or "unmotivated."

Engagement involves sensitivity to the thin line between persua-
sion and coercion and attention to the power differential between
the service provider and the client or potential client, as well as to
the ways these factors can undermine personal choice. Finally, methods of ensuring access and engagement are integrated within and are
part of, as opposed to adjuncts or qualifications to, providing good
clinical and rehabilitative care.

You will know that you are promoting access and engagement when:

1. The service system has the capacity to go where the potential
   client is, rather than always insisting that the client come to the
   service. Services and structures (e.g., hours of operation and
   locations of services) are designed around client needs,
   characteristics, and preferences.
2. The team provides, or can help the person gain swift access to,
   a wide range of services. People can access these services from
   many different points. In a "no wrong door" approach to
   providing an array of services, individuals can also self-refer to
   a range of service options (e.g., specialized rehabilitation
   supports) without the need for referral from a primary clinical
   provider. In addition, individuals can access rehabilitation
   programs and community supports without being mandated to
   participate in clinical care. However, self referrals will be
   subject to admission processes and need approval by a
   licensed entity to satisfy reimbursement and accreditation
   needs.

3. There is not a strict separation between clinical and case management functions, though there may be differences in expertise and training of the people providing these services. Services and supports address presenting clinical issues, but they are also responsive to pressing social, housing, employment, and spiritual needs. For example, employment is valued as a crucial element of recovery. Building skills and finding employment are competencies included in all staff job descriptions, including those of clinical providers, with only the most difficult-to-place clients being referred to specialized programs.

4. The assessment of motivation is based on a stages-of-change model, and services and supports incorporate motivational enhancement strategies that assist practitioners in meeting each person at his or her own level. Training in these strategies is required for all staff who work with people with serious mental illness in order to help move people toward recovery.

5. Staff and agencies look for signs of organizational barriers or other obstacles to care before concluding that a client is noncompliant with treatment or unmotivated for care—for example, meeting the child-care needs of women with children.

6. Agencies have "zero rejection" policies that do not exclude people from care based on symptoms, substance use, or unwillingness to participate in prerequisite clinical or program activities. For example, vocational rehabilitation agencies do not employ screening procedures based on arbitrary "work readiness" criteria, as such criteria have limited predictive validity regarding employment outcomes. Such procedures also are based on the assumption that individuals must attain, and maintain, clinical stability or abstinence before they can pursue a life in the community, when in fact employment and other meaningful activities often form a path by which people become stable in the first place.

7. Staff have an "open case" policy that dictates that a person's refusal of services, even despite intensive and long-term outreach and engagement, does not require that he or she be dropped from the "outreach" list. This person may still accept services at another time. Committee structures and supervision are in place to evaluate the fine line between assertive outreach versus potential harassment or coercion. In addition, the agency establishes guidelines regarding what defines an "active" versus

an "outreach" client and considers how such definitions impact program enrollment, documentation standards, dropout lists, case load definitions, and reimbursement strategies.

8. From an administrative perspective, the system builds on a commitment to and practice of motivational enhancement, with reimbursement for pre-treatment and recovery management supports. This includes flexibility in outpatient care, including low-intensity care for those who do not presently choose or benefit from high-intensity treatment.

9. Outpatient substance abuse treatment clinicians are paired with outreach workers to capitalize on the moment of crisis that can lead people with co-occurring disorders to accept treatment and to gain access to their appropriate level of care.

10. Mental health professionals, addiction specialists, and people in recovery are placed in critical locales to assist in the early stages of engagement—for example, in shelters, courts, hospital emergency rooms, and community health centers. The agency develops and establishes the necessary memoranda of agreement and protocols to facilitate co-location of services.

11. The team or agency employs staff with first-person experience of recovery who have enhanced credibility for making contact with and engaging people in services and treatment.

12. Housing and support options are available for those who are not interested in, or ready for, detoxification but who may begin to engage in their own recovery if housing and support are available to them. Practitioner ambivalence regarding harm-reduction approaches and the issue of public support for persons who are actively using must be addressed in relation to this point.

What you will hear from people when you are promoting access and engagement:

- *I didn't want nothing to do with them at first, but folks from the Center just kept showing up . . . they didn't drop me or let me get off on the wrong track . . . they didn't give up, they just stuck by me. They were like a velvet bulldozer.*

- *I hated going to their building. Everybody looked at me as I was walking up the block like, "Oh, I wonder if he's a patient there—crazy and on dope." So, I just never went. But they came to me on my own turn and my own terms. Today, I think my case manager is the reason I'm still alive.*

- *I got help with the kinds of things that were most important to me—like getting my daughter back, and putting food on the table for her. Since they were willing to help me with that stuff, I figured, "Hey, maybe I should listen to what they are telling me and try out that program they keep talking about." Today I've been clean for nine months . . . .*
- *Nobody wanted anything to do with me before. It was always, "Come back and see us when you get serious about your recovery . . . when you've got some clean urines." But then this program tried to help me out with getting this job I had wanted for a really long time. Now, I am working part time and I've finally got a reason to be sober every day.*
- *They knew when to take no for an answer. They didn't stay on my back all the time, but I knew they were always there for me if I needed them. Now I don't say no so often.*

C. Ensuring Continuity of Care

Recovery in mental health, in the sense in which we are using it in this book, refers to a prolonged or long-term process. That is, it does not refer to an acute phenomenon such as recovery from the flu or from a broken bone. This is not to say that mental illness cannot also be acute. Many people do, in fact, experience an isolated episode of mental illness and do not develop a prolonged condition.

For people experiencing only one acute and delimited episode of mental illness, however, the notion of recovery is unlikely to have much relevance. Such individuals are unlikely to consider or refer to themselves, for example, as being "in recovery" from a psychiatric disorder. In the face of the significant stigma and discrimination that continue to be associated with mental illnesses by the general public, these persons seldom disclose their psychiatric history or define themselves in terms of this isolated episode of illness, preferring to return quietly to the normal lives they led previously. Without giving much thought to the repercussions of their condition for their social role or sense of identity, such individuals are unlikely to describe themselves as being "in recovery" from anything.

For those individuals for whom being in recovery is a meaningful goal, their struggle with mental illness is likely to be sustained.

In such cases—which, it should be acknowledged, compose a significant segment of the population who receive care from public-sector systems—an acute model of care is neither the most useful nor most appropriate. Particularly in terms of system design, prolonged conditions call for longitudinal models that emphasize continuity of care over time and across programs. Consistent with the principles undergirding the "new recovery movement" in addictions, the long-term nature of serious mental illness suggests a number of parameters for developing new models of care that go beyond loosely linked acute episodes (White, 2001).

These models are based on the belief that full recovery is seldom achieved following a single episode of treatment, and that practitioners, as well as clients, families, and policy makers, should not be disappointed or discouraged by the fact that there are no quick fixes (White, 2001). Similar to (other) chronic medical illnesses, previous treatment of a person's condition also should not be taken to be indicative of a poor prognosis, of noncompliance, or of the person's not trying hard enough to recover. Exacerbations of psychiatric symptoms are to be viewed as further evidence of the severity of the person's condition rather than as causes for discharge (for example, we do not discharge a person from a cardiologist's care for having a second or third heart attack). All of these principles suggest that treatment, rehabilitation, and support are not to be offered through serial episodes of disconnected care by different practitioners, but through a carefully crafted system of care that ensures the continuity of the person's most significant healing relationships and supports over time and across episodes, programs, and agencies.

You will know that you are ensuring continuity of care when:

1. The central concern of engagement shifts from "How do we get the client into treatment?" to "How do we nest the process of recovery within the person's natural environment?" For example, people have often asked for meeting places and activities to be available on weekends, especially for individuals who are in the early stages of their recovery and for whom these times can be particularly difficult.
2. Services are designed to be welcoming to all individuals, and there is a low threshold (i.e., minimal requirements) for entry into care. There also is an emphasis on outreach and

pre-treatment recovery support services that can ensure that individuals are not unnecessarily excluded from care. If a person is denied care, he or she receives a written explanation as to why and is connected to appropriate alternatives, including appointments and transportation.

3. Eligibility and reimbursement strategies for this group of individuals (i.e., outreach and pre-engagement) are established and refined as necessary over time by administrative leadership.

4. People have a flexible array of options to choose from, and options are not limited to what "programs" are available. These options allow for a high degree of individualization and a greater emphasis on the physical/social ecology (i.e., context) of recovery.

5. Individuals are not expected or required to progress through a continuum of care in a linear or sequential manner. For example, individuals are not required to enroll in a group home as a condition of hospital discharge when this is determined solely by professionals to be the most appropriate level of care. Rather, within the context of a responsive continuum of care, individuals work in collaboration with their recovery team to select the services from the array that meet their particular needs and preferences at a given time.

6. In a recovery management model, an individual's stage of change is considered at all points in time, and the focus of care is on enhancing existing strengths and recovery capital. The assessment of problems and needs is consistently coupled with an assessment of resources and strengths in both initial and ongoing recovery planning. This is best achieved by including the person's family and kinship network and any natural supports he or she believes would be supportive of recovery.

7. Goals and objectives in the recovery plan are not defined by practitioners based on clinically valued outcomes (e.g., reducing symptoms, increasing adherence) but rather are defined by the client with a focus on building recovery capital and pursuing a life in the community.

8. The overall focus of care shifts from preventing relapse to promoting recovery. Services are not primarily oriented toward crisis or problem resolution (for example, detoxification and stabilization). There is a full array of recovery support services, including proactive, preventive supports and post-crisis, community-based resources such as adequate and safe housing,

recovery community centers operated by people in recovery, sustained recovery coaching, monitoring with feedback, and early reintervention if necessary. The concept of "aftercare" is irrelevant, as all care is considered continuing care and there is a commitment to provide ongoing, flexible support as necessary.

9. Valued outcomes are influenced by the system's commitment to ensuring continuity of care. For example, less emphasis is placed on a professional review of the short-term outcomes of single episodes of care (e.g., readmission or incarceration rates) and more emphasis is placed on the long-term effects of service combinations and sequences on the outcomes valued by the client, such as quality of life issues, including satisfaction with housing, relationships, and employment.

10. The range of valued expertise is expanded beyond specialized clinical and rehabilitative professionals and technical experts to include the contributions of many individuals and services. These individuals may include peers in paid or volunteer positions, mutual aid groups, indigenous healers, faith-community leaders, primary care providers, and other natural supports. Valuing and incorporating such community resources in ongoing care planning is viewed as essential to decreasing dependence on formal mental health care and assisting the person to develop a more natural recovery network. In this spirit, the community, rather than the clinic or agency, is viewed as the ultimate context for sustained recovery.

11. Individuals are seen as capable of illness self-management, and interventions support this as a valued goal of recovery-oriented services. People are actively involved in all aspects of their care, including policy development, assessment, goal setting, and evaluation. These different forms of involvement build capacity for independent community living and are powerful antidotes to the passivity and dependence that may have resulted from years of being a recipient of professionally prescribed and delivered care. In the process of decreasing the power differential that traditionally has characterized relationships between clients and practitioners, care is conceptualized within a partnership or consultant framework in which services—while available over the long-term—may be time-limited and accessed by the person when and as he or she deems necessary.

12. New technologies (e.g., tele-medicine and Web-based applications and self-help resources) are incorporated as service options to enhance illness self-management and collaborative treatment relationships.
13. Access to housing, employment, and other supports that make recovery sustainable is enhanced. This includes changing policies and laws that restrict people's access to employment and home ownership, such as having a criminal record for nonviolent, one-time, drug-dealing offenses or offenses related to mental illness.
14. Policy formulation and legislative advocacy at the administrative level are coupled with ongoing efforts to work collaboratively with a variety of state systems to ensure continuity of care—for example, with the Department of Corrections to put into place plans for re-entry, or with resources such as Oxford Houses and rental assistance for people with substance-abuse disorders coming out of jails and prisons.
15. In order to facilitate sustained recovery and community inclusion, advocacy efforts are extended beyond institutional policies and procedures to the larger community, including stigma-busting, community education, and community resource development activities.

What you will hear from people when you are ensuring continuity of care:

- *They were there for me—no strings attached. I didn't walk through the door and get a whole bunch of expectations dumped on me.*
- *People respected that I was doing the best I could. It was two steps forward, one step back for a long time, but overall I was moving in the right direction for the first time in as long as I could remember. But they stuck with me for the long haul. Now, I've been clean for 18 months, and someone still calls me every day to check in—even if it's just to say, "Hi, how ya' doin'?"*
- *I didn't get kicked out of the program because I had a dirty urine—it used to be that happened every week. This time, I had been clean for two months. My case manager reminded me of how good it was in those two months, and I wanted to get back there.*
- *It used to be I was terrified of leaving detox. I'd go back to the same crappy environment and be back out on the streets in a matter of days. But I got into some sober housing, and it changed my life.*

- *They knew I needed to work on my recovery AND my life at the same time. That meant getting a part-time job, paying off my debts, working on my marriage, and learning how to enjoy myself again and to do it all drug-free.*

D. Employing Strengths-Based Assessment

As described above, traditional mental health services were based on a narrow, acute-care model that perceived mental illnesses as diseases that could be treated and cured. While this approach works effectively for many people, for many others it primarily serves to add to their already heavy burdens. In these cases, practitioners have had an unfortunate tendency to overlook the remaining and coexisting areas of health, assets, strengths, and competencies that the person continues to have at his or her disposal—what remains "right" with people—by focusing on the assessment and treatment of their deficits, symptoms, and impairments—what is "wrong" with people. Emphasizing the negative in this way has led to a tremendous sense of hopelessness and despair among both clients and the mental health practitioners who serve them.

In addition, focusing solely on deficits in the absence of a thoughtful analysis of strengths disregards the most critical resources an individual has on which to build in his or her efforts to adapt to stressful situations, confront environmental challenges, improve his or her quality of life, and advance in his or her unique recovery journey. As the process of improvement depends, in the end, on the resources, reserves, efforts, and assets of and around the individual, family, or community, a recovery orientation encourages practitioners to view the glass as half full rather than half empty (Saleeby, 2001).

Following principles that have been articulated at length by Rapp (1998) and others, strengths-based approaches allow professionals to balance critical needs that must be met with the resources and strengths that individuals and families possess to assist them in this process. This perspective encourages practitioners to recognize that, no matter how disabled, every person continues to have strengths and capabilities as well as the capacity to continue to learn and develop. The failure of an individual to display competencies or strengths is therefore not necessarily attributed to deficits within the person but may rather, or additionally, be due to the failure of the service system or broader community to adequately elicit information in this area or to create the opportunities and support needed for these strengths to be displayed.

While system and assessment procedures have made strides in recent years regarding inquiry into the area of individual resources and capacities, simply *asking* an individual what strengths he or she possesses or what things the person thinks he or she may be "good at" may not be enough to solicit the information that is critical to the recovery planning process. For example, many people who have chronic conditions will at first report that they have no strengths. Such a response should not be taken at face value; rather, it should be seen as representative of the years of difficulties and failures they may have endured and the degree of demoralization that has resulted. Over time, it is not uncommon for such individuals to lose touch with the healthier and more positive aspects of themselves and become unable to see beyond their "patient" role.

When facing such circumstances, practitioners need to conceptualize one of their first steps as helping this person get back in touch with his or her previous interests, talents, and gifts. The guidelines below are intended to assist practitioners in conducting a comprehensive, strengths-based assessment that can help people rediscover themselves as capable individuals with a history, a future, and strengths and interests beyond their symptoms, deficits, or impairments.

You will know that you are providing strengths-based assessment when:

1. A discussion of strengths is a central focus of every assessment, care plan, and case summary. Assessments begin with the assumption that individuals are the experts on their own recovery and that they have learned much in the process of living with and working through their struggles. This strengths-based assessment is conducted as a collaborative process, and all assessments in written form are shared with the individual.

2. Initial assessments recognize the power of simple yet powerful questions such as "What happened?" "What have you found helpful in the past?" "What do you think would be helpful?" and "What are your goals in life?" Self-assessment tools rating the

level of satisfaction in various life areas can be useful ways to identify diverse goals for which supports can then be designed.

3. Practitioners attempt to interpret perceived deficits within a "strength and resilience" framework, as this will allow the individual to identify less with the limitations of the disorder. For example, an individual who takes medication irregularly may automatically be perceived as "noncompliant," "lacking insight," or "requiring monitoring to take meds as prescribed." This same individual, however, could also be seen as "making use of alternative coping strategies such as exercise and relaxation to reduce reliance on medications" or could be praised for "working collaboratively to develop a contingency plan for when medications are to be used on an 'as-needed' basis."

4. While strengths of the individual are a focus of the assessment procedure, thoughtful consideration also is given to potential strengths and resources within the individual's family, natural support network, service system, and community at large. This is consistent with the view that recovery is not a solitary process but rather a journey toward interdependence within one's community of choice.

5. The diversity of strengths that can serve as resources for the person and his or her recovery planning team is respected. Saleeby (2001), for example, recommends conceptualizing strengths broadly to include the following dimensions: skills (e.g., gardening, caring for children, speaking Spanish, creating budgets), talents (e.g., playing the bagpipes, cooking), personal virtues and traits (e.g., insight, patience, sense of humor, self-discipline), interpersonal skills (e.g., comforting the sick, giving advice, mediating conflicts), interpersonal and environmental resources (e.g., extended family, good neighbors), cultural knowledge and lore (e.g., healing ceremonies and rituals, stories of cultural perseverance), family stories and narratives (e.g., migration and settlement, falls from grace and redemption), knowledge gained from struggling with adversity (e.g., how one came to survive past events, how one maintains hope and faith), knowledge gained from occupational or parental roles (e.g., caring for others, planning events), spirituality and faith (e.g., a system of meaning to rely on, a declaration of purpose beyond self), and hopes and dreams (e.g., personal goals and vision, positive expectations about a better future).

6. In addition to the assessment of individual capacities, it is beneficial to explore other areas not traditionally considered "strengths"—for example, the individual's most significant or most valued accomplishments, ways of relaxing and having fun, ways of calming down when upset, preferred living environment, educational achievements, personal heroes, most meaningful compliment ever received, and so forth.

7. Assessment explores the whole of people's lives while ensuring emphasis is given to the individual's expressed and pressing priorities. For example, people experiencing problems with mental illness or addiction often place less emphasis on symptom reduction and abstinence than on desired improvements in other areas of life, such as work, financial security, safe and affordable housing, or relationships. For this reason, it is beneficial to explore in detail each individual's needs and resources in these areas.

8. Strengths-based assessments ask people what has worked for them in the past and incorporate these ideas in the recovery plan. People are more likely to use strategies that they have personally identified or developed than those that have been prescribed for them by others.

9. Guidance for completing a strengths-based assessment may be derived from certain interviewing strategies employed in solution-focused approaches to treatment. For example, DeJong and Miller (1995) recommend the following types of inquiry: exploring for exceptions (occasions when the problem could have occurred but did not); imagining a future when the problem has been solved and exploring, in detail, how life would then be different; assessing coping strategies—that is, asking how an individual is able to cope despite the presence of such problems; and using scaling questions (where the individual rates his or her current experience of the problem) to elucidate what might be subtle signs of progress.

10. Illness self-management strategies and daily wellness approaches such as wellness recovery action planning (WRAP) (Copeland, 1997) are respected as highly effective, person-directed recovery tools and are fully explored in the strengths-based assessment process.

11. Cause-and-effect explanations are offered with caution in strengths-based assessment, as such thinking can lead to

simplistic resolutions that fail to address the complexity of the person's situation. In addition, simplistic solutions may inappropriately assign blame for the problem to the individual, with blame being described as "the first cousin" of deficit-based models of practice. For example, to conclude that an individual did not pay his or her rent as a direct consequence of his or her "noncompliance" with medications could lead to an intrusive intervention to exert control over the individual's finances or medication. Strengths-based assessments respect that problem situations are usually the result of complex, multidimensional influences and explore with the person in more detail the various factors that led to his or her decisions and behavior (e.g., expressing displeasure with a negligent landlord).

12. Strengths-based assessments are developed through in-depth discussion with the individual as well as attempts to solicit collateral information regarding the person's strengths from the family and natural supports. Since obtaining all of the necessary information requires time and a trusting relationship with the person, a strengths-based assessment may need to be completed (or expanded) after the initial contact as treatment and rehabilitation unfold. While each situation may vary, the assessment is written up as soon as possible in order to help guide the work and interventions of the recovery planning team. Modular approaches to service delivery, billing, and reimbursement are considered by local and state leadership; for example, certain information is gathered in the first 24 hours, with additional factors being assessed by the end of one week, one month, etc.

13. Efforts are made to record the individual's responses verbatim rather than translating the information into professional language. This helps to ensure that the assessment remains narrative-based and person-centered. If technical language must be used, it is translated appropriately and presented in a person-first, nonoffensive manner—for example, one that avoids the language of dysfunction or disorder.

14. Practitioners are mindful of the power of language and carefully avoid the subtle messages that professional language has historically conveyed to people with psychiatric diagnoses or addictions, as well as to their loved ones. Language is used

that is empowering, avoiding the eliciting of pity or sympathy, as this can cast people with disabilities in a passive, "victim" role and reinforce negative stereotypes. For example, just as we have learned to refer to "people who use wheelchairs" as opposed to "the wheelchair-bound," we should refer to "individuals who use medication as a recovery tool" as opposed to people who are "dependent on medication for clinical stability." In particular, words such as "hope" and "recovery" are used frequently in documentation and delivery of services.

15. Practitioners avoid using diagnostic labels as catch-all means of describing an individual (e.g., "she's a borderline"), as such labels yield minimal information regarding the person's actual experience or manifestation of the illness. Alternatively, a person's needs are best captured not by a label but by an accurate description of his or her functional strengths and limitations. While diagnostic profiles may be required for other purposes (e.g., decisions regarding medication, justification of level of care), asset-based assessment places limited value on diagnosis per se. In addition, acknowledging limitations and areas of need are not viewed as accepting one's fate as being a chronically mentally ill person. Rather, identifying and accepting one's current limitations is seen as a constructive step in the process of recovery. Gaining perspective on both strengths and weaknesses is critical in this process, as it allows the person to identify, pursue, and achieve life goals despite the lingering presence of disability.

16. Language used is neither stigmatizing nor objectifying. At all times, "person-first" language is used to acknowledge that the disability is not as important as the person's individuality and humanity: for example, "a person with schizophrenia" versus "a schizophrenic," or "a person with an addiction" versus "an addict." Employing person-first language does not mean that a person's disability is hidden or seen as irrelevant; however, it also is not to be the sole focus of any description about that person. To make it the sole focus is depersonalizing and is no longer considered an acceptable practice.

17. Exceptions to person-first and empowering language that are preferred by some persons in recovery are respected. For instance, the personal preferences of some individuals with substance-abuse disorders, particularly those who work the

12 Steps as a primary tool of their recovery, may at times be inconsistent with person-first language. Within the 12 Step fellowships, early steps in the recovery process involve admitting one's powerlessness over a substance and acknowledging how one's life has become unmanageable. It is also common for such individuals to introduce themselves by saying, "My name is X and I am an alcoholic." This preference is respected as a part of the person's chosen recovery process, and it is understood that it would be contrary to recovery principles to pressure the person to identify as "a person with alcoholism" in the name of person-first language or principles. Use of person-first language is in the service of the person's recovery; it is not a superordinate principle to which the person must conform. While the majority of people with disabilities prefer to be referred to in first-person language, when in doubt ask the person what he or she prefers.

What you will hear from people when you are employing strengths-based assessment:

- *I used to think my life was over, but my illness isn't a death sentence. It's just one small part of who I am. Sometimes I forget about those other parts—the healthy parts of me. But my counselor always reminds me. You really need someone like that in your life.*
- *Being in recovery means that I know I have certain limitations and things I can't do. But rather than letting these limitations be an occasion for despair and giving up, I have learned that in knowing what I can't do, I also open up the possibilities of all I can do.*
- *I thought I was so alone in my problems. I may not feel as though I have much strength right now, but I realize I can draw strength from all the people around me— my friends, my neighbors, my pastor, and my counselors here at the Center.*
- *When they asked me about what I was good at and what sorts of things in my life made me happy, at first I didn't know who they were talking to. Nobody ever asked me those kinds of questions before. Just sitting through that interview, I felt better than before I had walked through the door!*
- *No one here treats me like a label. Just because I have schizophrenia, that doesn't tell you a whole lot. My roommate does too, but we couldn't be more different. Folks here take the time to get to know lots of things about me, not just the things that go along with my diagnosis.*

E. Offering Individualized Recovery Planning

In accordance with the relevant federal and state statutes, as well as the guidelines of the Joint Commission for the Accreditation of Healthcare Organizations (JCAHO), the Commission for the Accreditation of Rehabilitation Facilities (CARF), and other accrediting bodies regarding the need for individualized care, all treatment and rehabilitative services and supports to be provided shall be based on an individualized, multidisciplinary recovery plan developed in collaboration with the person receiving these services and any others that he or she identifies as supportive of this process. While based on a model of collaboration and partnership, significant effort will be taken to ensure that individuals' rights to self-determination are respected and that all individuals are afforded maximum opportunity to exercise choice in the full range of treatment and life decisions. The individualized recovery plan will satisfy the criteria of treatment, service, or care plans required by other bodies (e.g., the Centers for Medicaid and Medicare Services) and will include a comprehensive and culturally sensitive assessment of the person's hopes, assets, strengths, interests, and goals in addition to a holistic understanding of his or her mental health conditions and other medical concerns within the context of his or her daily life.

Typical examples of such life-context issues include employment, education, housing, spirituality, social and sexual relationships, and involvement in meaningful and pleasurable activities. In order to ensure competence in these respective areas, including competence in addressing the person's cultural background and affiliations, the multidisciplinary team will not be limited to psychiatrists, nurses, psychologists, and social workers but may also include rehabilitative and peer staff and, wherever possible, relevant community representatives and/or others identified by the client.

Building on the strengths-based assessment process, individualized recovery planning both encourages and expects the person to draw upon his or her strengths to participate actively in the recovery process. It is imperative throughout this process that practitioners maintain a belief in the individual's potential for growth and development, up to and including the ability to exit successfully from services. Practitioners also solicit the person's own hopes, dreams, and aspirations, encouraging individuals to pursue their preferred goals even if doing so presents potential risks or challenges.

For example, many people identify returning to work as a primary recovery goal. It is not uncommon for practitioners to advise against this step, based on their assumption either that an individual is not "work ready" or that employment will be detrimental to his or her recovery, whether because the stress of working could precipitate symptoms or relapse or because the new income could endanger the person's disability benefits. While such advice is rooted in good intentions, it sends a powerful message to the individual and can reinforce self-doubts and feelings of inadequacy. Rather than discouraging the person from pursuing this goal, the practitioner can have a frank discussion with the person about his or her concerns while highlighting the strengths that the individual can draw upon to take the first step toward achieving this goal.

In this vein, individualized recovery planning explicitly acknowledges that recovery entails the person's taking risks to try new things and is enhanced by the availability of opportunities for the person to learn from his or her own mistakes and their natural consequences. This is an important source of progress in the person's efforts to rebuild his or her life in the community that—similar to exercising one's muscles—cannot proceed without an exertion of the person's own faculties.

You will know that you are offering individualized recovery planning when:

1. Core principles of "person-centered" planning are followed in the process of building individualized recovery plans. For example:
   1.1. Consistent with the "nothing about us, without us" dictum, practitioners actively partner with the individual in all planning meetings and/or case conferences regarding his or her recovery services and supports.
   1.2. The individual has reasonable control as to the location and time of planning meetings, as well as to who is involved, including conserved persons who wish to have an advocate or peer-support worker present. Planning meetings are conducted and services are delivered at a time that does not conflict with other activities that support recovery, such as employment. The individual can extend an invitation to any person he or she believes will be supportive of his or her efforts toward recovery. Invitations extended are documented in the recovery plan. If necessary,

the person (and family as relevant) is provided with support before the meeting so that he or she can be prepared and participate as an equal.

1.3. The language of the plan is understandable to all participants, including the focus person and his or her nonprofessional, natural supports. Where technical or professional terminology is necessary, it is explained to all participants in the planning process.

1.4. When individuals are engaged in rehabilitation services, the rehab practitioners are involved in all planning meetings (at the discretion of the individual) and are given copies of the resulting plan.

1.5. Within the planning process, a diverse, flexible range of options are available so that people can access and choose those supports that will best assist them in their recovery. These choices and service options are clearly explained to the individual, and documentation reflects the options considered.

1.6. Goals are based on the individual's unique interests, preferences, and strengths, and objectives and interventions are clearly related to the attainment of these stated goals. In the case of children and youth, the unique goals of the family are also considered, with the youth increasingly driving the process as he or she approaches the age of maturity. In cases in which preferred supports do not exist, the recovery team works collaboratively with the individual to develop the support or to secure an acceptable alternative.

1.7. Planning focuses on the identification of concrete next steps, along with specific timelines, that will allow the person to draw upon existing areas of strength in order to move toward recovery and his or her vision for the future. Individuals, including unpaid, natural supports who are part of the planning process, commit to assist the individual in taking those next steps. The person takes responsibility for his or her part in making the plan work. Effective recovery plans help people rise to this challenge regardless of their disability status.

1.8. A discussion of strengths is a central focus of all recovery plans (See Section D). Assessments begin with the assumption that individuals are the experts on their own recovery and that they have learned much in the process of working through their struggles.

1.9. Information on rights and responsibilities of receiving services is provided at all recovery planning meetings. This information should include a copy of the mechanisms through which the individual can provide feedback to the practitioner and/or agency, such as the protocol for filing a complaint or compliments regarding the provision of services.

1.10. The individual has the ability to select or change his or her service providers within eligible guidelines and is made aware of the procedures for doing so.

1.11. In the spirit of true partnership and transparency, all parties have access to the same information so that people may embrace and effectively carry out responsibilities associated with the recovery plan. Clients are automatically offered a copy of their written plans, assessments, and progress notes. Knowing ahead of time that a copy will be shared is a simple but powerful strategy that can dramatically impact both the language of the plan and the content of its goals and objectives.

1.12. The team reconvenes as necessary to address life goals, accomplishments, and barriers. Planning is characterized by celebrations of successes, and meetings can occur beyond regular, established parameters (e.g., six-month reviews) and crises (e.g., "all-treaters" meetings to address hospitalization or relapse).

2. A wide range of interventions and contributors to the planning and care process are recognized and respected. For example:

2.1. Practitioners acknowledge the value of the person's existing relationships and connections. If it is the person's preference, significant effort is made to include these "natural supports" and unpaid participants, as they often have critical input and support to offer to the team. Interventions should complement, not interfere with, what people are already doing to get and keep themselves well, such as drawing support from friends and loved ones.

2.2. The plan identifies a wide range of both professional supports and alternative strategies to support the person's recovery, particularly those that have been helpful to others with similar struggles. Information about medications and other treatments is combined with information about self-help, peer support, exercise, nutrition, daily maintenance activities, spiritual practices and affiliations, homeopathic and naturopathic remedies, and so on.

2.3. Individuals are not required to attain or maintain clinical stability or abstinence before being supported by the planning team in pursuing such goals as employment. For example, in some systems access and referral to vocational rehabilitation programs may be controlled by a clinical practitioner, and people are often required to demonstrate "work readiness" or "symptomatic stability" as a prerequisite to entry. In addition to an abundant literature that has shown that screening procedures and criteria have limited predictive validity, this structure also neglects that fact that activities such as working are often the paths by which people become clinically stable in the first place.

2.4. Goals and objectives are driven by the person's current values and needs and not solely by commonly desired clinical/professional outcomes; for example, recovery is a process that may or may not begin with the individual understanding or appreciating the value of abstinence or of taking medications.

3. Community inclusion is valued as a commonly identified and desired outcome. For example:

3.1. The focus of planning and care is on how to create pathways to meaningful and successful community life and not just on how to maintain clinical stability or abstinence. Person-centered plans document areas such as physical health, family and social relationships, employment/education, spirituality, housing, social relations, recreation, community service and civic participation, and so forth, unless such areas are designated by the person as not being of interest. For example, traditional planning has often neglected the spiritual and sexual aspects of people's lives. Achieving interdependence with natural community supports is a valued goal for many people in recovery who express a strong preference to live in typical housing; to have friendships and intimate relationships with a wide range of people; to work in regular employment settings; and to participate in school, worship, recreation, and other pursuits alongside other community members. Such preferences often speak to the need to reduce time spent in segregated settings designed solely to support people labeled with a mental illness.

3.2. Recovery plans respect the fact that services and practitioners should not remain central to a person's life over time, and exit criteria from formal services are clearly defined. However, given the unpredictability of illness, and of life more generally, readmission must also be uncomplicated, with its avenues clearly defined when people are discharged from services.

3.3. Recovery plans consider not only how the individual can access and receive needed supports from the mental health system and the community but also how the individual can, in turn, give back to others. People have identified this type of reciprocity in relationships as being critical to building recovery capital and to the recovery process as a whole. Therefore, individuals should be encouraged to explore how they can make meaningful contributions in the system or in the community, such as through advocacy, employment, or volunteering.

3.4. A focus on community is consistent not only with person-centered care principles but with the need for fiscal efficiency. Practitioners and people in recovery should be mindful of the limited resources available for specialized services and should focus on community solutions and resources first by asking, "Am I about to recommend or replicate a service or support that is already available in the broader community?" At times this has direct implications for the development of service interventions within recovery plans, for example, creating on-site health and fitness opportunities such as exercise classes without first exploring to what extent that same opportunity might be available in the broader community through public recreational departments, YMCAs, and so on. If natural alternatives are available in the community, individuals should be informed of these opportunities, and to the extent that what is offered is culturally responsive and accessible, individuals should be supported in pursuing activities of their choice in integrated settings.

4. The planning process honors the "dignity of risk" and "right to fail" (Deegan, 1992) as evidenced by the following:

   4.1. Prior to appealing to coercive measures, practitioners try different ways of engaging and persuading individuals in ways that respect their ability to make choices on their own behalf.

   4.2. Unless determined to require conservatorship by a judge, individuals are presumed competent and entitled to make their own decisions. As part of their recovery, they are encouraged and supported by practitioners to take risks and try new things. Only in cases involving imminent risk of harm to self or others is a practitioner authorized to override the decisions of the individual. Person-centered care does not take away a practitioner's obligation to take action to protect the person or the public in the event of emergent or crisis situations; instead it limits the authority of practitioners to specifically delimited circumstances involving imminent risk as defined by relevant statutes.

   4.3. In all other cases, practitioners are encouraged to offer their expertise and suggestions respectfully within the context of a collaborative relationship, clearly outlining for the person his or her range of options and possible consequences. Practitioners support the dignity of risk and sit with their own discomfort as the person tries out new choices and experiences that are necessary for recovery.

   4.4. In keeping with this stance, practitioners encourage individuals to write their own crisis and contingency plans (such as psychiatric advanced directives or the crisis plans of the WRAP model). Ideally, such plans are directed by the individual but developed in collaboration with the entire team so as to share responsibility and resources in preventing or addressing crises. Such plans provide detailed instructions regarding preferred interventions and responses in the event of crisis, and they maximize an individual's ability to retain some degree of autonomy and self-determination at a time when he or she is most likely to have these rights taken away. This plan is kept in an accessible location and can be made available for staff providing emergency care.

5. Administrative leadership demonstrates a commitment to both outcomes and process evaluation. For example:

    5.1. Outcomes evaluation in a provider-driven paradigm is typically limited to change in specific agency functions (e.g., length of hospital stays) and by the need to protect the image of the agency (e.g., consumer satisfaction). In a consumer or family-driven paradigm, in contrast, evaluation is a continuous process, and expectations for successful outcomes in a broad range of quality-of-life dimensions (e.g., in areas such as employment, social relationships, and community membership) are high. The maintenance of clinical stability alone is not accepted as the desired treatment outcome, as the experience of recovery is about much more than the absence of symptoms or distress.

    5.2. There is a flexible application of process tools, such as the "Assessment of Person-Centered Planning Facilitation Integrity" questionnaire (Holburn, 2001), to promote quality service delivery. Assuming attention is paid to the larger organizational culture, process tools can be helpful in defining the practice and then monitoring its effective implementation.

What you will hear from people when you are offering individualized recovery planning:

- *It's amazing what you can do when you set your mind to it— especially when you're no longer supposed to have one!*
- *It made such a huge difference to have my pastor there with me at my planning meeting. He may not be my father, but he is the closest thing I've got. He knows me better than anyone else in the world, and he had some great ideas for me.*
- *I had been working on my recovery for years. Finally, it felt like I was also working on my LIFE!*

- *Not everybody thought it was a good idea for me to try to get my daughter back. But they realized that without her, I didn't have a reason to be well. So, we figured out a plan for what to do if I couldn't handle the stress, and my whole team has stood beside me every step of the way. Was it "too stressful" at times? You bet! But every day is a blessing now that I wake up and see her smiling face!*

F. Functioning as a Recovery Guide

The sentiment that "we're not cases, and you're not managers" (Everett & Nelson, 1992) has been accepted increasingly as a fundamental challenge to the ways that mental health care is conceptualized within a recovery-oriented system. During this time, the predominant vehicle for offering services to many adults with serious disabilities has evolved from the team-based and in vivo approach of intensive case management to the introduction of strengths-based and rehabilitative forms of case management that attempt to shift the goals of care from stabilization and maintenance to enhanced functioning and community integration.

From the perspective of recovery, however, even these inherited models of case management limit the progress that otherwise could be made in actualizing the shift from a deficit- and institution-based framework to a recovery paradigm. This paradigm calls for innovative models of community-based practice that move beyond the management of cases, and beyond merely semantic changes that introduce new terms for old practices, to the creation of a more collaborative model that respects the person's own role in directing his or her life and, within that context, his or her own treatment (in much the same way that people, in collaboration with their health care professionals, make decisions about their own medical care for other conditions such as hypertension). One such model that is emerging, and which is described in more detail in the next chapter, is that of the community or recovery guide.

Rather than replacing any of the skills or clinical and rehabilitative expertise that practitioners have obtained through their training and experience, the recovery guide model offers a useful framework in which these interventions and strategies can be presented as tools that the person can use in his or her own recovery. In addition, the recovery guide model offers both practitioners and people in recovery a map of the territory they will be exploring together.

Prior to attempting to embark with a client on his or her journey of recovery, however, practitioners appreciate that the first step in the process of treatment, rehabilitation, or recovery is often to engage in a relationship with a reluctant and disbelieving, but nonetheless suffering, person. Practitioners accept that most people with serious mental illness will not know that they have a psychiatric disorder at first, and therefore frequently will not seek help on their own. The initial focus of care is thus on the person's own understanding of his or her predicament (not necessarily the events or difficulties that brought him or her into contact with care providers) and on the ways the practitioner can be of assistance in addressing this predicament, regardless of how the person understands it at the time.

It also is important to note that within this model, care incorporates the fact that the lives of people in recovery did not begin with the onset of their disorder, just as their lives are not encompassed totally by psychiatric treatment and rehabilitation. Based on recognition of the fact that people were already on a journey prior to the onset of their disorder, and therefore prior to coming into contact with care, the focus of care shifts to the ways that this journey was impacted or disrupted by each person's condition(s).

For example, practitioners strive to identify and understand how the person's mental illness has impacted on or changed the person's aspirations, hopes, and dreams. If the person appears to be sticking resolutely to the hopes and dreams he or she had prior to onset of the disorder, and despite or without apparent awareness of the disorder and its disabling effects, then what steps need to be taken for him or her to get back on track or to take the next step or two along this track? Rather than the reduction of symptoms or the remediation of deficits—goals that we assume the person will share with care providers—it is the person's own goals for his or her life beyond or despite his or her disability that drive the treatment, rehabilitation, and recovery planning and efforts.

You will know that you are functioning as a recovery guide when:

1. The primary vehicle for the delivery of most mental health care is the relationship between the practitioner and the person in

recovery. The care provided must be grounded in an appreciation of the possibility of improvement in the person's condition, offering people hope and/or faith that recovery is "possible for me." Practitioners convey belief in the person even when he or she cannot believe in himself or herself and offer gentle reminders of his or her potential. In this sense, staff envision a future for the person beyond the role of "mental patient" based on the person's own desires and values, and they share this vision with the person by communicating positive expectations and hope.

2. Practitioners assess where each person is in relation to the various stages of change (e.g., precontemplation, preparation, etc.) with respect to the various dimensions of his or her recovery. Interventions are appropriate to the stages of change relevant to each focus of treatment and rehabilitation (e.g., a person may be in an action phase related to his or her substance abuse disorder but be in precontemplation related to his or her mental illness).

3. Care is based on the assumption that as a person recovers from his or her condition, the mental illness becomes less of a defining characteristic of self and more simply one part of a multidimensional sense of identity that also contains strengths, skills, and competencies. Services elicit, flesh out, and cultivate these positive elements at least as much as, if not more than, assessing and ameliorating difficulties. This process is driven by the person in recovery and his or her hopes, dreams, talents, and skills, as well as by the person's response to perhaps the most important question: "How can I be of help?"

4. Interventions are aimed at assisting people in gaining autonomy, power, and connections with others. Practitioners regularly assess the services they are providing by asking themselves, "Does this person gain power, purpose (valued roles), competence (skills), and/or connections (to others) as a result of this interaction?" and, equally important, "Does this interaction interfere with the acquisition of power, purpose, competence, or connections to others?"

5. Opportunities and supports are provided for the person to enhance his or her own sense of personal and social agency. For example, practitioners understand that medication is only one tool in a person's "recovery toolbox" and learn about alternative

methods and self-management strategies in which people use their own experiences and knowledge to apply the wellness tools that work best for them. "Sense of agency" involves not only feeling effective and able to help oneself but also being able to positively impact the lives of others. Practitioners can promote this by thoughtfully balancing when to do "to" or "for" someone against when to let someone do for himself or herself. Knowing when to hold close and support and protect, when to encourage someone while offering support, when to let someone try alone and perhaps stumble, and when to encourage a person strongly to push himself or herself is an advanced but essential skill for practitioners to develop. While these are intuitive skills that all practitioners must struggle to refine over time, prior to taking action it is always beneficial for practitioners to ask the question, "Am I about to do for this person something he or she could manage to do more independently?" Strong messages of low expectations and incapability are given, and reinforced, every time unnecessary action is undertaken for a person instead of with him or her.

6. Individuals are allowed the right to make mistakes, and this is valued as an opportunity for them to learn. People in recovery report that they have found meaning in adverse events and failures and that this has subsequently helped them advance in their recovery. In accordance with this, practitioners recognize that their role is not necessarily to help people avoid adversity or to protect them from failure. For example, the reexperiencing of symptoms can be viewed as a part of the recovery process and not necessarily a failure or setback. The "dignity of risk" ensures the following of a thoughtful and proactive planning process in which practitioners work with individuals to develop relapse-prevention plans, including advance directives that specify personal and treatment preferences in the event of future crises.

7. People are allowed to express their feelings, including anger and dissatisfaction, without having these reactions be attributed to symptoms or relapse.

8. Care not only is attentive to cultural differences of race, ethnicity, and other distinctions of difference (e.g., sexual orientation) but incorporates this sensitivity at the level of the individual. Only an individual-level process can ensure that practitioners avoid stereotyping people based on broad or

inaccurate generalizations (e.g., what "all lesbians" want or need) and enable them instead to tailor services to the specific needs, values, and preferences of each person, taking into account each individual's ethnic, racial, and cultural affiliations.

9. Rather than dwelling on the person's distant past or worrying about the person's long-term future, practitioners focus on preparing people for the next one or two steps of the recovery process by anticipating what lies immediately ahead, by focusing on the challenges of the present situation, and by identifying and helping the person avoid or move around potential obstacles in the road. Although the practitioner deemphasizes the person's early personal history (because it may not be relevant) and long-term outcome (because it cannot be predicted), either of these perspectives may be invoked should they prove useful in the current situation. Especially as these issues pose barriers to recovery, practitioners utilize appropriate clinical skills within the context of a trusting relationship in order to enhance the person's capacity to overcome, compensate for, or bypass these barriers (see Section H).

10. Interventions are oriented toward increasing the person's recovery capital as well as decreasing his or her distress and dysfunction (see sections C and H). Grounded in a person's "life-context" (Davidson & Strauss, 1995), interventions take into account each person's unique history, experiences, situations, developmental trajectory, and aspirations. In addition to culture, race, and ethnicity, this includes less visible but equally important influences on each person's development, including both the traditional concerns of mental health practitioners (e.g., family composition and background, history of substance use and relapse triggers) and less common factors such as personal interests, hobbies, and role models that help define who each person is as an individual and as a member of his or her network.

11. Practitioners are willing to offer practical assistance in the community contexts in which their clients live, work, and play. In order to effectively address "individuals' basic human needs for decent housing, food, work, and 'connection' with the community," practitioners are willing to go where the action is;

that is, they get out of their offices and go out into the community (Curtis & Hodge, 1994). They are prepared to go out to meet people on their own turf and on their own terms, and to "offer assistance which they might consider immediately relevant to their lives" (Rosen, 1994, p. 55).

12. Care is not only provided in the community but is also oriented toward increasing the quality of a person's involvement in community life. Thus the focus of care is considered more important than the locus, or where it is provided. The focus of care includes the process of overcoming the social and personal consequences of living with psychiatric and/or substance abuse disorders. These include gaining an enhanced sense of identity and meaning and purpose in life and developing valued social roles and community connections despite a person's continued symptoms or disability. Supporting these goals requires that practitioners have an intimate knowledge of the communities in which their clients live, the community's available resources, and the people who are important to them, whether they be a friend, parent, employer, landlord, or grocer. Practitioners also are knowledgeable about informal support systems in communities, such as support groups, singles clubs, and other special interest groups, and they actively pursue learning about other possibilities that exist to help people connect.

13. Efforts are made to identify sources of incongruence between the person and his or her environment and to increase person–environment fit. This is done both by helping the person assimilate into his or her environment (through symptom management, skill acquisition, etc.) and by helping the community better accommodate people with disabilities (through education, stigma reduction, the creation of niches, etc.), with the common goal being to develop "multiple pathways" into and between members of communities.

14. In order to counteract the often hidden effects of stigma, practitioners explicitly draw upon their own personal experiences when considering the critical nature of various social roles in the lives of all individuals (e.g., being a parent, a worker, a friend), continuing to view people in recovery squarely within the context of their daily lives (i.e., as opposed to within institutional settings).

15. Community-focused care supplements, and is not meant to be a substitute for, the practitioner's existing expertise and services. Rather than devaluing professional knowledge and experience, the "recovery guide" approach moves psychiatry much closer to other medical specialties in which it is the health care specialist's role to assess the person, diagnose his or her condition, educate the person about the costs and benefits of the most effective interventions available to treat his or her condition, and then provide the appropriate interventions. There is an expectation that practitioners will engage in continuing professional education so that they are aware of, and can deliver, a wide range of evidence-based and emerging practices. But no matter how expert or experienced the practitioner, it is ideally left up to the person and his or her loved ones to make decisions about his or her care.

16. Recovery is viewed as a fundamentally social process, involving supportive relationships with family, friends, peers, community members, and practitioners. Interventions serve to minimize the role that professionals play in people's lives over time and maximize the role of natural supports. While the provider–client relationship can be a powerful component of the healing and recovery process, individuals must also develop and mobilize their own natural support networks to promote sustained recovery and independent community life.

What you will hear from people when you are functioning as a recovery guide:

- *She believed in me, even when I didn't believe in myself. Hope was the biggest gift she could have given me . . . and it saved my life.*
- *When he asked me, "So, how can I best be of help?" I thought, "Oh, great, I've really got a green one. You are supposed to be the professional—you tell me!" But I get it now. I need to decide what I need to move ahead in my recovery. And I needed to know it was O.K. to ask people for that. That was the key.*
- *When she even showed up on my doorstep with a bag of clothes so my baby could start kindergarten, I knew this one was different. I couldn't care about myself or my recovery until I knew my kids were O.K. She*

didn't pity me or look for a pat on the back. She just knew this was what I needed, and it made all the difference in my recovery.

- *I was terrified of going back to that hospital. My case manager couldn't guarantee me that it wouldn't happen again. But we sat down together and did a plan for how to make things different if there ever was a "next time." Knowing my dog would get fed, making sure somebody talked to my landlord so I wouldn't get evicted, and being able to write down how the staff could help me if I lost control—all those things made the idea of going back less scary.*

G. Community Mapping and Development

Given its focus on life context, one tool required for effective recovery planning is adequate knowledge of the person's local community, including its opportunities, resources, and potential barriers. This knowledge is to be obtained and updated regularly at a community-wide level for the areas in which a program's service recipients live, but it also is to be generated on an individual basis contingent on each person's interests, talents, and needs.

Historically falling under the purview of social work and rehabilitation staff, the function of identifying, cataloging, and being familiar with community resources both within and beyond the formal mental health system can be carried out by staff from any discipline with adequate training and supervision. In most cases, however, this expertise will reside with local community-based practitioners rather than with inpatient or residential staff located at a distance from the person's community of origin. In such cases, close coordination between inpatient/residential and outpatient staff will be required to obtain and integrate this information into the individualized recovery plan. Regardless of how it is provided, a comprehensive understanding of the community resources and supports that are available to address the range of a person's needs as he or she identifies them is essential to the recovery planning process across the continuum of care.

Asset-based community development is one essential strategy for developing this comprehensive understanding of local resources and supports. Based on the pioneering work of Kretzmann and McKnight (1993), asset-based community development (ABCD) is a widely recognized capacity-focused approach to community development that can help open doors into communities for persons who have been labeled or otherwise marginalized, and through which people in recovery can build social capital and participate in community life as citizens rather than clients.

Through the cultivation of mutually beneficial relationships, ABCD has been shown to be an effective technology for capitalizing on the internal capacities of low-income urban neighborhoods and rural communities, particularly as the depth and extent of associational life in these communities is often vastly underestimated. Whereas community development has historically been deficit- or problem-based and fueled by "needs assessments" and "needs maps," ABCD operates on the premise that every person in a community has gifts, strengths, skills, and resources to contribute to the community and that community life is shaped, driven, and sustained by the contributions of an involved and interdependent citizenry. Capacity, strengths, and resources are also derived from community associations (religious, civic, recreational, political, social, etc.) and from community institutions (schools, police, libraries, parks, human services, etc.).

ABCD is a fully participatory process that involves all persons in mapping the resources and capacities of a community's individuals, its informal associations, and its structured institutions, as a means of identifying existing but untapped or overlooked resources and other potentially hospitable places in which the contributions of people with disabilities will be welcomed and valued (McKnight, 1992). Information about individuals, community associations, and institutions is collected through the sharing of stories and in one-on-one interviews that foster the development of personal relationships.

The relationships, resource maps, and capacity inventories that result from this process serve to guide ongoing community development and provide a means by which people can expand their existing social networks and involvement in community activities. Pride in past achievements is strengthened, new opportunities for creative endeavors are discovered, resiliency is experienced, and hope is sustained. It is important to note that the primary producers of outcomes in this process are not institutions but individuals strengthened by enhanced community relationships. ABCD ultimately helps people in recovery derive great benefit from access to a range of naturally occurring social, educational, vocational, spiritual, and civic activities involved in their return to valued roles in the life of their community.

You will know you are engaged in community mapping and development when:

1. People in recovery and other labeled and/or marginalized persons are viewed primarily as citizens and not as clients, and they are recognized for the gifts, strengths, skills, interests, and resources they have to contribute to community life.
2. Community leaders representing a range of community associations and institutions work together with people in recovery to carry out the process of community development.
3. People in recovery and other community members experience a renewed sense of empowerment and social connectedness through voluntary participation in civic, social, recreational, vocational, religious, and educational activities in the community. Therefore, opportunities for employment, education, recreation, social involvement, civic engagement, and religious participation are regularly identified and are compiled in asset maps, capacity inventories, and community resource guides. These informational resources are made available to individuals on their initial agency orientation and are updated over time as knowledge about the local community grows.
4. Asset maps and capacity inventories created collaboratively by actively involved community stakeholders reflect a wide range of natural gifts, strengths, skills, knowledge, interests, values, and resources available to a community through its individuals, associations, and institutions. In other words, they are not limited to social and human services or professional crisis or emergency services.
5. High value is placed on the less formal aspects of associational life that take place, for instance, in neighborhood gatherings, block watch meetings, coffee klatches, salons, barbershops, book groups, knitting and craft circles, restaurants, pubs, diners, and so forth.
6. Institutions do not duplicate services that are widely available in the community through individuals and associations.
7. Community development is driven by a creative, capacity-focused vision identified and shared by community stakeholders. It is neither deficit-oriented nor driven solely by needs assessments and needs maps.
8. The relational process of gathering information about community assets and capacities through personal interviews

and sharing of stories is recognized as being as important as the information that is collected.

What you will hear from people when you are engaged in community mapping and development:

- *I just wanted to get back to my life: my friends, and my job, and my church activities. My recovery was important, but it didn't matter so long as I didn't have those things in my life to look forward to. It was those things that kept me going in my darkest days.*
- *Just having a place to hang out, where I blend in with the crowd . . . where no one knows me as a patient on the ACT team. That is when I am most peaceful.*
- *It wasn't enough for me to just get better. I appreciated everyone's help, but I felt like such a charity case all the time. What really made a difference was when my counselor helped me to get a volunteer position at the local nursing home. Sometimes I read to the folks, or we play cards. It may not be fancy, but it feels right to me. I don't just have to take help from everybody else, I have valuable things to give back in return.*
- *I knew all about the places where folks could go to get help if they had a problem with drugs or mental illness. What I had forgotten about was how to have FUN! My case manager gave me this terrific list of low-cost activities that happen right around the corner from my apartment, and I never even knew this stuff was right under my nose. It's opened up a whole new world for me. I made some great friends, and one of them is even looking for some part-time help in her art store—so I'm gonna get a job out of it, too! Things happen in the strangest ways sometimes. . . .*
- *My yoga class at the mental health center got cancelled, and instead they gave us a coupon to try out some free lessons at the city Rec Department. At first I was so disappointed, but once I tried it out, I loved it. I now take Pilates in addition to yoga, and I also joined a hiking club. I feel healthier physically and mentally . . . .*

H. Identifying and Addressing Barriers to Recovery

To this point, our guiding assumption has been that mental illnesses are illnesses like any others, and that, with few exceptions, seeking and receiving care for these disorders should resemble the process involved with other medical conditions. Although we have made a point of stressing the need for outreach and engagement to ensure access to care, we otherwise may have given the reader the impression that people with serious mental illness are educated consumers of health care and that they will naturally act on their own behalf to make appropriate choices in this and other domains.

Experienced practitioners will no doubt consider such a perspective simplistic and naïve and will suggest that up to 80% of the work entailed in treating serious mental illnesses is devoted to helping people to arrive at a position of being willing to receive care for their condition. Once a person accepts that he or she has a mental illness and agrees to participate in treatment and/or rehabilitation, the bulk of the more difficult work may appear to be done. We appreciate this sentiment and agree that it may take a generation or more before many more people experiencing these conditions will be able to access and benefit from care in a more straightforward and uncomplicated manner.

For the foreseeable future, there will continue to be two major sources of complications—and of considerable suffering—that make accessing and benefiting from care a labor-intensive and difficult process. These two types of barriers to recovery reside both external to the person, in societal stigma and discrimination and in the ways in which care has historically been structured and provided, and internal to the person, intrinsic to the nature of the illnesses themselves. In order to promote recovery, practitioners must be able to identify and address the variety of barriers encountered in each of these domains.

In terms of external barriers, there currently are elements and characteristics of the service delivery system and the broader community that unwittingly contribute to exacerbating symptoms and creating and perpetuating chronicity and dependency in individuals with serious mental illness. Foremost among these is the discrimination that continues to affect people with mental illness in society at large and, even more importantly, within the mental health system itself.

This discrimination results in people with mental illness being viewed and treated as second-class citizens in a variety of life domains. One by-product of repeated discrimination is that people come to view and treat themselves as second-class citizens as well. What advocates within the mental health community have come to call "internalized stigma" presents a significant obstacle to recovery, undermining the self-confidence and self-esteem required for the person to take steps toward improving his or her life. The demoralization and despair that are associated with internalized stigma and feelings of inferiority also sap the person's sense of hope and initiative, adding further weight to the illness and its effects.

Beyond the impact of stigma and discrimination, there are a variety of ways in which the health care system and the broader community make recovery more difficult. These range from the lack of affordable housing and accessible, high-quality medical care to the employment disincentives built into entitlement programs, to the punitive aspects of some care settings and programs (e.g., in which people are discharged for manifesting the symptoms of their illness). Identifying and assisting the person to overcome these barriers to the degree possible is an important component of the work of the recovery-oriented mental health care practitioner.

In terms of internal barriers, there are several aspects of serious mental illnesses and their place within contemporary society that complicate and undermine a person's efforts. For example, while trauma may not be intrinsic to mental illness per se, there is considerable evidence that suggests that people experiencing serious mental illness at the present time have a greatly increased chance of having experienced trauma earlier in their lives, as well as of being at increased risk for exposure to trauma and victimization currently.

Perhaps more directly as a consequence of the illness itself, there also are symptoms of mental illness that pose their own barriers. The hallucinations and delusions often found in psychotic illnesses, for example, may compete as a source of information with health care practitioners, thereby discouraging the person from taking prescribed medications or otherwise participating in treatment or rehabilitation. The heightened senses of creativity and self-importance that often accompany episodes of mania similarly may lead a person down a path that diverges from the one preferred by his or her loved ones and care providers. As destructive as they may appear to the person's loved ones or care providers, giving up delusions or mania often comes with its own costs. As the young man with schizophrenia described in the last chapter, who was struggling with believing either his voices and delusions or his doctors, once poignantly asked: "If you had the choice between being a CIA operative or a mental patient, which would you choose?"

Accepting that these and other elements associated with the disorders themselves undermine a person's efforts to cope with his or her illness, recovery-oriented practitioners become familiar with these issues and adept in working proactively with the person to overcome or bypass their destructive impact. Many of the skills and techniques traditionally utilized by clinicians within the context of office-based practice find their greatest utility and effectiveness in this domain, whether offered inside or outside of the office.

You will know you are addressing external and internal barriers to recovery when:

1. There is a commitment at the local level to embrace the values and principles of recovery-oriented care and to move away from the dominant illness-based paradigm. The practices identified throughout this book can only grow in a culture that fully embraces recovery principles and values. Systemic changes that reflect this paradigm shift include the following:

    1.1. Stakeholders understand the need for recovery-oriented system change as a civil rights issue that aims to restore certain elementary freedoms (e.g., self-determination, community inclusion) to American citizens who have been diagnosed with mental illnesses.

    1.2. Stakeholders work together to move away from the criteria of "medical necessity" and toward "human need" (Tondora, Pocklington, Gorges, Osher, & Davidson, 2005), from managing illness to promoting recovery, from deficit-oriented to strengths-based, and from symptom relief to personally defined quality of life. Perhaps most critical is the fundamental shift in power involved in realigning systems to promote recovery-oriented care—the shift away from prioritizing expert knowledge over respect for personal autonomy and self-determination.

    1.3. The possibility of recovery, and the responsibility to deliver recovery-oriented care, must be embraced by all stakeholders at all levels of the system. While many exciting things are occurring in agencies across the country, recovery-oriented change tends to occur in a fairly fragmented manner, with a relatively small number of progressive practitioners or advocates taking on a large amount of responsibility for carrying out the recovery mission. For example, certain programs and staff in mental health systems (e.g., peer or rehabilitation practitioners, community-based case managers) are uniquely positioned to be leaders in the mission to provide recovery-oriented care, and the contributions of these programs should be respected and capitalized upon. Taking a lead in the recovery mission is a natural fit for such programs for a variety of reasons, including their structure as private nonprofit entities, their rehabilitation expertise, lower pressure and demands to deliver only medically necessary care, and their direct affiliations with the state or national consumer/recovery movement. However, agencies and systems must guard against the complacency that results when recovery is seen as being a "nice add-on" but "not part of my job" or as being manifest only in "special" (i.e., token) programs that are split off from the functioning of the agency as a whole. Recovery-oriented system change will only take hold and thrive if it is understood that it is the shared mission of all stakeholders and that the task of promoting recovery—as the overarching aim of all mental health care—is everyone's job. Resources and guidelines are emerging that define exactly what that job is, depending on what one's role is as a practitioner (e.g., primary clinician, peer specialist, supported employment specialist) within the system.

2. Systemic structures and practices that inhibit the adoption of recovery-oriented practices are identified and addressed. Representative change strategies in this area include the following:

   2.1. Well-intentioned efforts to provide a full "continuum" of care have led to a system in which people are sometimes expected to enter and progress through a range of services in a sequential fashion as they "stabilize" and move toward enhanced functioning and greater independence. The misapplication of this model has led to systems of care in which individuals are then expected to jump through hoops in order to earn their way into less restrictive settings (e.g., an expectation that they prove they can prepare three meals a day or keep their living space clean before they can move out of a group home) or to earn the right to participate in preferred services (e.g., an expectation that they comply with medication or outpatient psychotherapy groups before they will be referred to a supported employment program). In addition to there being an accumulating body of evidence that demonstrates the failure of such a continuum approach (Breakey & Fischer, 1995; Drake, Becker, Clarke, & Mueser, 1999; Ridgway & Zipple, 1990; Tsemberis, 1999), this sequential movement through a preexisting continuum of supports is inconsistent with the civil rights perspective noted above and contradicts current knowledge suggesting that recovery is neither a linear process nor a static end product or result. Rather, it is for many a lifelong experience that involves an indefinite number of incremental steps in various life domains, with people moving fluidly between the various domains over time (as opposed to moving through these dimensions in a systematic, linear process). Rather than a preestablished continuum of services, what is necessary is a flexible array of supports that each person can choose from at different points in time depending upon his or her phase of recovery and unique needs and preferences. This array should be constantly evolving based on the input of persons in recovery, the experience of practitioners, and the research literature.

2.2. There is often a lack of clarity regarding system priorities when agencies attempt to implement numerous initiatives simultaneously—for example, evidence-based practice versus recovery-oriented programming. While such initiatives may not be incompatible, competing demands—and even complementary ones—can diffuse the effort and resources of the agency and inhibit the adoption of any new practices. It is critical that there be coordinating structures to attend to both the prioritization and the integration of new initiatives, policies, and procedures.

2.3. The structure of certain outcome indicators places significant pressures on agency staff to operate in a manner that they see as inconsistent with recovery-oriented care.

For example, staff might like to support persons in making choices regarding their housing preferences, such as moving to a less intensive level of supported housing. They may legitimately be concerned, however, that they will be held accountable should the result of such a choice ultimately be a negative one. This accountability is not limited to the potential adverse events themselves; it is further accentuated through the agency's collection of mandatory performance data, such as statistics regarding the number of individuals who move from "housed" to "homeless." The resulting need to portray the agency's performance on such indicators as positive creates a strong incentive for the maintenance of stability as a desired outcome in and of itself.

In contrast, a desired goal of recovery-oriented care is to promote growth, independence, and wellness—goals that at times involve the taking of reasonable risks that may result in interim setbacks. At both the agency and system level, quality management tools and outcome indicators should be examined, and mechanisms should be built in to track the trade-off that sometimes exists as we support individuals in taking risks to grow and advance in their recovery.

2.4. Processes for continual quality assurance and independent audits by people in recovery and families trained in recovery-oriented care need to be funded and coordinated. Outcomes and assessment of quality should focus not solely on the rating of services/supports but also on whether the choices people make are personally meaningful and whether recovery-oriented care leads to a valued community life.

2.5. Initial placement and service design currently is driven by practitioners' assessments of what the individual seeking services needs. While this assessment should remain a critical element of the referral process, it should be coupled with questions, directed to the person and answered in his or her own words, that solicit the individual's perception of what services and supports would be most helpful. Individuals must be engaged as active partners in their care from the outset. This can only be achieved with greater transparency in the system of care as a whole and with greater involvement of the person and family in all important decision-making processes, including the decision about the initial level of care and team/program assignment.

2.6. Recovery plans respect the fact that services and practitioners should not remain central to a person's life over time. Currently, many mental health systems lack clearly defined exit criteria, and it is not uncommon for individuals to feel as if they will be attached to the formal system for life following their entry into care. This perpetuates a sense of chronicity through which individuals lose hope that they will be able to resume a meaningful and productive daily life beyond treatment. In contrast, exit criteria should be established and used to engage people in a collaborative decision-making process regarding the potential advantages and risks of moving to a lower level of care, with an effort being made to respect the individual's desire to "graduate" whenever possible. When an individual is strongly advised by the recovery team against "graduation," there should be evidence in the recovery plan of concrete steps being taken by the individual and the team to reach this ultimate goal. In establishing exit criteria, agencies must take caution to avoid punitive measures by which individuals are discharged from services for displaying symptoms of their illness or addiction.

2.7. Despite legislative advances in the past decade, the structure of federal and state disability, benefits, and vocational programs continues to impede the wish of many individuals to enter, or reenter, the workforce, thereby excluding them from an activity which many have described as a cornerstone of recovery. Rigid definitions of disability, earnings limits that perpetuate poverty, a lack of supported employment programs, and complex referral procedures drastically reduce the likelihood that individuals will access necessary services and return to meaningful employment. To integrate employment within the larger system of care, the task of assisting people in entering employment and education must be inherent in the responsibilities of the entire practitioner network, including those not specifically charged with work service or supported education activities.

3. The implementation of recovery-oriented care is facilitated, rather than impeded, by funding, reimbursement, and accreditation structures. Intrinsic to any dialogue regarding systemic barriers to recovery-oriented care is the need to address funding structures that recognize a limited range of clinical interactions as reimbursable services, as well as documentation requirements that hinder creative formulation of recovery-oriented goals and objectives. Necessary change strategies to address these barriers include the following:

   3.1. Rules and regulations dictating eligibility and reimbursement for Medicaid and other public supports must be adapted at the federal and state level over time for greater relevance to innovative, recovery-oriented approaches. Even though Medicaid is funded by federal dollars, it remains primarily a state-administered program, and considerable flexibility exists already in using these dollars to support innovative, community-based, recovery-oriented services and supports.

   3.2. Within existing funding structures, training and technical assistance can be provided to practitioners attempting to implement recovery-oriented practices to assist them in learning how to translate the wishes of people in recovery into reimbursable service goals and to describe their interventions in a manner that will legitimately generate payment.

   3.3. Operating in this manner is consistent with the growing understanding that recovery-oriented practices cannot be an add-on to existing care for which additional funding must always be secured. Rather, recovery-oriented care begins with discovering ways to be creative and flexible within the constraints of existing resources. In some cases, for example, merging funds may enable collaborations to move beyond funding silos to provide people with flexible, highly individualized services (Osher, Dwyer, & Jackson, 2004). Programs that successfully utilize such alternatives must be explored for expansion (Blessing, Tierney, Osher, Allegretti-Freeman, & Abrey, 2005).

   3.4. Self-directed funding opportunities should be considered both on a collective basis and through individualized budget programs. The Florida "Self-Directed Care" initiative is an example of a program that shifts fiscal control from the hands of service providers to the hands of service users. Within this program, participants are given control of their service dollars and then are free to shop around to weave together the type and frequencies of services that may best respond to their individual interests and preferences. While this approach has proponents, there is also an inherent tension and uncertainty about whether there is any guarantee that high-quality services will be available to purchase if there are no consistent fiscal underpinnings. A robust practitioner network is needed, and it must be easily accessible (Jonikas, Cook, Fudge, Hiebechuk, & Fricks, 2005).

4. Training and staff development are prioritized as essential functions to increase individual practitioners' competency in providing recovery-oriented care. Necessary change strategies to address this issue include the following:

   4.1. As consensus emerges regarding the knowledge and skills needed to implement recovery-oriented care, this information must lead to the development of competency models, and these models must be disseminated broadly as guidance for training programs and licensing bodies that prepare and accredit future providers of mental health care. For example, competency models regarding the delivery of recovery-oriented care should be used to address training gaps in pre-certification curricula as well as ongoing professional development activities.

   4.2. Once established, competency models—which are largely underutilized in general in mental health—should be incorporated in all human resource activities (e.g., hiring, routine performance evaluation, promotion decisions, staff development targets) as a means of promoting accountability and quality improvement.

   4.3. An analysis of staff's current competencies and self-perceived training needs should guide the development of ongoing skill-building activities at the agency level. For example, practitioners are frustrated by the fact that they are overwhelmed by a constant stream of change mandates for which they receive little or no training or support. There are beneficial, self-reflective tools, such as those in the Appendix (e.g., the Recovery Self-Assessment [RSA] and Recovery Knowledge Inventory [RKI]; Campbell-Orde, Chamberlin, Carpenter, & Leff, 2005), that can be used to conduct a training-needs analysis that identifies both strengths and areas in need of improvement as they relate to the provision of recovery-oriented care. Gaps in skill sets can be identified and prioritized for development by training administrators.

4.4. Training alone will not allow practitioners to develop the enhanced skill set and the increased sense of efficacy that will allow them to carry out the complex responsibilities and roles of the recovery-oriented practitioner. Competency-based training must be coupled with ongoing mentor support, enhanced supervision, recovery-oriented case conferences, and opportunities for peer consultation.

4.5. Directors of clinical services and agency leaders should be involved in ongoing training initiatives so that there is consistency in proposed recovery-oriented practices and the system's administrative structures. This allows direct care staff to feel supported and respected, and it affords agency leadership the opportunity to actively identify and address any systemic barriers that prohibit the adoption of recovery-oriented practices.

4.6. Training and staff development activities must be sensitive to the role confusion that can result from the adoption of recovery-oriented practice. Recovery-oriented care does *not* imply that there is no longer any role for the practitioner to play in the treatment and recovery process. Rather, the practitioner's role has changed from that of all-knowing, all-doing caretaker to that of coach, architect, cheerleader, facilitator, mentor, or shepherd (Adams & Grieder, 2005; Davidson, Tondora, et al., 2006)—roles that are not always consistent with one's clinical training or experiences. One effective educational strategy may be using a combination of literature, outcomes/efficacy data, and personal accounts such as recovery dialogues to help practitioners learn the new roles of advisor, mentor, or supports broker (Jonikas et al., 2005). Furthermore, those involved in educating practitioners about self-determination and recovery-oriented care have found that acknowledging staff's fears and doubts, rather than dismissing them or shaming the staff, is more likely to lead them to accept a new role in their clients' lives (Holburn & Vietze, 2002). The application of sophisticated and effective clinical practices in the larger context of collaborative partnerships and self-determination is a training area that requires attention.

4.7. No matter how competent the workforce, no matter how ripe the culture, and no matter how compatible the funding mechanisms, recovery-oriented care will not become a reality unless people in recovery and their families understand it, are supported in using it, and come to demand it as a basic expectation of quality care. It is imperative that training initiatives regarding recovery-oriented care not neglect the need of people in recovery and families to develop their own capacity to self-direct their treatment and life decisions. Some may already do this with great skill and acumen. Others may be reluctant to assume the seat of power, having been socialized by their culture (Harry, Kalyanpur, & Day, 1999) or taught by professionals and agencies that their proper role is one of deferential compliance (Katz & Danet, 1973). Ideally, training initiatives put all stakeholders, including people in recovery, families, and practitioners, at the same table.

5. Forces at the societal level (e.g., stigma, discrimination, lack of basic resources) that undermine recovery and community inclusion are identified and addressed. Necessary change strategies to address this issue include the following:

5.1. A lack of basic resources and opportunities (e.g., jobs, affordable housing, medical care, educational activities) in the broader community significantly complicates the task of recovery for persons with serious mental illness. This lack of resources and opportunities often stems from inadequate knowledge and skills on the part of community organizations regarding how to create welcoming and accessible environments for all people. Mental health practitioners have significant expertise to address this skill and knowledge gap, and they should be prepared to offer supportive guidance and feedback at both the individual and the community level. For example, consultation with a community employer regarding the impact of a certain medication on an individual's stamina can lead to a reasonable accommodation in the workplace that allows greater productivity and success on the job—an outcome which is ultimately beneficial to both the individual and the employer. Provided with appropriate support and consultation, many community members are excellent collaborators and can become facilitators of the recovery and community inclusion process.

5.2. Despite the promise of such collaborations, discrimination against people with mental illness will most likely continue for the foreseeable future. Community collaborations and education must therefore be coupled with efforts by mental health practitioners to recognize instances of discrimination, to understand relevant disability legislation (e.g., the Americans with Disabilities Act), and to effectively utilize state and local resources (Offices of Protection and Advocacy, the Equal Opportunity Employment Commission, advocacy organizations, etc.). This type of knowledge also must be built within the consumer community so that people in recovery can protect themselves by recognizing and rectifying experiences of discrimination.

5.3. Agencies are cautioned to avoid the establishment of "one-stop shopping" service programs. In an effort to respond to individuals' multidimensional needs while also protecting them from the experience of stigma and discrimination, agencies tend to develop "in-house" alternatives to community activities based on concern that the community will never accept or welcome individuals with mental illness. As a result, agencies often create in artificial settings activities that already exist in the natural community—for example, developing in-house medical clinics, movie nights, General Equivalency Diploma classes, social events, and so on. Agencies that fall into this trap of providing a one-stop shop for the needs of people with mental illness inadvertently contribute to the development of chronic "patienthood" as well as the perpetuation of discriminatory and unethical practices by community members. We must continue to work with community partners to uphold their obligation to respect people with mental illness as citizens who have the right to be treated according to the principles of law that apply to all other individuals (NCD, 2000).

5.4. A focus on promoting access to community opportunities is consistent not only with recovery-oriented principles but also with the need for fiscal efficiency. Professionals and service recipients should be mindful of the limited resources available for specialized services and should focus on community solutions and resources first, by asking, "Am I about to recommend or replicate a service or support that is already available in the broader community?" At times, this has direct implications for the development of service interventions within recovery plans (for example, creating on-site health and fitness opportunities such as exercise classes without first exploring to what extent that same opportunity might be available in the broader community through public recreational departments, YMCAs, and so forth). If natural alternatives are available in the community, the individual should be informed of these opportunities and then supported in accessing them based on his or her preferences.

6. Certain internal barriers unique to mental illness are identified and addressed. Necessary change strategies to address these barriers include the following:

6.1. It is important to acknowledge that people with mental illness may be reluctant to assume some of the rights and responsibilities promoted in recovery-oriented systems. They may initially express reluctance, fears, mistrust, and even lack of interest when afforded the right to take control of their treatment and life decisions. It is critical to explore and address the multiple factors influencing such responses, as they often result from a complex interaction of the person's condition and his or her past experiences in the mental health care system. As suggested by Jonikas and colleagues (2005), there are many factors involved when people in recovery "resist" recovery-oriented system change, including a lack of trust that human service systems or various care providers will cede control; service eligibility criteria that require an emphasis on illness and crisis in order to receive assistance; learned helplessness consequent to years of dependency (especially for those in institutional settings); an inability to express, or discomfort with articulating, personal preferences and ideas; and feelings of pressure that they must "get it right the first time" or else be blamed for their failures when assuming greater control in the recovery process. Significant training and skill building within the recovery community is necessary to address this internal barrier and to support people as they embrace expanded roles and responsibilities. Education and ongoing support and mentoring are perhaps best offered through mental health advocacy organizations and peer-run programs.

6.2. Individuals with serious mental illness often have histories of trauma that impact on treatment and recovery. As mentioned earlier, while trauma may not be intrinsic to mental illness per se, there is considerable evidence that suggests that people living with serious mental illness at the present time have a greatly increased chance of both having experienced a history of trauma earlier in their lives and being at risk for future victimization (Sells et al., 2003). Evidence also suggests that the failure to attend to a person's history of sexual and/or physical abuse will seriously undermine the treatment and rehabilitation enterprise, leading to a poor prognosis, while approaches that are responsive to trauma significantly improve treatment effectiveness and outcomes. Similar processes resulting from patterns of relating in a person's family context or immediate social environment may pose additional barriers to the person's recovery. Within the context of urban poverty and violence, for example, the only "incentive" offered by abstinence may be a decreased immunity to the horrors that a person faces on a daily basis.

6.3. The above barriers represent more of an interaction between a person's condition and his or her experiences in the mental health system and the community at large. In addition, the symptoms of certain illnesses themselves may also pose direct impediments to the recovery process. As we described above, for example, hallucinations and delusions may compete with the information a person is receiving from health care professionals, thereby discouraging the person from taking prescribed medications or participating in other treatment or rehabilitation. Similarly, impairments in such areas as working memory, executive processes, language, attention and concentration, and problem solving can undermine a person's abilities to articulate and assert his or her personal wants, needs, and preferences in the context of a relationship with a clinical practitioner. Such cognitive impairments may be further aggravated by negative symptoms that are currently considered to be among the most unremitting and malignant of the impairments associated with psychosis. These include a lack of goal-directed activity, withdrawal, apathy, and affective flattening, all of which can create the impression that individuals are not interested in taking an active role in their care, thereby placing them at increased risk of being underestimated and undervalued as partners in the recovery planning process.

In certain conditions, the elimination or reduction of symptoms may also come with great ambivalence. For example, while episodes of mania can be destructive, they may include a heightened sense of creativity, self-importance, and productivity that is difficult to give up. Being able to identify and address this and other sequelae requires knowledge and skill on the part of the clinical practitioner. There must be a commitment to continuing professional development regarding emerging evidence-based and recovery-oriented practices that allow people to manage, or bypass, their symptoms to build a personally gratifying life in the community.

What you will hear from people when you are addressing external and internal barriers to recovery:

- *My mental illness was the least of my worries when it came to getting back to work after I got discharged from the hospital. I was terrified about losing my benefits, and my employer gave me a really hard time when I asked if I could come in a half-hour late one morning in order to see my doctor. My therapist and I sat down, and he helped me sort out what would happen to my benefits and gave me some great information about how I could talk to my boss and request some accommodations that would help me be successful on the job. I have been back now for almost a year, and I just got the Employee of the Month Award.*

- *I used to get so pissed when I got asked to sign off on the treatment plans my doctor had to send to the insurance company. Half the time, I could barely tell that it was MY plan. It didn't reflect any of the things I had said were important. My new doctor explained to me how the insurance and billing things work, and then we worked on the plan together. It still wasn't perfect, but at least I kind of knew where he was coming from and that he really HAD heard what I was trying to say.*

- *All those years I spent in social skills groups, I met the same 20 people I knew from Clozaril clinic and the clubhouse. It didn't exactly expand my social horizons! Now I am playing basketball in one of the city leagues, and there is this girl I've got my eye on who comes to the games. My therapist and I have been talking a lot about how I could strike up a conversation with her.*

- *The thought of getting discharged was so terrifying to me I almost didn't want to get well. But my case manager and I made sure that I had people and places I could go to for support when I needed it—and these folks had been involved in our work all along. It made a huge difference in my feeling good about taking the next step.*

- *I just didn't buy it when my clinician started talking to me about this thing called "consumer-driven care" . . . But she proved to me that she was for real in terms of making some changes in how we worked together— even referred me to a local self-advocacy center. I had been sitting back, letting other folks call the shots, and then complaining when things got messed up. A peer specialist at the advocacy center called me out on it. I realized that I had gotten real comfortable letting other folks make decisions for me, and I know now that I gotta take charge of my own recovery, and the peers at the Center are helping me to do that.*

Discussion

It should be readily evident from these standards that the introduction of recovery-oriented care in no way diminishes or devalues the role of professional intervention in mental health. To the contrary, we hope that we have provided ample examples and illustrations of the ways in which recovery-oriented practice requires not only sophisticated

clinical and technical skills but additional skills in community resource development, mapping, and collaboration. As the distinction
between *recovery* as pertaining to what the person does and *recovery-
oriented care* as pertaining to what practitioners offer remains both
crucial and confusing to many practitioners, we choose to close this
chapter with a brief elaboration of this point.

We begin with the fact that the centrality of the client's role in
recovery neither originated with nor is restricted to mental health.
In other medical specialties, however, there does not seem to be
such persistent confusion about the respective roles of patient and
practitioner, nor does accentuating the role of one appear to come
at the cost of sacrificing the other. When we suggest, for example,
that someone who has been in an accident follow a graduated plan
of convalescence and exercise in order to regain his or her physical
functioning, we do not thereby diminish the importance of the orthopedist's role in assessing the impact of the trauma, setting the
broken bones, and prescribing an exercise plan, which may then
need to be implemented with the assistance of a physical therapist
and the support of the person's family.

We know that while broken bones may heal of their own accord—with or without detriment to the person's functioning—they
are more likely to heal completely with timely and effective care.
Similarly, while the person might eventually regain his or her functioning following an accident without a graduated exercise plan or
physical therapy, he or she is more likely to do so in an expedient
and uncomplicated fashion, and is less likely to suffer unexpected
setbacks, with the guidance of competent and experienced healthcare practitioners. Based on these considerations, we reject both of
the following univocal assertions: (1) the person will not benefit from
professional intervention and (2) the orthopedist is responsible for
the person's recovery. Although it is unquestionably each person's
own recovery, this recovery can be substantially supported and facilitated by the assistance of competent and experienced practitioners.
The fact that we find it necessary to make this point repeatedly de-
rives mostly from the history of stigma, discrimination, and prejudice against people with serious mental illness rather than from any
wish to devalue or diminish the role of mental health practitioners.
Drawing again from the orthopedic analogy, the person will need
to exercise and resume use of those faculties most directly affected
by his or her trauma. In the case of mental illness, these faculties

include the person's cognitive, social, and emotional life as well as his or her sense of self, personal and social identity, and belonging within his or her community. If a person with a broken leg does not try to walk again, he or she will not regain the use of the leg that was broken. If a person with a mental illness does not try to reclaim responsibility for his or her life, he or she will be unable to regain functioning. This fact poses a fundamental challenge to the provision of recovery-oriented care.

Like the proverbial horse that cannot be made to drink, recovery-oriented practitioners can create or enhance access for people in recovery to a variety of educational, vocational, social, recreational, and affiliative activities in the community. They cannot, however, make the decisions *for* the person as to which, if any, of these activities he or she will participate in and find enjoyable or meaningful. But the challenge confronting recovery-oriented practitioners may not, in this way, be unique to mental health. Cardiologists, for example, cannot make their patients stick to a heart-healthy diet any more than oncologists can keep some of their patients from smoking. What complicates the picture in the case of mental health is the perception that the person's decision-making capacity is itself among the faculties most directly affected by the illness.

As mental illnesses are currently viewed primarily to be diseases of the brain, such a concern is understandable. In and of itself, however, this concern cannot be taken to lead inevitably to the conclusion that other, well-intentioned people must therefore step in and make decisions for the person. In certain, limited circumstances, practitioners are legally authorized, if not also obligated, to do so. These circumstances include imminent risk of harm to the person and/or others (i.e., homicidality, suicidality, grave disability). In most other circumstances, however, practitioners are left in the difficult position of having to honor—if not actively support—the person's decisions, even in cases in which the practitioner is persuaded that it is the illness, rather than the person's best judgment, that is driving the decision-making process.

In the absence of conservatorship, guardianship, or other legal mechanisms, practitioners can educate, inform, discuss, debate, and attempt to persuade the person to embrace some options rather than others. If the person is ever to regain his or her functioning, however, in the end he or she will have to be accorded the "dignity of risk" and the "right to failure." As is true in most components of recovery-oriented care, it requires concerted effort and reflection—and perhaps supervision—as well as compassion for mental health practitioners to continue to view and treat the person as sitting in the driver's seat of his or her own life. Given the damage that these disorders can do to the person's self-esteem and confidence, though, it is difficult to imagine how recovery can be achieved through other means.

5   The Role of the Recovery

Guide

A Recovery-Oriented

Alternative to Clinical Case

Management

We have defined and discussed the nature of various notions of
recovery, grappled with the implications of a recovery vision for
mental health system transformation, and begun to draw the out-
lines of a transformed system. Now we can turn to the question of
how such services and supports can actually be offered to people
who need them. Here we propose what we call the *recovery guide
model.* Analogous to the role currently played by case management,
the recovery guide model is an organizing vehicle by which practitioners can offer a range of services and supports to people, either
directly or through others. As with case management, the intensity,
scope, focus, and duration of a recovery guide's work with a person
will depend on that person's needs, preferences, life circumstances,
and goals at a given point in his or her unique recovery journey.

In this chapter we describe the basic aims, tenets, and tools of this
approach. First, though, we offer a brief review of advances in mental
health case management that preceded and led up to the concept of
recovery guides, including the present recognition that, in a recovery-
oriented system of care, people with serious mental illness can no longer
be considered "cases" that others manage (Everett & Nelson, 1992).

Recent Advances in Mental Health Case Management

With the failure of a combination of Thorazine and psychotherapy to achieve the aims of deinstitutionalization (Johnson, 1992), case management became the predominant service that mental health systems offered their clients with serious mental illness (Sledge, Astrachan, Thompson, Rakfeldt, & Leaf, 1995). In addition to being inadequately funded, community-based systems of care that were developed to enable people with serious mental illness to leave state hospitals were fragmented and uncoordinated "non-systems" of care (Hoge, Davidson, Griffith, & Jacobs, 1998). As it was practically impossible for people seeking care to navigate these complex and unintegrated health and social service systems on their own, the case manager role was created to identify and coordinate the provision of services to meet their multiple needs in the community (Hoge, Davidson, Griffith, Sledge, & Howenstine, 1994; Sledge et al., 1995). Case managers' primary responsibility was to assess people's needs, link them to services, and monitor their service use and outcomes.

When it became apparent that lone case managers could not ensure access to or coordination among services over which they had no administrative or fiscal authority, team-based approaches to case management were developed. In these approaches, mental health practitioners could provide care directly or "broker" services from other agencies and practitioners (Hoge et al., 1994). The most well articulated and rigorously evaluated team-based approach to intensive case management was the Program for Assertive Community Treatment (PACT), developed in the 1970s (Stein and Test (1980). PACT, or ACT (Assertive Community Treatment), as it has since come to be known, and other versions of team-based intensive case management are characterized by the provision of comprehensive care in natural community settings, with lower client-to-staff ratios, caseloads that are shared by teams of practitioners, 24-hour emergency coverage, and time-unlimited services (Bond, 1991; Mueser, Bond, Drake, & Resnick, 1998). This shift to team and outreach-based care gave the first impetus to the recovery guide model of practice.

In a related development, assertive mental health outreach to homeless persons, or "homeless outreach," a practice modeled in good measure on ACT, emerged in the early 1980s as practitioners learned that many homeless persons with mental illness shun traditional community mental health clinics because of previous negative experiences with them (Segal, Baumohl, & Johnson, 1977); clinic requirements that applicants disclose personal information and acknowledge having a mental illness in order to receive help; medication and other treatment side effects; difficulty negotiating mental health clinic or center bureaucracies; and the exigencies of homeless life, such as having to choose between eating at a soup kitchen and keeping an appointment with a clinician (Dennis, Buckner, Lipton, & Levine, 1991; Koegel, 1992). Given their mandate to engage these individuals in care, mental health outreach staff have had to be creative and resourceful in finding ways to address, bypass, or overcome these factors to connect with clients "where they are" both geographically and existentially. An outreach worker described his way of connecting with a homeless client who initially spurned his help:

> I observed his survival tactics. I noticed that he picks up bottles. One of the things I did was collect some bottles. . . . I observed that he had ripped-up blankets, so I offered him a blanket. Every time we got together I had something to offer him. . . . I never asked him for anything, I always brought something to him. When he had been approached on the street they always wanted something from him. (quoted in Rowe, 1999, p. 63)

Homeless outreach strategies include not requiring people to acknowledge having a mental illness or accept mental health treatment in order to get help with other needs. Outreach workers "engage," or build trust and a connection with, homeless persons through helping them with basic needs such as food, emergency shelter, and clothing and offering them a range of services such as housing, medical care, substance abuse treatment, and help in obtaining jobs or income supports. Over time, outreach workers try to persuade their clients to accept mental health treatment (Brickner, 1992; Morse et al., 1996; Susser, Goldfinger, & White, 1990; Swayze, 1992).

Simultaneously with these advances, concerns that community mental health services emphasized the deficits and problems of persons with serious mental illness over their strengths and interests gave rise to both strengths-based and rehabilitative approaches to case management (Mueser et al., 1998). These approaches incorporate many of the principles of psychiatric rehabilitation (Anthony, 1993), emphasizing the importance of skill building as a way to promote community tenure. They also allow for more client input and direction as opposed to being driven by mental health practitioners with an accumulated body of knowledge. Finally, they stress that the community, where most of the contact between case managers and clients takes place, offers resources for, and can present obstacles to, people's growth and development.

The question we are left with after this brief review is, "To what degree are these approaches based on or oriented toward promoting the person's recovery?" In homeless outreach, for example, people can be engaged gradually in a trusting and helpful relationship through assistance with meeting their basic needs, with the ultimate goal of getting them off of the streets or of keeping them out of the hospital or jail. From the perspective of a recovery guide model, the main question is, "To what degree were these goals the person's own goals, and to what degree did the outreach worker act as a guide, rather than as a manager, in helping the client achieve them?"

Top 10 Principles of Recovery-Oriented, Community-Based Care

Before describing the practices entailed in this model, we want to review the principles that underlie them. In contrast to the continued debate and lack of clarity over what the concept of "recovery" means in relation to serious mental illnesses, a considerable amount of consensus has emerged on core principles of recovery-oriented care (e.g., Anthony, 2000; Davidson, Stayner, et al., 2001; Jacobson & Greenley, 2001; Ridgway, 2001). Based on our reviews of this literature (e.g., Davidson, O'Connell, et al., 2005; O'Connell, Tondora, Evans, Croog, & Davidson, 2005), we have distilled the following top 10 principles. Although the principles overlap, each one addresses a unique and important dimension of recovery-oriented care. Taken together, they describe the domain and central strategies for the recovery guide's work.

Principle 1: Care Is Oriented to Promoting Recovery

As we suggest in the preceding section, this principle is neither as obvious nor as straightforward as it may sound at first. Promoting recovery is not synonymous with reducing symptoms, increasing insight or medication adherence, ameliorating deficits, enhancing community tenure, or preventing hospitalizations, all of which have been seen as aims of mental health care in the past. Since the 1999 Surgeon General's Report on Mental Health, the field has been encouraged to accept that "all services for those with a mental disorder should be consumer-oriented and focused on promoting recovery" (DHHS, 1999, p. 455). That is, all mental health care should be driven by the client's own goals, grounded in an appreciation of the possibility and the nature of recovery, and oriented to facilitating each person's efforts toward recovery in whichever form it takes at the time.

These statements stand in stark contrast to much of the last 150 years of mental health policy and practice, an era based on a maintenance and stabilization framework at best, or on a belief in the progressive deterioration of persons with serious mental illness at worst. The notion that many people can recover from a serious mental illness is still relatively new, and the notion that they can enter into and pursue recovery even while they remain disabled is newer still. We are just beginning to identify the implications of these recognitions for practice. One implication of this shift in focus, however, is that people need to be offered hope for a renewed sense of self and purpose in their lives. Hope may come from others who believe in the person's potential or from the person's religious faith, even when he or she lacks that hope (Davidson, Stayner, et al., 2001; Deegan, 1996a; Fisher, 1994; Jacobson & Curtis, 2000; Mead & Copeland, 2000; Smith, 2000). As described by Jacobson and Greenley (2001), "Hope sustains, even during periods of relapse. It creates its own possibilities. Hope is a frame of mind that colors every perception. By expanding the realm of the possible, hope lays the groundwork for healing to begin" (p. 483).

In addition to hope, being in recovery involves a process of overcoming some of the consequences of illness; gaining an enhanced sense of identity, empowerment, and meaning and purpose in life; and developing valued social roles, citizenship, and community connections in spite of having symptoms, deficits, or continued disability (Cooke, 1997; Davidson et al., 2001; Deegan, 1996a). A recovery vision requires that care be based explicitly on a belief in people's potential to manage and improve their lives over time. Recovery-oriented care thus includes practices that help people gain connections with and autonomy in relation to others, aid in skill development as well as symptom management and treatment, focus on abilities and strengths rather than deficits, and are guided by the person in recovery. It includes asking clients questions about their hopes, dreams, interests, talents, and skills and, perhaps most important, asking "How can I help?" in addition to asking about and assessing their problems. Given the focus of recovery-oriented care on fostering a functional sense of agency in the person himself or herself, practitioners ask themselves, in particular, "Does this person *gain* power, purpose, competence, or connections to people as a result of this interaction?" and, conversely, "Does this interaction *interfere* with this person's acquisition of power, purpose, skills, or connections to others?" (Carling, 1995).

Principle 2: Care Is Strengths-Based

Traditional mental health services have been organized around a medical model that perceives mental illness as a disease that must be "treated" and "cured" (Corrigan & Penn, 1998). By focusing on the assessment and treatment of deficits, aberrations, and symptoms— all the things that are "wrong" with people—practitioners may overlook all that remains "right" with people—their remaining, coexisting areas of health, assets, strengths, and competencies (Davidson & Strauss, 1995). Because no "cure" for mental illness is available at present, emphasizing the negative leads to a sense of hopelessness and despair among both clients and mental health practitioners. A recovery orientation encourages us to see that "all people have . . . strengths and capabilities as well as the capacity to become more competent" (Grills, Bass, Brown, & Akers, 1996, p. 129; Rapaport, 1981).

As a result of this recognition, we come to appreciate that "the failure of a person to display competence is not due to deficits within the person but rather to the failure of . . . social systems to provide or create opportunities for competencies to be displayed or acquired" (Grills et al., 1996, p. 130). By focusing on strengths rather than deficits, people can begin to identify and develop greater competencies, assets, and resources upon which to expand their opportunities (Rapp, 1993; Rapp & Wintersteen, 1989). This focus promotes the development of an upward positive spiral of competence, leading to increased health, which leads to increased competence (Davidson, 2003). The story of Tyrese is illustrative of this principle.

Tyrese was a man in his 40s who spent the majority of his days sitting in a chair or on a couch at the drop-in center, smoking cigarettes and watching television. While he conversed with others on occasion, he seemed just as happy to sit by himself, lost in his thoughts, his cigarette smoke, or the television show that happened to be on at the moment. His appearance was disheveled, and he would occasionally blurt out something that appeared to be in response to hallucinated voices. In this respect, Tyrese was perhaps not as alone as he appeared. Although this drop-in center had a fairly lenient policy regarding "hanging out," the staff eventually became concerned about Tyrese and what, if anything, he was getting from his visits to the drop-in center. He repeatedly turned down invitations to participate in activities and responded to the suggestions of his peers and the staff about what else he might do with disinterest. He appeared to be stuck, and the staff began to feel stuck with him as well.

When it came time for his service review, the only goal of interest that Tyrese could identify was finding a job. He had no work history, had not graduated high school, had no identifiable skills, and could not—or would not—state any more clearly what kind of job he might be interested in. All of the efforts the members and staff of the drop-in center made to involve Tyrese in activities were fruitless. Everyone appeared to have run out of ideas and figured that it was least better for Tyrese to come to the drop-in center every day, even if he did nothing, than to remain at home alone.

Shortly after the staff became resigned to viewing the drop-in center as a better alternative for Tyrese than his staying home alone, it occurred to a staff member to wonder what Tyrese's home life was like. Where, in fact, did he live? With whom? Either it had not occurred to them to ask or, when they did ask, Tyrese had not been forthcoming with answers. No one seemed to know much about his life outside of the drop-in center. With this recognition, one staff member—the one who first wondered about what Tyrese did outside of the drop-in center and with whom—decided that this was a mystery that could be solved. He decided to spend more time with Tyrese and try to learn more about his life. Tyrese, however, would not answer the usual questions about whom he lived with, where, etc. Finally, more out of desperation than anything else, the staff member asked Tyrese, "Well, how do you get here every day?" At this question, and to the staff member's surprise, a small light shone in Tyrese's eyes and he responded, "I take the bus." "Which bus?" the staff member persisted. After further discussion it emerged that Tyrese in fact took two buses to the drop-in center each day, that he lived on the other side of town, and that he did not mind the 45-minute bus ride; in fact, he enjoyed the rides back and forth as much as his time at the drop-in center.

Tyrese, it turned out, enjoyed buses and riding buses, and he knew more about the bus system in his city than just about anyone else outside of the bus company. When the staff member asked to accompany Tyrese home from the center one day, Tyrese talked nonstop throughout the 45-minute ride and change of buses about the different routes, the different schedules, and how he had learned over the years to be able to get from any point in the city to any other point by taking no more than three buses. The staff member also noticed that while he was on the bus, Tyrese appeared to be animated, attentive, and interested. He didn't have time to entertain or respond to voices, as he was busy greeting the bus driver, explaining the routes to his fellow rider, and savoring each moment of the ride. At the end of their first ride together, it came as no surprise to the staff member that Tyrese confided to him that what he liked most about the drop-in center was the fact that it provided bus tokens at a reduced rate (and had a wide-screen television).

The staff member shared his experiences with Tyrese and his new insights into Tyrese's life outside the drop-in center with the staff, but no one had any immediate ideas about what to do with this information. Then, when budget cuts came down from the state and the program had to give up its van and transportation service, the staff had to brainstorm and problem-solve about how some clients would be able to get to the center. During this discussion, one staff member initially quipped that perhaps Tyrese could teach other members how to use the bus service. What started out as a joke quickly was turned into a proposal, however, and Tyrese was approached with the idea. Would he be interested in teaching other members about the city's bus system, and would he be willing to ride with them and show them the routes until they became comfortable themselves?

To the staff's surprise, Tyrese's eyes again lit up, and he responded with excitement. The fact that the staff were willing to pay him for this service did not seem to be as important to him as the fact that he was being seen, and valued, for what he had to offer. While becoming the "bus trainer" did not stop his voices or initially improve his hygiene, it did engage Tyrese in the life of the center, enable him to make friends among his peers, and get him up off the couch. Over time, however, he did wash and cut his hair so that he could wear a new baseball cap he had bought with the word "Conductor" on the front.

As might eventually happen in Tyrese's case, for many people, rediscovering their remaining areas of health and their talents, gifts, and possibilities makes it easier for them to acknowledge and accept the limitations imposed by the illness (Hatfield, 1994; Munetz & Frese, 2001; Smith, 2000; Sullivan, 1994; Young & Ensing, 1999). This acknowledgment and acceptance does not mean accepting one's identity as a "mentally ill person," however, but rather has to do with redefining how one thinks about and understands life's challenges (Ridgway, 2001). Deegan (1996b), for example, describes the "paradox of recovery . . . that in accepting what we cannot do or be, we begin to discover who we can be and what we can do." Gaining perspective on one's strengths and weaknesses allows one to identify, pursue, and achieve life goals despite the lingering presence of disability (Deegan, 1988, 1993; Hatfield, 1994; Munetz & Frese, 2001; Ridgway, 2001; Sayce & Perkins, 2000; Smith, 2000; Sullivan, 1994; Young & Ensing, 1999). Within this view, limitations become the "ground from which spring our own unique possibilities" (Sayce & Perkins, 2000, p. 74). As a person enters into and pursues recovery, the illness becomes less a defining characteristic of self than a part of a multidimensional self that also contains strengths, skills, and competencies. Care, to be recovery-oriented, must elicit, flesh out, and cultivate these positive elements at least as much as it assesses and attempts to ameliorate difficulties.

Principle 3: Care Is Community-Focused

Following the early years of deinstitutionalization, the National Institute of Mental Health recognized that the multiple needs of people with serious mental illness living in the community were not being addressed by existing care. The Institute thus designed and disseminated a model of community treatment that focused on housing, income maintenance, medical care, and rehabilitation in addition to traditional mental health services (Turner & TenHoor, 1978). Turner and Schifren (1979) described the resulting Community Support Program initiative of the 1970s as promoting the development of a "network of caring and responsible people committed to assisting a vulnerable population meet their needs and develop their potentials without being unnecessarily isolated or excluded from the community" (p. 2). Somewhere along the way, however, care that was designed to be community-focused became confused with care that was simply community-based, with the *focus* of care being replaced by the *locus* of care (Stein, 1989).

In addition to being provided outside of hospital settings, true community-focused care is provided in a person's natural environment, facilitates the development of relationships with other community members, helps people develop citizenship and roles that are of value to their community, and works with members of the general community to combat stigma and increase access to resources. Community-focused care views the incongruence between people and their environment as the target for intervention. It helps people assimilate into their environment through symptom management, skill acquisition, and other means, and helps the community accommodate people with disabilities through education, stigma reduction, the creation of valued roles and niches, and other means. Taken together, this dual focus helps to develop "multiple pathways" into and among members of communities (Dailey et al., 2000).

Principle 4: Care Is Person-Driven

American society places tremendous value on the freedom to exercise choice in everyday life. Constrained only by their access to resources, adults have the right and responsibility to make their own decisions about where they live, what they do, and how they want to be treated as long as these decisions do not infringe on other people's rights. During a century of institutional care, these rights and responsibilities were denied to asylum inmates, who were seen as incapable of taking care of themselves. Unfortunately, this view did not disappear altogether with the downsizing of state mental hospitals; instead it has been carried, to various degrees, into community treatment settings, recreating an "institution without walls" in the community (Davidson, 1997; Estroff, 1995). Continuing to be viewed as largely incapacitated by their psychiatric disorder, people with serious mental illness have yet to be accorded the same rights to autonomy and self-determination, or the same responsibilities for self-care, as the general public.

A person-driven model of care is one that the person with the disability directs. It reflects his or her own wants, needs, and preferences; involves primary relationships as sources of support; focuses on capacities and strengths; and accepts risks, failures, uncertainties, and setbacks as natural and expected parts of learning and self-determination (Gerteis, Edgman-Levitan, Daley, & Delbanco, 1993; O'Brien & Lovett, 1992). In this model, practitioners learn to "do nothing without the client's approval, involving clients in decisions regarding every step of the process." In addition, according to this model, "opportunities to move each client closer to being the director of the case management scenario [are to] be found, created, and exploited" (Rapp, 1998, p. 374).

For this model to be effective, of course, people with disabilities need to feel like members of society despite their disability status, as opposed to being subsumed by their illness or diagnostic label. When illness robs people of their personhood and all of the socially valued roles that accompany it, the patient role is one of the few that remain (Estroff, 1989)—illness takes on what sociologists call a "master status," and the main form of membership in society, for many, becomes that of "program citizenship" (Rowe, 1999). As Deegan observes, when the person's "identity [becomes] synonymous with a disease, then there is no one left inside to take on the enormous work of recovery" (1996b, p. 12). By contrast, "the process of rediscovering and reconstructing an enduring sense of self as an active and responsible agent provides an important and perhaps, crucial, source of improvement" (Davidson & Strauss, 1992).

Following the client's lead in this regard is not always a straightforward or uncomplicated affair, of course. People with serious mental illness will occasionally make bad choices or prefer things that others know are not in their best interest—just like everyone else. In this case, however, staff feel an ethical and moral obligation to protect people from their own poor judgment or from activities, relationships, or roles they fear might exacerbate the person's illness. This, for example, is often the reason given for why staff do not always help people get jobs when they express an interest in working, the fear being that working will be stressful. In addition to overlooking the fact that unemployment and poverty are sure to be equally, if not more, stressful, staff are not in a position to know what is best for another person. Robert's situation exemplifies this lesson, and gives us pause in thinking that we always, or ever, know best.

> Robert was a man in his early 30s from an Irish background who had grown up in a small town outside of Boston. As do many people when they develop a serious mental illness, Robert had moved to the city and had unfortunately become disconnected from his family. Also like many first-generation Americans, Robert had been expected to finish school and acquire a profession, to help support his large family. While his three brothers had gone on to college

and took secure, well-paying jobs, Robert had dropped out of school, wandered around the country, and refused to work—even in the family business. Eventually his parents insisted that he move out, and Robert landed in a working-class neighborhood in Boston, alone, on disability, and with not much to live for.

Robert appeared to have few, if any, goals, except for wanting a girlfriend and a car. His case manager did not know what to do for him, as he was already connected to services, dutifully took his medication, and maintained his one room within an SRO Housing unit not far from the clinic. Otherwise, Robert remained aloof and suspicious, and would not divulge much information about his history or interests. Based on Robert's few expressed goals, the case manager explained that if Robert wanted a car he should get a job so that he could afford to buy and maintain one, and that if he wanted a girlfriend he should find places to hang out where he might meet women. In response to these suggestions, Robert initially looked puzzled and then explained to the case manager that he already had a place to hang out where there were plenty of women, at least on the weekends, but that he couldn't meet or attract them because he didn't have a car. The problem was not access or proximity but not having his own wheels. "What self-respecting woman," he asked, "would go out with a 33-year-old man who didn't have his own car?"

Rather than pressing the point about getting a job to be able to afford a car, the case manager focused on the fact that Robert did indeed have a place to "hang out." Apparently, Robert spent most afternoons and evenings sitting at the bar of a neighborhood pub, chatting with the bartender and other regulars and watching sports on one of the several television sets suspended above it. He was a Red Sox, Patriots, and Celtics fan, and he often stayed until the bar closed around 2:00 A.M. and then returned to his room to sleep well into the late morning. After lunch at the social club and attending to any errands, appointments, or laundry, Robert would then return to the pub for the remainder of the day. All that he needed, as far as he was concerned, was a car and girlfriend.

When the case manager discussed this new information with Robert's psychiatrist, they both became concerned about Robert spending all of his time at a bar and wondered how much he was drinking and what effect his drinking was having on the efficacy of his medications. Perhaps Robert was not benefiting as much as he might from the medicine, and perhaps his progress was stalled, because he was drinking too much, perhaps even on a daily basis. They agreed that what Robert needed was to start attending AA meetings or, if he did not agree to that, perhaps to join the dual-disorder group at the clinic. Robert, they surmised, was one of those people who had had an undetected co-occurring addiction and needed more intensive treatment.

When the psychiatrist and case manager tried to discuss these concerns with Robert, he denied drinking alcohol at all and insisted that he was a "teetotaler." When they expressed doubts about the veracity of this Robert became angry, shouting at the two of them that they could come with him to the pub if they wanted to and find out for themselves if they didn't believe him. Then he promptly stormed out of the office. Robert then didn't show up for his regular appointments with the case manager for several weeks and repeatedly hung up on him when he called, insisting that the case manager was "in cahoots" with his parents and could no longer be trusted.

After several weeks and several offers, Robert finally agreed to meet the case manager at the pub. The case manager explained that he was willing to take Robert up on his offer and to find out for himself, as long as Robert would agree to his doing so. They met at the pub the next afternoon, and Robert proudly introduced the case manager to the bartender and some of the other customers, saying that he was an "old friend" visiting from out of town. The case manager was impressed with the familiarity with which Robert addressed and chatted with the people there and his level of apparent comfort, wondering what had happened to Robert's usual aloof and suspicious demeanor. It then occurred to the case manager that he had never seen Robert outside of the clinic before, and that perhaps his paranoia was increased when he was in such a setting. His medical record, after all, noted that Robert had had several involuntary hospitalizations in the past, and perhaps he was not comforted by being in a mental health setting. He did appear to be comforted, however, by being in a pub.

When the case manager commented on how "at home" Robert appeared to be in the pub, Robert explained that it should be no surprise, as he was virtually raised in a pub. The family business, as it turned out, was a neighborhood pub, and all family activities and events revolved around the pub. He did his homework at the pub, had his meals at the pub, brought his dates to the pub, and, eventually, got kicked out of the pub. His fond reminiscences of family life quickly turned sour as he related that his father and three brothers were all "drunks—respectable, responsible drunks, perhaps, but drunks nonetheless. He had never fit in, and when he reached 16 and still wouldn't join them in drinking, tensions between him and his family only increased.

Robert was clearly spent after disclosing so much personal information to the case manager, and he quickly turned his attention to the horse race on ESPN. The case manager took the opportunity to jokingly inquire of the bartender about Robert's preferred beverages and found out that Robert did, in fact, drink a lot of tea, along with a fair amount of club soda. Armed with lots of new, rich, and interesting information about Robert to ponder, and to discuss with the psychiatrist, the case manager left the pub that afternoon wondering why he didn't leave his office, and the clinic, more often.

Principle 5: Care Allows for Reciprocity in Relationships

The recovery process entails regaining a sense of agency in one's life and a sense of belonging and self-worth within one's community and society at large (Davidson, Stayner, et al., 2001). We have long known that it is therapeutic to give of oneself to others (Biegel & Tracy, 1994; Riessman, 1990). However, many persons with psychiatric disabilities have become so accustomed to *receiving* help and having decisions made for them that they feel they have little of value to share. They may also be accustomed to having their offers of reciprocity rejected because traditional client–clinician therapeutic boundaries and roles forbid such a two-way street. When asymmetrical and largely unidirectional relationships exist between practitioners and clients, "staff hold the power to allocate or give based on their judgment" (Curtis & Hodge, 1994, p. 25). This also may contribute to passivity in clients, and may carry over into their other, more naturally occurring, relationships (Davidson, Stayner, & Haglund, 1998).

Practitioners can help clients gain a sense of agency and self-worth by treating them as equals, accepting their appropriate gestures of reciprocity, and encouraging their participation in self-help (Mead & Copeland, 2000). The development of valued social roles and involvement in meaningful activities are cornerstones of the recovery process. They give people a sense of self-worth and purpose in their lives (Anthony, 1993; Davidson, Stayner, et al., 2001; Ridgway, 2001; Young & Ensing, 1999). It's hard to have a sense of belonging to your community without a sense of what you can contribute to it. As Jacobson and Greenley put it, "To connect is to find roles to play in the world" (2001, p. 483). Preferably, these roles will benefit others as well as oneself, a principle we noted in Chapter 2 and which was articulated eloquently by Tom, a participant in one of our earlier studies, who continued on to explain more fully:

I could choose to be a nobody, a nothing, and just [say] "the hell with it, the hell with everything, I'm not going to deal with anything." And there are times when I feel like that. And yet, I'm part of the world, I'm a human being. And human beings usually kind of do things together to help each other out, that type of thing. And I want to be part of that. . . . If you're not part of the world, it's pretty miserable, pretty lonely. So I think . . . [it's] important . . . involvement in some kind of activity. Hopefully an activity which benefits somebody. I have something to offer . . . that's all I'm talking about. And I think [this project] made it a little bit easier for me to think in those terms, to not be afraid to give things to people, and not be afraid to take things from people in return. (quoted in Davidson, Haglund, et al., 2001, p. 288)

Principle 6: Care Is Culturally Responsive

As documented in the supplement to the Surgeon General's report on mental illness entitled *Mental Health: Culture, Race, and Ethnicity* (DHHS, 2001), people from ethnic and racial minority groups are both overrepresented *and* underserved among recipients of public-sector mental health care. While the prevalence of psychiatric disorders may be comparable across cultural and racial groups, access to care, service use, and health outcomes are not. Few, if any, effective services are tailored and responsive to the unique social and cultural backgrounds of people of color, and some forms of traditional treatment may be less effective or even detrimental when used with ethnic minority populations. Spanish-speaking families, for example, have been found to have more symptoms when treated with highly structured family therapy and fewer symptoms when receiving less structured case management services (Telles et al., 1995). In addition to a mistrust of the mental health system among persons of color (Becerra, Karno, & Escobar, 1982; Grier & Cobbs, 1968; Gutierrez, Ortega, & Suarez, 1990; Neighbors, Elliott, & Gant, 1990), some characteristics of traditional services run counter to the values of these communities. For both African and Hispanic Americans, for example, these characteristics include a reliance on agencies as opposed to personal relationships and extended peer and family networks, and a focus on the individual as opposed to the group (Butler, 1992; Grier & Cobbs, 1968; Gutierrez et al., 1990; Neighbors et al., 1990).

The lack of congruence between cultural values and traditional mental health services, in combination with disparities in service access, utilization, satisfaction, and outcomes, prompted the Surgeon General to call for expanded research to clarify when and how traditional treatments ought to be adapted, or new ones developed, to meet the needs and preferences of people of color. When developed, these services can be oriented to the local community and can draw on local resources as well. It is difficult, however, even for culturally responsive programs to be tailored to the unique cultural identities of individuals. We know from research on ethnic identity development, for example, that not all individuals from a particular ethnic background, or even from the same specific subgroup (e.g., Afro-Caribbean or Chilean), will identify to the same degree and in the same ways with their cultural heritage and its traditional values (Casas & Pytluk, 1995; Pope-Davis, Liu, Ledesma-Jones, & Nevitt, 2000; Vandiver, 2001). Based on a number of factors, such as length of time in the United States and family context, tremendous variability can be found within even the smallest enclaves of minority communities.

In addition, common experiences among persons of different racial, ethnic, or cultural backgrounds may make for greater "cultural-experiential" solidarity, at a given time and under certain circumstances, than these persons share with their own ethnic or other group. Two people spending time with and protecting each other as street homeless persons sleeping under highway bridges may feel that they share an intense and particular lived experience that brings them closer to each other than factors of race or ethnicity could.

As a result, recovery-oriented care not only needs to attend to cultural differences across race, ethnicity, and other distinctions such as sexual orientation but must incorporate this sensitivity at the level of the individual client in order to avoid stereotyping people ("what all lesbians want or need," for example), and instead to tailor services to the needs, values, and preferences of each person.

Principle 7: Care Is Grounded in the Person's
Life-Context

Care that is grounded in a person's "life-context" acknowledges, builds on, and appreciates each person's unique history, experiences, situations, developmental trajectory, and aspirations (Davidson & Strauss, 1995). In addition to culture, race, and ethnicity, there are less visible but perhaps equally important influences on each individual's development, including both traditional concerns of mental health practitioners such as family composition and background and history of symptoms and hospitalizations, and less common factors such as personal interests, hobbies, and role models that help define who people are as individuals.

Just as many people find that a serious mental illness may subsume who they were as individuals prior to becoming ill, we at times fall into viewing people as if they were born with a mental illness and did not have a life beforehand (Davidson & Strauss, 1995). Due in part to such perceptions and the corresponding treatment by others, many people with mental illness become accustomed to living an invisible life on the margins of society. Practitioners must understand the impact that marginalization has had on their clients and their expectations and encourage them to reconnect to the persons they *used* to be as one possible bridge to becoming who they *want* to be, despite the limitations imposed by their disability. Appreciation of an individual's life-context is an underdeveloped dimension of recovery-oriented care that we discuss further in a later section through the lens of the recovery guide.

Principle 8: Care Addresses the Socioeconomic Context of the Person's Life

The context of poverty and disconnection from material resources and opportunities such as education, work, and strong social networks both exacerbates and interacts with marginalization, invisibility, and the "distorted visibility" of mental illness. Mental health outreach workers, for example, learn that the life context of the person they are trying to help is also the context of poverty and homelessness. An outreach team director in New Haven, Connecticut, stated this principle eloquently:

> If someone walks in for an appointment, the clinician will do an intake evaluation. The clinician never puts in their mind, "What is the experience like, living at Columbus House Shelter?" They lose that from the entire interview, something that's central to the client's life. I think some of the clinical success has been internalizing "What does it mean to be homeless?" You meet the client on a different level. (quoted in Rowe, 1999, p. 90)

If, as outreach workers learn, engagement with the person first—as opposed to engagement with the patient—is critical in establishing the trust and relationship from which worker and client move forward, then such awareness of the person also helps make workers aware of their client's need for housing, income, social supports, and other material and social needs that are necessary, although not sufficient, conditions of full membership in society (Rowe, 1999). The helping relationship and socioeconomic context meet, for clients, in the conviction that their outreach workers see and regard them as full human beings, and understand the barriers of poverty they face, along with the challenges of mental illness, stigma, and isolation. These two—helping relationship and context—also meet, for workers, in the principles of not making promises they cannot keep and keeping the promises they do make. When a resource such as housing is not available, the worker's promise to continue to work with the client and see him or her through this difficulty helps sustain the relationship until the resource does become available.

Principle 9: Care Is Relationally Mediated

Recovery is a fundamentally social process (Jacobson & Greenley, 2001; Mezzina et al., 2006). Supportive relationships with family members, friends, practitioners, community members, and peers allow individuals to become interdependent in a community that can both share in their disappointments and pain and revel in their joy and successes (Baxter & Diehl, 1998; Fisher, 1994; Jacobson & Greenley, 2001; Mead & Copeland, 2000; Ridgway, 2001; Smith, 2000; Sullivan, 1994; Young & Ensing, 1999). People in recovery often attribute their recovery to someone "really believing in me" or "seeing something inside me that I couldn't see" (Davidson, Stayner, et al., 2001; Ragins, 1994).

Regardless of the number of tools or interventions a practitioner uses, the heart of any effective intervention is the relationship between the practitioner and the client (Anthony, 1993). Like other caring people in the person's life, mental health practitioners must believe in their clients even when the clients cannot believe in themselves and must remind them gently of their potential. To promote recovery, practitioners must be able to envision a future for their clients, one based on clients' own desires and values, and they must share this vision with them through communicating positive expectations and hope.

Consistent with this principle, the establishment of trusting, supportive relationships through persistence and consistency is considered by some to be the most fundamental requirement of recovery-
oriented care. In the presence of such relationships, the illness no
longer remains the primary focus of the person's life, and the person is able to move on to other interests and activities (Anthony,
1993). With such encouraging support, people may be able to take
risks they have not taken before. To fully realize the benefits of this
process, practitioners must be more than just "case managers." They
must also be willing to fill gaps in needed service areas and "to assist
clients in developing their own individual visions and journeys of
recovery through the process of defining meaning and purpose in
their lives" (Lunt, 2000, p. 402). Unfortunately, the development of a
genuine relationship between the practitioner and the client has been
missing in the conceptualization of most case management models.

Principle 10: Care Optimizes Natural Supports

Traditional mental health systems have been described as tending
to "surround people with serious mental health problems with a sea
of professionally delivered services . . . which stigmatize them and set
them apart from the community" (Nelson, Ochocka, Griffin, & Lord,
1998, p. 881). A recovery-oriented model of care helps minimize
the role that practitioners play in clients' lives over time and maximize the role of natural supports such as friends, family, neighbors,
and other community members. Rather than substituting for such
networks and, in effect, offering their clients "program citizenship"
through the mental health system, practitioners assist their clients
in regaining citizenship in the sense of access to the rights, responsibilities, roles, and resources that society offers to its members through
public institutions and associational life (Rowe, 1999; Rowe, Kloos,
Chinman, Davidson, & Cross, 2001). Practitioners help people mobilize their own support networks through developing new ties and
strengthening old ones (Biegel & Tracy, 1994). One strategy for expanding relationship networks is to tap into and "place a premium
on the use of existing available community resources like families,
volunteer opportunities, neighbors, junior colleges, sports leagues,
YMCAs, faith communities, and arts centers" (Rapp, 1998, p. 371).
    In order for mental health practitioners to help people make
these connections, they must know the community their clients live

in and the resources available in it. They must also know what people are important to them, whether parent, friend, landlord, or grocer. Practitioners also must be knowledgeable about informal community support systems such as support groups, singles clubs, and other special interest groups and be willing to learn more about other possibilities that exist to help people make new connections. This kind of knowledge does not come from sitting in an office. Similarly, the process of connecting people often cannot be managed through referral or brokering processes. Helping people increase their natural supports often means that practitioners have to make those connections themselves, be familiar with resources and friendly spots in the community, and be involved in the community. Where pathways to community life seem largely absent, practitioners must develop active relationships with a range of community members and resources so that those clients can gain entrée to a range of "normal" activities and socially valued roles, and so they can leave behind the identity of "mental patient" and internalize a more positive identity in the community (Gilmartin, 1997; Rappaport, 1995). Doing so requires practitioners to avoid the temptation of recreating within the mental health system opportunities that could exist in the broader community, as suggested by Jan's story. (In this case, Jan is this young man's actual name; he has joined the user movement in Sweden and is very public in telling his recovery story, including publishing it as a book [in Swedish].)

> Jan is a young Vietnamese immigrant to Sweden who has battled schizophrenia for over 10 years. He has been seriously disabled by the illness and hospitalized on numerous occasions when he has been unable to take care of himself. He credits the turning point in his recovery to his discovery of a bowling alley in Stockholm, where he developed an intensive interest in both the sport and the life of the bowling alley. Initially he was a leisure bowler. Very quickly, however, he fell in love with the sport and began to spend many hours bowling by himself. Through what then became a hobby, he made friends at the bowling alley among the staff and other regular bowlers and, after a while, took a job cleaning the lanes and balls and doing general trouble-shooting. He reinvested his new earnings back into the bowling alley, buying his own ball and shoes and joining a league. Within a few years of intensive training and daily practice, he became the country's Amateur Bowler of the Year, missing a perfect 300 game by one pin.

Jan has been very eager and articulate in talking about his experiences with both schizophrenia and bowling, and he participated in our multinational study of recovery. When he described the meaning and role of bowling and the bowling alley in his recovery, he clearly pointed out that it was crucial that he was able to take up bowling, join a league, and excel as an ordinary citizen rather than as a user of mental health services. His experience would not have been the same had he bowled as a member of the mental health social club or only with other "users" (i.e., consumers). This is because it was bowling that first gave him a positive sense of identity apart from his illness and his involvement in mental health care. As he described it, "At the bowling alley it doesn't matter if you're mentally ill, if you're a foreigner, an asthmatic, a dyslexic—just as long as you bowl as many strikes as you can you are just like everyone else. So when I'm playing a match I'm worth just as much as anyone else, maybe even more. . . . In a bowling match everyone's a bowler. It's the number of strikes that counts, nothing else." (quoted in Davidson, Borg, et al., 2005, p. 196)

The Job of the Recovery-Oriented Practitioner

Even after reading these principles, some practitioners may still view them as somehow applying to someone else. Most graduate programs outside of psychiatric rehabilitation, for instance, continue to train people to conduct thorough assessments, offer accurate diagnoses, and provide effective treatments, but not to deal with clients' housing or employment goals, and seldom to ensure that their clients are involved in meaningful activities or having fun or gaining pleasure.

One implication of our 10 principles is that in order to address "individuals' basic human needs for decent housing, food, work, and 'connection' with the community," practitioners must be willing to go where the action is; that is, they must get out of their offices and out into the community (Curtis & Hodge, 1994, p. 15). They must be prepared to go out to meet people on their own turf and on their own terms, and to "[o]ffer assistance which they might consider immediately relevant to their lives. . . . [It is] to draw all the fragments of services and resources which we find in the community into a system and safety net around the service user, and even to recreate asylum, in the best sense, in the community; that is, a haven of safety and a harbor from which to set out again" (Rosen, Diamond, Miller, & Stein, 1993, pp. 134, 148). This safety net includes the need for supportive family and social relationships; meeting basic survival needs such as food, clothing, and safe housing; and securing employment and other socially valued roles, as well as access to appropriate and needed psychiatric and physical health care.

Fifty years of largely office-based practice, however, have contributed to a gradual distancing between practitioners and the problems that persons with serious mental illnesses confront in their day-to-day lives (Rosen, 1994). This distancing from the person's own lived experiences—in combination with stigma and mentalism—has led at times to a loss of the personhood of people with serious mental illness. Having difficulty viewing the client's predicament as one which we could be facing in our own lives ("there but for the grace of God . . .") results in our grasping "a clear picture of neither the problems nor the solutions" (Deitchman, 1980, p. 788). Vocational rehabilitation provides one example of this process. Through the distancing entailed in our making referrals to vocational rehabilitation programs, we have demonstrated an unfortunate tendency to divorce the meaning of work for people with serious mental illness from the meanings that work has for the rest of us. In an earlier publication (Strauss & Davidson, 1997), we noted that this tendency has had a dehumanizing impact not only on our clients but also on us:

> Work has been viewed primarily as adjunctive or as a support to treatment, with the expectation that recovery or cure will have to take place before work can return to playing a central role in the person's life. This view neglects the fact that the disabled person continues to live his/her life despite . . . the disorder, and that major dimensions of life such as work and social relationships may retain the meaning they had for the person prior to the onset of his/her illness . . . As soon as we turn our back on the body of first-person knowledge, the guide derived from our own lives, we start talking about "schizophrenics" or "manic-depressives" or "borderlines". . . . Work loses its fundamental meaning and importance in human existence and comes to be seen as an adjunct or support to a person's "real" treatment. [In contrast,] work should be viewed as the bridge across which a person can travel in leaving serious mental disorder and becoming an increasingly competent, intact, human being. (pp. 107–108)

In order to avoid this distancing and dehumanizing tendency, we recommend that practitioners draw upon their own experiences when considering the critical nature of the worker role—or of any other socially valued role, for that matter—for all people, continuing to view clients within the context of their daily lives (Strauss & Davidson, 1997). In other work, we have called this function "social imagination."

> Social imagination starts with an ability to cross cultural barriers by drawing upon our own experiences and imaginatively inserting ourselves into the situation of others. Having taken this leap, social imagination then involves working with others to achieve certain negotiated goals. By this definition and in this context, fantasy and the projection of our own desires and fears onto others are debased forms of imagination that keep others at bay and protect us from having to acknowledge our frightening kinship with and difference from them. (Rowe, 1999, p. 116)

A concrete example of social imagination at work may be more helpful. The following is the story of an outreach worker's one-night brush with homelessness:

> I worked at Bloomingdale's and I had a financial mishap which left me homeless in New York for one night. . . . I didn't have enough money to get my car out of the garage. I didn't want to bother my family. I said, "I don't have to work the next day, I'm getting paid, I'll hang in New York for the night." I went to the New York Public Library. It closed about 9 p.m. I only had a few bucks, so went to Popeye's Fried Chicken. New York prices, it didn't go far . . . I went to Port Authority bus station. . . . The rule of thumb was you could not sleep. Once you dozed you were out. . . . About two that morning they made everybody leave, all the homeless people. Homeless people seem to migrate to some coffee shop. You're part of this migration. It was dark, the feeling. . . . The coffee shop threw everybody out about three. . . . I was homeless for one night and it felt like forever, it felt like forever. (quoted in Rowe, 1999, pp. 56–57).

Social imagination requires a strong dose of humility. Without it, this worker might have persuaded himself, for example, that one night of homelessness was all he needed to get the experience down pat. Used with humility, though, it can be another tool in the recovery-oriented practitioner's tool kit.

Considering the impact of the illness and various life circumstances on the person extends to medications as well. That is, the prescription and monitoring of medications necessarily extends beyond the person's symptoms to the impact of those symptoms and the medications on the person's overall life. Recovery-oriented practitioners attend to how medications will affect such important dimensions of the person's life as a job or an intimate relationship, for example, and talk with the client about how medications can be a tool in his or her recovery. One client who is taking a risk by starting a new job may need to increase his medication to offset his increased anxiety, while another client starting a new job may need to decrease her medication to overcome its sedating effect so she can get out of bed on time. Similarly, a client taking risks in developing a new relationship may be concerned about a medication's effect on his or her sexual functioning.

As it cannot be anyone other than the psychiatrist or nurse practitioner whose job it is to explore and understand these issues in order to prescribe medications effectively (Noordsy et al., 2000), it also cannot be anyone other than the recovery guide's job to explore and understand the many other facets of the client's life in the community. Within a recovery orientation, there is no other job.

The Emerging Model of Recovery Guide

Since the introduction of Stein and Test's Program for Assertive Community Treatment (ACT) in the 1970s, intensive, team-based models of community-based practice have been the service of choice for people seriously disabled by mental illness, particularly for those who have been "difficult to engage" in or have not derived benefit from conventional care (Bond, 1991). A major advance of the ACT approach that makes it a good point of departure for the development of recovery-oriented care is the provision of skills training and other direct mental health services "in vivo"—that is, in the natural community settings where they are needed as opposed to in a clinician or case manager's office. We suggest that this shift from office-to community-based practice, initiated with ACT, is a work in progress, with several additional steps needed to fulfill the promise of the new paradigm we argue for here.

Adherents and practitioners of the ACT approach began to articulate some of these implications by contrasting the traditional role of case managers, whom they likened to "travel agents," to their new role as outreach-based practitioners, which they conceptualized as that of "traveling companions":

> The client in the community needs a traveling companion, not a travel agent. The travel agent's only function is to make the client's reservation. The client has to get ready, get to the airport, and traverse foreign terrain by himself. The traveling companion, on the other hand, celebrates the fact that his friend was able to get seats on the plane, talks about his fear of flying, and then goes on the trip with him, sharing the joys and sorrows that occur during the venture. (Deitchman, 1980, p. 789)

ACT staff cannot be content with being "brokers" of services, sitting behind their desks and making appointments for their clients, since their clients may frequently fail to show up for such appointments. Similarly, practitioners cannot be content with making suggestions regarding steps their clients may need to take in their lives, such as seeking employment, since clients may then either disregard or be unable to follow those suggestions on their own. Rather than waiting for clients to show up at their office, practitioners must meet them where they are in the community and encourage their participation in job hunting and other activities, even accompanying them to these activities if necessary.

The traveling-companion metaphor is a good first step toward a new model for community-based practice, but there are some problems with it. The traveling-companion image suggests that the staff and client share a relationship similar to that of two friends traveling together. This image fails to capture the fact that practitioners are responsible for assessing and addressing the client's needs and are paid for their services, and it implies a false reciprocity between the two parties. It also suggests a lack of attention to differences in power between practitioners and clients. Practitioners have access to resources and social status and serve, to some degree, as agents of the state, with the power and obligation to intervene on behalf of the person and the community. Clients, on the other hand, often have few resources, low status, and limited power to refuse or resist the services being "offered" to them.

As argued by Rosen (1994) and Rosen, Diamond, Miller, and Stein (1993)—experienced ACT proponents all—ACT staff should no more be confused with friends or peers than should traditional office-based case managers. For this reason, they suggest the image of a tour guide as opposed to that of a traveling companion. The tour-guide metaphor preserves the staff member's status as a care provider and the asymmetrical nature of the relationship, and it shares much with the "community guide" proposed by McKnight in his work with adults with developmental disabilities. Community guides "assume a special responsibility for guiding excluded people out of service and into the realm of the community" (McKnight, 1992, p. 59).

In addition to providing a service they are paid for, community guides learn "that in order for the fullness of community hospitality to be expressed and the excluded person to be wholly incorporated as a citizen they must leave the scene" (McKnight, 1992, p. 59). In other words, rather than becoming an enduring figure in the person's life, community guides play a transitional role in facilitating the person's engagement into social relationships with peers in the community. They are neither peers nor friends but facilitators and, in a sense, willing tools for people to use in reconnecting to the things that matter to them.

The notion of a tour or community guide represents a step beyond that of a traveling companion, yet even this revision falls short of capturing the full flavor of recovery-oriented practice, as most people with serious mental illness do not readily or willingly seek out the assistance of a guide. The journey of mental illness is not a trip that anyone wants to take, is prepared for, or has much information about in advance. Thus it is a journey people are unlikely to contact mental health practitioners for help with, at least in the early phases of the illness. Instead, the early phases of mental illness are characterized by confusion, cognitive interference, withdrawal, and shock. Due to the stigma that continues to cling to mental illness, the lack of education or information provided to the lay public regarding mental illness, and the denial and disbelief that often accompany the onset of the illness, people often struggle with serious mental illness for many years before coming to understand that what they are struggling with *is* a mental illness. Another prolonged period may follow before they can muster the courage and trust to accept

their need for treatment and support. As a result, we should not expect clients to seek guidance from a mental health expert or, for
that matter, from a community guide, just as we should not expect
clients to be appreciative of practitioners' efforts to offer to help
them when they do not yet recognize that they need it.

If a person with a serious mental illness willingly seeks out a
guide for help in navigating the complex health and social systems
required to gain access to services or to reclaim a life in the broader
community, the guide's job is made considerably easier. Early in the
course of illness, however, this is more the exception than the rule.
The rule suggests instead that the first job of the practitioner is to
engage a reluctant, disbelieving, suffering person in care. We charac-
terize the term "recovery guide" as an expansion upon the tour or
community guide through explicit recognition and incorporation
of the need for engagement as the first step in developing a trusting
relationship that then can be put to use in guiding the person along
the path of recovery.

Building on this foundation, we then elaborate the concept of
guide by appealing to the metaphor of hiking. We have chosen the
hiking metaphor because it represents a sphere entirely separate
from mental illnesses and the services associated with them, and because it offers practitioners the opportunity to underscore how the
recovery journey must lead beyond illnesses, symptoms, deficits, and
service systems toward "ordinary" life lived among friends and family in local neighborhoods. By using this metaphor, we can evoke life
beyond the disability service system and in the direction of the wider
world and community.

Just as in recovery-oriented practice, hiking guides begin by helping the people they are guiding to recognize and take account of
their strengths, skills, and positive experiences. We speak of this aspect of recovery as "examining your backpack." What do you bring
to the journey of recovery that will help you in your exploration?
What interests, goals, and aspirations motivate you and can help to
sustain you during the setbacks, mishaps, and difficulties that you
will confront on the trail? One poignant reminder of the central
importance of these goals was evident in our early efforts to help
people gain needed skills in accessing and navigating an urban bus
system. People showed little interest in the subject until we realized
they needed to be asked where they would like to go before learning how to get there on a bus. They had no desire to learn how to

ride a bus for its own sake, only as a means of getting to and from places and activities they were interested in.

Once people have begun to explore their strengths, skills, interests, and goals, however, it also becomes important to recognize personal limitations that can affect the pace of the hike or the path and type of terrain that is chosen. As captured in Deegan's "paradox of recovery," such recognition of personal limits and challenges may liberate and empower people to progress further on their recovery journey. While this journey can seem abstract, everyone understands the importance of taking into account one's level of fitness or a health challenge such as high blood pressure when planning a hike. Thus, the hiking metaphor helps individuals reframe the challenges that confront them in their journey, from all-encompassing experiences of deficiency and dependence to specific and circumscribed personal limits they must take into account when planning their hike, including the duration and pace of travel and the kinds of help they need. This reframing facilitates constructive conversations with people about using tools and supports, including prescribed medications and therapy, to help them with their recovery journey rather than to be subsumed or coerced by them.

As in recovery, those who aspire to be good hiking guides must earn the trust of those they help, not only through their ability to listen accurately and empathically but also by offering a variety of choices, opportunities, and decisions to the hikers themselves. Hikers need to recognize and make choices at the outset of the guiding relationship, and the importance of making these choices increases exponentially when challenges and difficulties arise. At the same time, good hiking guides can help hikers recognize their skill level, experiences, and limitations so that they can build a legacy of successes.

Early on in the process, hikers may choose to travel in groups with an experienced guide, after which they gradually move on to more challenging terrain. They may also travel in smaller groups or pairs before they decide to go solo. Good hiking guides have a knack for suggesting experiences that are challenging and that call on the novice hikers' inner strengths and skills, as well as their desire and motivation, but that are not beyond their reach. At the same time, they are not afraid to allow hikers to experience frustrations and failure, as long as they are gradually gaining forward momentum. As in hiking, the best recovery guides help people match their self-chosen goals with their own interests, strengths, and capacities; with opportunities and resources in the community around them; and with natural supports that can help them sustain their progress.

As in recovery, successful hiking guides encourage mutual feedback and experiences of reciprocity among hikers, so that each learns to know all the others as individuals with unique preferences who, for example, like to leave at the break of day or only after two cups of coffee. While the role of guide remains distinct, a natural sense of reciprocity allows hiker and guide to appreciate each other's humanity, along with its challenges and its causes for celebration.

In summary, hiking can be used as an effective heuristic in training recovery guides and as a metaphor that can help people in recovery see the recovery journey as anchored in practical, everyday realities of living rather than as subsumed by deficit-oriented service systems and interventions. Even the idea of urban hiking (as opposed to rural) is potentially helpful, since destinations in the local community often hold their own challenges, risks, and potential rewards for people with serious mental illness who have been forced out to the margins of their communities. In all of this work, it is just as crucial in recovery-oriented practice as it is in hiking that the guide have accumulated his or her own experience and wisdom to be offered to the person in recovery in credible and useful ways. It is extremely difficult, if not impossible, to guide another person's hike from the clinic or office. The value of personal, as well as professional, experience in these domains—the idea and experience of having "been there" oneself—is one of the considerations that contributes to making people who are themselves in recovery especially well-suited for this role.

With this background and metaphor in mind, we continue our exposition of the roles and responsibilities of the recovery guide with a set of lessons to be learned in working with people with serious mental illness.

Lesson 1

Meet the client where he or she is, not only geographically or materially but also personally, socially, and emotionally.

Most people will not know that they have a serious mental illness at first, and therefore they will not seek help on their own. The initial focus of care thus should be on the person's understanding of his or her predicament and on the ways in which the practitioner can be helpful in addressing this predicament. Recovery guides need to take prospective clients' perception of their difficulties as the starting point for developing a trusting relationship that then can serve as the cornerstone for other helping efforts.

We learned this lesson first in conducting outreach to homeless persons, when outreach staff, as noted earlier in this chapter, began to realize that people were more responsive to offers of coffee and a sandwich, concrete assistance with securing housing, or meeting other basic needs than to offers of psychiatric treatment or medication. Extrapolating from this rather extreme situation to more common ones, practitioners need to attend to what prospective clients are concerned about most, regardless of its relationship to the illness per se.

Practitioners can't assume that people with mental illness experiences their illness in the same way or have had experiences of seeking or receiving help. People have different ways of accounting for the unusual experiences, disruptions, interruptions, and difficulties their illness brings on, ranging from believing that others are conspiring against them to their relationship to God, to punishments for earlier sins, to the effects of previous accidents or substance abuse. Rather than viewing these beliefs as further evidence of the client's illness, we suggest that it is more useful to view them as representing people's best efforts to make sense of their own experiences (Davidson, 2003).

If Joanna, a client, says that she lives in Florida with her children when Nancy, the worker, knows she lives in a local supported housing program and that the state took her children away from her 20 years ago, Nancy has at least two choices. She can regard the client as delusional, or she can reflect that, while delusional thought may be present, the client is expressing, concretely, the truth behind the cliché, "Home is where the heart is." If she proceeds on this latter possibility, she may find new ways to engage with Joanna and may come to understand, after the fact, that Joanna was actually trying to engage with her as well (by sharing what is most important to her, even if it has long since been lost).

In addition, clients' attitudes toward us and the kind of help we offer will be shaped by their previous experiences with psychiatric treatment and the mental health system as a whole, particularly if they have had experiences of involuntary commitment or forced medication. Despite our most benevolent intentions, a legitimately earned skepticism regarding practitioners' motives may contribute to making the engagement process complicated and protracted.

In prior research involving interviews with clients of an assertive community treatment team (Chinman et al., 1999), we learned that clients may resist the engagement efforts and guidance of ACT staff if they see staff as strangers who have not taken the time to get to know them but have the chutzpah (the nerve) to ask them to do things anyway. This research suggested that while problem-specific psycho-education and other clinical interventions are valuable, there is equal, if not more, value in getting to know the individual first, independently of his or her illness. The person may be an accomplished pianist, a lover of pepperoni pizza, or a nervous mom worried about losing custody of her children. Engaging the person around one of his or her interests or concerns may prove to be the key to establishing oneself in the client's eyes as an individual who is genuinely interested in and concerned about his or her well-being.

In addition to meeting clients where they are and showing genuine interest in them as persons, efforts with prospective clients who have come to mistrust the mental health system and its practitioners must be repetitive and persistent over time. Persistence, however, should not supersede the overarching goal of establishing a trusting relationship with clients at a pace that is comfortable for them. The recovery guide must be careful to respect clients' right to decline their overtures, advice, and other interventions. In the study mentioned above, one ACT staff member coined the notion of a "velvet bulldozer" approach (Chinman et al., 1999) to capture the gentle but persistent way in which he had had to pursue one of his particularly reluctant clients. From the client's perspective, the velvet bulldozer approach involves the sense that the staff person is "sticking by me" or "not giving up on me" (Davidson, 2003).

> When a research interviewer asked the person just quoted what she thought had been most helpful about the ACT team she'd been assigned to after years of rejecting treatment, she explained, "They kept showing up . . . they didn't drop me or let me get off the medications . . . they didn't give up, they just stuck with me." It was only after several months of repeated efforts to engage this client that she began to have some trust in the staff's concern and intentions toward her. Further, it was not until she began to feel understood

by the staff, after several more months, that she began to listen to what they were saying and consider their recommendations, loosening her hold on the isolation and her substance use. Eventually she revealed that she had been a practicing architect before the onset of her affective disorder. She showed the staff some of her sketches as she began to take on a more active role in her own recovery.

It is important to note that the kind of patience and persistence this work requires means that it is not for everyone. Estroff suggests that it "appeals to people who do not know the meaning of the word 'no.' They don't like the status quo; they will try anything to help their clients and they are not loyal to institutions or to centers, only to the people they are working with" (Rosen, 1994, p. 61). In this regard, program leaders must select staff for this work carefully and pay attention to matching roles and responsibilities, as well as clients, with particular staff members' personal strengths, interests, and limitations.

Lesson 2

Recognize that the client had already embarked on his or her own journey before meeting you.

Once the recovery guide has developed, with the client, an initial sense of trust and engagement, he or she can move to the components of the work that are more consistent with the guide metaphor. It is important to remember, however, that the client was already on his or her journey before the onset of the illness, and before coming into contact with the guide. As much as having a serious mental illness may have interrupted or interfered with the client's aspirations and plans, the journey that follows still has to be connected in meaningful ways to what came before. Clients' lives did not begin with the onset of their illness, any more than their lives can or should be subsumed by psychiatric treatment and rehabilitation.

Social imagination, which we discussed earlier, may provide some help to the tour guide who meets for the first time a disheveled older man rambling incoherently. How many of us have had a family member or a friend whom we knew first as that family member or friend and much later on as a person who had a "psychotic break"? Do we not remember and know that person first as the family member and friend we grew up with, and grieve that others see only the disorganized, disheveled person he or she has become?

Following a talk we gave not long ago on the various roles and resources of the tour guide, one experienced clinician objected by saying, "That all sounds fine and good, but what if the client won't get on the damn bus?!" It is not the recovery guide's job to get the client to agree to "get on the bus." Not only might clients prefer to take a taxi, ride a bicycle, or walk, but more importantly clients are already on journeys of their own when we meet them. It is we who need to join their journey, get on *their* bus, so to speak, rather than try to persuade them to get on ours.

Once we recognize that the client was already on a journey prior to the onset of his or her illness and prior to meeting us, the focus shifts to the ways in which mental illness has challenged or changed the person's aspirations, hopes, and dreams. If the person appears to be sticking resolutely to the hopes and dreams he or she had prior to onset of the disorder, and despite or in denial of the illness and its disabling effects, then what steps can help him or her get back on track? Rather than the reduction of symptoms or the remediation of deficits, goals we assume the client will share with us, it is the client's own goals for his or her life, beyond or despite mental illness, that need to drive the treatment planning and rehabilitation efforts.

Once these goals have been identified and articulated, recovery guides have a number of tools at their disposal to help the client make progress toward achieving them. The recovery guide's training and knowledge provide some of these tools, helping the client work toward recovery by providing education about serious mental illnesses, the recovery process, coping strategies, and the person's options, and by translating mental health procedures, services, and language into understandable and usable information. This expertise, however, does not substitute for knowing the needs, interests, and strengths of the client.

The guide cannot impart his or her expertise to the client in a simple or straightforward manner, as if giving a person cognitive strategies or telling a person what to do inevitably leads to significant personal change. Instead, the client's experiences, preferences, and concerns must determine the content and course of the journey. The client, in consultation with the guide, can choose where to go, when, and in what manner, and whether to stroll leisurely through scenic routes or charge ahead on a more direct but rocky path. This is partly because the client will have a better sense of his or her own stamina and energy level, ability to tolerate frustration and setbacks, and degree of comfort with a given pace of change. It also is due to the fact that it is the client's life that ultimately has to change to support recovery, and thus it is the client who must do much of the hard work of recovery.

Lesson 3

Rather than dwelling on the client's distant past or worrying about the client's long-term future, recovery guides focus on the next several steps of the journey and on the sites that lie ahead.

Psychodynamic approaches to psychotherapy and clinical case management have long been criticized for focusing on clients' pasts rather than on their present circumstances and needs. In the course of the ACT study described earlier, one participant reported that she stopped seeing an office-based psychotherapist for her affective disorder and alcohol dependence when this therapist only wanted to focus on her childhood memories and their presumptive effects on her, despite the fact that she, the client, had pressing concerns in her day-to-day life: "She kept telling me that I hadn't gotten over my father's death. Like whoever does?" When this clinician sent her a letter informing her that she was going to be discharged from treatment for missing too many appointments, the woman reported wanting to frame the letter as her "graduation diploma," feeling that this was the only way she would be able to leave the mental health system behind.

In the opposite direction, clinical psychiatry has made profound and far-reaching mistakes in telling clients and their families that illnesses such as schizophrenia or bipolar disorder were death sentences from which they would never recover (e.g., North, 1987). Although they perhaps no longer suggest that families grieve for the loss of their adult child recently diagnosed with a serious mental illness, it is still routine for practitioners to inform clients that they will have to take their psychiatric medications "for the rest of your life, just like you would have to take insulin for diabetes." Not only do we lack credible evidence on which to base such statements— many people stop taking their medications later in the course of their recovery without undue ill effects—but long-term pronouncements of any sort are typically not very helpful to anyone, including people receiving mental health services.

Finally, as we now know that there is vast heterogeneity in outcome for serious mental illnesses and that diagnosis can no longer predict prognosis (e.g., Carpenter & Kirkpatrick, 1988; Davidson & McGlashan, 1997; Harding, Zubin, & Strauss, 1987; McGlashan, 1988), practitioners should refrain from making long-term predictions regarding their client's future when we have yet to discover an accurate crystal ball.

In this respect, among others, the recovery guide model can be particularly helpful in directing the practitioner's attention toward the "sights" and "sites" their clients are likely to be most interested in. Tour guides neither dwell on their clients' histories prior to their current excursion nor worry about what their clients will be doing when they return home following the trip. In addition, while they may provide some overall information about the entire trip at its inception, such as listing the historical sites they will be visiting, good guides focus primarily on the next one or two sites coming up, both to hold their clients' interest and to avoid inundating them with too much information. If the bus is on the way to the Eiffel Tower, the guide does not drone on about the Notre Dame cathedral or bestow praises on the Arch of Triumph, or prepare riders for the next leg of their trip by recounting the history of the Roman Colosseum while they are still in Paris.

The recovery guide helps to prepare clients for the *next one or two steps* of the recovery process by anticipating what lies ahead in the near future, focusing on the characteristics and challenges of the present situation, and identifying and helping clients avoid or move around potential roadblocks. Although the recovery guide deemphasizes early personal history (because it may not be relevant) and long-term outcomes (because they cannot be predicted), he or she may invoke either of these perspectives should they prove useful in the present. Clients who become stuck in patterns of failing at certain tasks may need help liberating themselves from the legacy of their past. Demoralized and hopeless clients who view mental illness as a death sentence may need information about the heterogeneity of long-term outcomes and their chances for improvement. In general, however, recovery guides have their hands full focusing on supporting the client's efforts in the present. This forward-looking orientation requires that the recovery guide provide a context for the new experiences and learning of the client, but with a clear awareness that the journey is guided by the preferences, goals, and interests of the client rather than by an ideal of normalcy to which the client should aspire (Davidson & Strauss, 1995).

Lesson 4

Your credibility and effectiveness as a recovery guide are enhanced to the degree that you are familiar with and able to anticipate interesting sites, common destinations, and important landmarks along the way.

Given the importance of focusing on the next one or two steps in the client's journey, it is helpful for recovery guides to be familiar with the recovery territory in general and to be able to anticipate interesting sites, common destinations, and important landmarks that most clients are likely to encounter along their way. This is not to contradict the highly personal nature of each individual's journey. Despite the unique characteristics of each individual's struggle, there remain issues and concerns that people who face challenges of coping with and compensating for their illness have in common. Examples of such shared concerns include health services such as medication options and medical treatment for other illnesses, social services such as applying for entitlements or getting support for parenting issues, learning skills for independent living such as finding safe and affordable housing and managing the responsibilities of being a tenant, and dealing with developmental issues of separation and individuation delayed or prolonged by the onset of the illness. Self-help and peer support groups might be included as a way for clients to share common experiences and gain the support of others who are working on the same issues.

Other landmarks may include finding opportunities to socialize outside of mental health centers or clubhouses. Involvement in meaningful activities such as work or education, or doing something creative and beyond the scope of traditional treatment, can help clients move beyond the relationship with the recovery guide and into the broader community, the destination of choice for most people. These common destinations are outlined in Figure 5.1, along with the range of resources and tools that recovery guides have at their disposal in helping clients explore these and other sites of interest.

We do not mean to discount the resources and tools of professional training and experience that recovery guides have. There are many other resources and tools that guides have at their disposal,

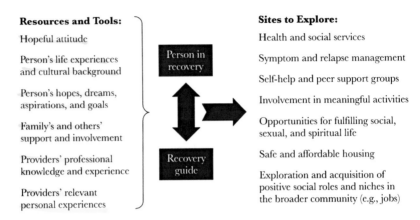

Resources and Tools:

Hopeful attitude

Person's life experiences and cultural background

Person's hopes, dreams, aspirations, and goals

Family's and others' support and involvement

Providers' professional knowledge and experience

Providers' relevant personal experiences

Person in recovery

Recovery guide

Sites to Explore:

Health and social services

Symptom and relapse management

Self-help and peer support groups

Involvement in meaningful activities

Opportunities for fulfilling social, sexual, and spiritual life

Safe and affordable housing

Exploration and acquisition of positive social roles and niches in the broader community (e.g., jobs)

Figure 5.1 Common components of the Recovery Guide Model.

however, that have not been emphasized as much in previous approaches. These include a hopefulness toward clients and their potential for improving their lives; the client's own aspirations, assets, interests, and goals that drive the recovery and care planning process; the observations, input, and resources of family members and other important people in the client's life and community; and the recovery guide's own life experiences, particularly when he or she is a member of the same community as his or her clients.

This last point is worth noting, as it is one of the resources that are related directly to the notion of the guide. In psychoanalytic training, for example, much is made of the trainee's need to be in psychoanalysis in order to become familiar with his or her own blind spots and to become immersed in the analytical process. McKnight (1992) makes a parallel point about the need for community guides to have an active investment in and extensive familiarity with their local community in order to make use of these resources in their work with clients. "Most effective guides," writes McKnight, "are well connected in the interrelationships of community life. They have invested much of life's energy and vitality in associational activity. Based upon these connections, they are able to make a variety of contacts quickly because 'they know people who know other people'" (pp. 59–60).

In addition to the client's assets, interests, and goals, the resources and input of his or her natural supports, and the guide's own professional knowledge and personal experience, it is useful for the guide to be familiar with and able to anticipate concerns and questions that commonly arise for people in different phases of recovery. Early in the course of illness and treatment, for example, people often ask themselves the following questions:

- What is happening to me?
- How can I get rid of whatever this is that is happening to me? How can I make it stop?
- What can I tell my parents and other people who care about me?
- How can I catch up to my peers?
- How can I have a normal life?
- How can I keep this from happening again?

Guides can anticipate such questions as part of the preparation for the upcoming trek. Acting on the knowledge that these issues may be on a client's mind will enhance the client's trust in the guide. Similarly, it is common later in the course of the recovery process for the following questions to emerge as people try to make sense of their past and create a new future:

- What happened to me?
- Why did it happen? Why did it happen to *me?*
- What is possible for me now?
- How can I get there from here?

These are difficult, sometimes impossible, questions to answer. They are the kinds of questions, however, that lie at the heart of the journey of recovery. To be able to share these concerns with their guides, clients need to have a sense that they are on the guide's radar and must be able to trust that guides have their best interests at heart. The guide can earn this trust by not giving false information about the language or customs of the country they are visiting together, by respecting the client and his or her central role in the recovery process, and by inviting, rather than discouraging, exploration of these kinds of "existential" questions. This trust also includes faith in recovery guides' professionalism and competence, which clients develop over time as they become confident that these guides will act in an ethical and knowledgeable way, have the power and knowledge to open doors and make things work, and are aware of and open to a range of options from which the client can make meaningful choices. Without these forms of trust, clients are un-likely to invite guides to join them on the next leg of their journey.

Once the journey is underway, recovery guides must be able to assess and follow the interests and preferences of the client. Just as it would be inappropriate for a tour guide to take you to France if you want to go to India, so too would it be counterproductive and inappropriate for the recovery guide to try to get a client a job at Wendy's when he or she expresses an interest in working at Macy's. Once client preference has been made clear, the recovery guide must be willing to engage and join with the client in pursuit of his or her goals. This may mean investigating employment opportuni-ties, helping the client to enroll in classes or become involved in community activities, helping to navigate the Medicaid system, or working with family members to create an understanding and sup-portive recovery environment. Through these and other joint explo-rations, the process is oriented toward helping the client create a life outside of or beyond his or her disability. Through this process, the client may or may not then conclude on his or her own that a job at Wendy's may be useful for the sake of work experience, inter-acting with other employees and the public, and having some extra income while preparing or waiting for an opening at Macy's.

Throughout this entire process, the issues of client choice and self-determination remain key. Offering clients meaningful choices and respecting and honoring those choices, however, can pose di-lemmas for recovery guides. What if the person refuses to choose to go along with his or her physician's recommended treatment regi-men? What if he or she continues to refuse all services, or insists on choosing to disregard the guide's efforts, showing what the guide considers "poor judgment"? The first step that the guide will need to consider in such circumstances is to reconsider what is being of-fered or recommended from the client's perspective. What is en-tailed for the client in following the recommended regimen? Does it move the client in the direction of his or her own goals and inter-ests? Is it consistent with the client's own beliefs, goals, hopes, and strengths? In short, is it a tour or leg of the client's journey that he or she deems worth taking?

If the guide remains convinced of the value of the options not taken, then he or she may need to consider the possibility that the client has already embarked on a different leg of the journey that may not be obvious to others. Again, the guide needs to consider whether what he or she is offering will impede or facilitate the journey that the client has already begun. In the end, it is ultimately the client's life and the client's journey, so it must be the client's decision which paths to follow and which to ignore, pass by, or file for possible use at a later time. In circumstances that do not pose serious and imminent risks to self—active suicidal ideation with intent, for example—or to others, as with assaultive behavior, clients should have the opportunity and freedom to make and learn from their own mistakes.

This is, of course, easier said than done, as exemplified in the following story:

> Yolanda, a 30-year-old woman living in a supportive housing program, came to a consultant's attention because she had a troublesome habit of leaving the building in the middle of the night and wandering around the downtown area of her small city. The staff had tried in vain to convince Yolanda to stop her late-night walks, at first trying to persuade her that it was too dangerous for her to be out alone at night in the city. When persuasion did not work, the staff established program parameters and rules which stipulated that Yolanda would not be allowed out of the building after 10:00 P.M., as she could not be trusted to cease this activity on her own and did not appear to appreciate the danger to which she was exposing herself. These efforts were in vain also, however, as Yolanda continued to "slip out" at night and disregard the new program rules no matter what consequences were put into place. The program was voluntary and the building was unlocked, and the staff had no way of preventing her from leaving short of physically blocking her way. They brought this situation to the attention of the program consultant, who had been stressing the need for client choice and self-determination in helping the program adopt a more recovery-oriented approach.
>
> Initially the consultant asked the staff if they knew why Yolanda left the building in the middle of the night; did they know what she was after? She wondered with the staff what Yolanda was trying to accomplish during her late-night walks and whether this same agenda could be pursued in other, less dangerous ways. Yolanda, for her part, however, was not interested in such discussions. At this point in time, she was not willing (or able?) to disclose to the staff where she went or why, and she was not willing (or able?) to consider other alternatives because she saw no reason to curtail her walks. The staff were torn between their wish to respect Yolanda's right to make her own decisions and choices and their strong desire and need to keep her safe. Arguments and disagreements

broke out between staff who took up either side of this debate, with some blaming others for being paternalistic and others responding by faulting their colleagues for being careless, irresponsible, and even unethical. What were they to do?

After many lengthy and heated discussions about the issue, and after many conversations with Yolanda exploring her reasons for leaving the building and assessing her understanding of the degree to which she was exposing herself to risk, the staff finally agreed to a middle road. They reasoned that they could respect Yolanda's choices without necessarily abandoning her to the ravages of illness or the dangers of the street. After having determined that Yolanda appreciated the risk she was taking each night that she left the building after dark, the staff brainstormed with her what steps could be taken to minimize the risks she took in doing so. What did other women do who needed to be out by themselves after dark? First, the staff took Yolanda to a store so that she could buy a rape whistle and a can of pepper spray. Once she realized that the staff were taking her wish to continue to take late-night walks seriously, Yolanda shared with them that she was in fact frightened at times and that she would like to know how to take better care of herself in such situations. As a next step, Yolanda asked the staff if they would transport her to a self-defense course for women at the local YWCA, for which she promptly registered.

While her late-night walks did not stop, the staff felt better about having done everything that they could think of and that was within their power to ensure Yolanda's safety while honoring her autonomy. As a result of these efforts, Yolanda's levels of trust in the staff and engagement in the program increased, she acquired new skills in self-defense, and she met potential new friends outside of the mental health system. For their part, the staff channeled their continued fears for Yolanda's safety and their anxieties about the liability they bore by making sure that they documented their conversations with Yolanda, her decisions, and the steps they had taken in all the appropriate places and, with Yolanda's permission, by discussing her situation with the local police and asking them to keep an eye out for her on their late-night rounds. While she still will not tell the staff where she goes at night or why, she does report that she has become somewhat friendly with the cops who are on the night shift.

Lesson 5

Guides prepare for the journey by acquiring tools that will be effective in helping the client address or bypass symptoms and other sequelae of the illness that act as barriers to his or her recovery.

A final area of focus for the recovery guide involves assessing the potential obstacles that might lie in the client's path and working with him or her to address, overcome, or bypass these barriers as they arise. Many conventional clinical and psychotherapeutic skills can be incorporated into this component of the recovery guide's backpack, as long as the guide has the requisite training and supervisory resources available to deliver these interventions competently. We have found that moving what traditionally have been office-based practices into community settings requires, if anything, more clinical skill, sophistication, and supervision than office-based practice, not less. The challenges of adopting more flexible boundaries and enabling the development of a less unidirectional relationship while continuing to act in the client's best interest raise many thorny ethical and practical issues, which have yet to be fully and adequately addressed. Without these skills and the ability to use them effectively in reducing, overcoming, or bypassing barriers to the client's recovery, the recovery guide will have a significantly diminished backpack and thus a significantly depleted capacity for helping clients on their journeys.

Far from simply transferring these skills from the office to the recovery guide's backpack, preparing clinical skills for use "on the street" requires a shift in perspective. This shift entails focusing less on symptom reduction and more on assessing, anticipating, and addressing barriers that get in the way of what the client wants to do. This requires having a sense both of what the client is trying to accomplish and of how specific symptoms, cognitive deficits, stigma, or other barriers get in the way of pursuing these goals.

While it is true that conventional clinical practice has emphasized the promotion of health and competence as well as symptom and deficit reduction, it also is true that most models of serious mental illness assume that a person's symptoms and other areas of dysfunction need to be reduced or contained *before* he or she can resume normative activities such as attending school, obtaining and maintaining competitive employment, and living independently. We now know, however, that many people can live independently, attend school, work, and have gratifying personal relationships *even while* continuing to experience symptoms and other sequelae of their illness (Davidson, Stayner, et al., 2001). Our previous research also has suggested that to the degree that these issues are addressed, clients will be better prepared and more motivated to take an active role in their own treatment, rehabilitation, and recovery (e.g., Davidson et al., 1997). On both humanitarian and clinical grounds, then, recovery guides must understand that people need not wait until their illness has been effectively treated to pursue their personal goals and aspirations or to derive meaning from and take pleasure in life.

As we noted above, for example, within a recovery perspective, medications are taken not simply to treat an illness, as antibiotics are taken to treat an infection, but to help the person work, concentrate in the classroom, or keep an apartment (Davidson & Strauss, 1995). Similarly, cognitive-behavioral interventions for delusions (e.g., Kingdon & Turkington, 1994; Fowler, Garety, & Kuipers, 1998) are offered not only to decrease the suffering from paranoid and persecutory ideas but also to help clients develop and maintain satisfying relationships with their peers, including peers who do not have a mental illness, rather than be shunned because of their alienating behaviors.

As another example, an increase in symptoms can often be taken as an indication of a significant event or challenge occurring in the person's life, and may need to be attended to as a factor influencing the pace of the journey or the person's need to stop at certain landmarks for rest and replenishment. It is equally important to appreciate, however, that symptoms alone can no longer be the cause for cancellation of the journey altogether or lead to indefinite delays in resuming the trek. On the contrary, people have been incredibly creative in finding their own ways to manage the symptoms and other sequelae of their illnesses. Recovery guides need to be familiar with such coping strategies so that they can offer them to their clients along the way.

In addition to addressing the direct effects of the illness as obstacles in the person's path, recovery includes recovery from the collateral damage left in the wake of mental illness. Often this can mean recovering from the effects of life in the mental health system and having been socialized into the role of "mental patient." It may also entail dealing with the indirect effects of mental illness, including poverty, discrimination, and fear. "Having a life" costs money, and poverty is a major barrier to effective integration into the community. Addressing the issues of fear, stigma, and discrimination requires a constant awareness of their existence and of the ways in which they marginalize people with mental illness. The role of the recovery guide involves figuring out with the client how to open doors to community involvements while remaining attentive to the ways in which stigma, discrimination, poverty, and fear arise and need to be addressed in the process of community inclusion. To the degree that this at times requires broader community education, advocacy becomes an accepted part of the recovery guide's scope of responsibility.

Identifying and helping clients to overcome the many obstacles to recovery originating from both inside and outside of the illness is an integral part of recovery guides' work. In order to do this work effectively, guides must be familiar with the territory and anticipate those obstacles. Just as a hiking guide would need to know how trails are laid out, how they are affected by various weather conditions, and how to do an on-the-spot assessment of whether it is safe to proceed on a given path (ideas suggested by a previous, anonymous reviewer), our guide needs to be familiar with a variety of sources of information that speak to the common challenges and areas of increased vulnerability that people with serious mental illness experience, and he or she needs to be able to determine when he or she may be impacting a client's condition or chances for success. In addition to the professional knowledge base they accrue in their training, they must develop a familiarity with, and seek ways to apply, available literature on adolescent and adult development; family systems; and first-person accounts of illness, discrimination, and recovery. Common issues of loss and grief, separation and individuation, and the need for valued social roles add to this body of knowledge.

Finally, recovery guides, as mentioned above, need to know about community resources that may benefit or interest their clients. These include informal support systems in the community that exist outside of the formal mental health system. The standard of care to which recovery guides aspire includes knowing the territory of recovery; the various paths up and down the mountain, including those specific to each client; and ways to translate this knowledge effectively into practical strategies that restore hope and functioning.

Discussion

In this chapter we have presented the recovery guide as a useful framework through which mental health practitioners can understand their role as facilitators of recovery and community integration.

We have focused primarily on the ways in which the role of the recovery guide differs from traditional practitioner roles, and on how this role affects the nature of the helping relationship with persons with serious mental illness. In closing, it also is important to look beyond the immediate practitioner–client relationship and consider how systemic factors can either support or impede the client's journey.

Training and clinical supervision are areas in which mental health systems can have a significant impact on practitioners' professional development. The recovery guide model incorporates case management within the context of a clinical relationship with relaxed boundaries that must shift to accommodate each person and his or her unique recovery journey. The guide might be called upon to help one client find furniture for a new apartment, offer testimony before the legislature, purchase a dress for Sunday services, or take a bus to visit an elderly parent. Each new situation can present a range of ambiguous and complex boundary dilemmas. In fact, such dilemmas are so inherent to community-based clinical practice that Curtis and Hodge (1993) have suggested that practitioners who do not face such boundary issues in their daily work are probably not doing their jobs.

At the same time, the mental health field lacks clear guidelines for what is professional and appropriate behavior for community-based practitioners (Carey, 1998), and "relaxing the boundaries" goes against the very grain of what most staff are taught in training programs and clinical supervision. The adoption of the recovery guide model thus necessitates new standards, not only for mental health practitioners but also for the institutions and supervisors that prepare them for clinical practice. Training programs must counter the pessimistic messages that are often sent to students regarding the chronic course of mental illness by presenting narratives of, and forums with, people in recovery as well the results of clinical research studies that show that partial to full recovery (in the more traditional sense of becoming free from symptoms) is possible for at least one-fourth, and up to two-thirds, of people with schizophrenia and other serious mental illnesses. Similarly, the notion of "recovery," and the practitioner's role in promoting it, must be expanded beyond clinical stability and maintenance to incorporate the pursuit of a meaningful life and a positive sense of belonging in the community.

Clinical supervisors and managers in mental health systems can reinforce this perspective and support recovery guides by helping them transfer their skills and knowledge from the classroom to the community. Often this involves drawing on their own experiences as community-based practitioners or sharing the stories of people in recovery who speak and write about the types of relationships and services that are helpful and not helpful. For example, mental health practitioners, as noted before, are frequently taught to maintain professional distance from their clients as a means of retaining objectivity in the helping relationship. Yet, while there are certainly negative consequences of overinvolvement for both the staff and clients, people report that "greater damage may be done by rigid enforcement of the traditional connotation of professional distance" than by some boundary violations (Curtis & Hodge, 1994, p. 24). Supervisors must therefore allow recovery guides to reflect upon the "getting to know" aspect of their work (Andres-Hyman, Strauss, & Davidson, 2007). It is this aspect—the trusting relationship between guide and client— that often makes practitioners uncomfortable because they might simply not know how to go about it (Chinman et al., 1999).

Individual and group supervision in which recovery guides share their experiences with one another and have an opportunity to give and receive feedback are venues through which guides can process the range of complex issues that accompany community-based practice. Supervision may include such issues as (1) how to conduct meetings and interactions in a wide range of settings such as coffee shops, soup kitchens, and emergency shelters, in such a way that both the guide and the client feel, and are, reasonably safe; (2) when and how to introduce the client to a social circle, such as a religious parish, that you may already be connected to as a member of the same community; (3) how to decide when it may be appropriate to use your personal resources to assist a client, as in driving a client to her daughter's kindergarten graduation when the agency van is not available; and (4) which type of personal information, such as the guide's own disability status, can be shared, and when, in the name of establishing and maintaining a genuine and empathetic helping relationship. Supervision must address all of these bends in the road of the recovery journey as well as the guide's own personal anxieties about the demands of the trek, especially in light of the fact that traditional training programs often do not adequately prepare practitioners for this type of work.

Finally, while clinical supervision can be a critical piece in assisting the guide in becoming comfortable in his or her role as an individual practitioner, it cannot, in and of itself, address larger, systemic obstacles that may impede recovery. These obstacles—which we tried to address in some detail in the preceding chapter—include eligibility or entry criteria for admission into certain services, such as "work readiness" as a criterion for vocational rehabilitation; funding structures that recognize a limited range of medically necessary interactions as reimbursable services; inadequate community resources, including a lack of affordable housing; high caseload sizes that prevent the development of responsive relationships; and entrenched policies and procedures, such as a rigid agency policy against accepting gifts from clients, that prohibit the cultivation of such relationships even where caseload sizes would allow them.

When such obstacles are encountered on an individual's pathway to recovery, it is the guide's job to work in collaboration with the client to identify the roadblock and to find routes under, around, over, or through it. This may mean encouraging the client to challenge the rules by becoming active in the agency's or the system's various decision-making bodies, or the guide's becoming active in this way himself or herself. Where such efforts fail, the recovery guide and client may even be tempted at times to break the rules to get around the roadblocks described above (Borg & Topor, 2002). In our opinion, however, the recovery guide model we are proposing should stimulate the field as a whole to ask instead, "Isn't it time for new rules altogether?" We hope that future volumes will flesh these solutions out in more depth and detail.

Appendix

As we noted in our Introduction, much of the work we have carried out to date has been in collaboration with the State of Connecticut's Department of Mental Health and Addiction Services. More recently, however, we have been invited to assist other systems in moving forward with their own transformation efforts. Rather than taking a "one size fits all" approach, we have tried to model in our work with these differing systems the same values of the recovery-oriented approach we described earlier (inclusion, collaboration, responsiveness, etc.). In doing so, we have increasingly found the principles of the emerging science of "technology transfer" to be helpful in stimulating the widespread organizational change necessary for effective, recovery-oriented systems of care to evolve. In addition to requiring a highly flexible approach that can be tailored to local conditions, we have taken the science of technology transfer to suggest that the existing gap between what we know and what we do can only be bridged by employing a combination of multifaceted knowledge-dissemination tools (Bero et al., 1998; Brown & Flynn, 2002).

Among the variety of mechanisms available to facilitate the evolution of care is the capacity of an organization to make use of ongoing technical assistance and consultation. By forging collaborative partnerships with stakeholders at all levels, we can create a vehicle through which information can be gathered, evaluated, and fed back to an organization for the purpose of program development, adjustment, and improvement (Borich & Jemelka, 1982; Chinman, Weingarten, Stayner, & Davidson, 2001; Hatry, Newcomer, & Wholey, 1994; Rouse, Toprac, & MacCabe, 1998). In order to develop tools for the collection and use of such information, we have been challenged to operationalize the characteristics of recovery-oriented care in as clear and concrete a manner as possible. We have then used this work to provide organizations and systems with specific tools that they can use to self-evaluate and inform corrective actions, such as training and supervision, in their own transformation efforts.

Prior to describing some of these tools, we would like to stress the importance of three basic assumptions which have guided this work and which we consider crucial to its success.

The first assumption, which we tried to justify in our first chapter, is that choice and self-determination among adults with serious mental illness are first and foremost legal and civil rights issues, not clinical, functional, or treatment issues. That is, unless, until, and only for as long as we have evidence to believe that persons are posing serious and imminent risks to themselves or others do we have the legal authority to interfere with their personal sovereignty. Bluntly stated, it is not up to a mental health professional to decide when others are stable enough, well enough, in their "right mind" enough, etc., to make their own decisions. That is their fundamental right as the citizens of a free and democratic society, unless, until, and only for as long as there are persuasive reasons to determine otherwise. While the case for such intervention might be made by a mental health professional, the ultimate authority in determining its legitimacy remains with a judge. How this important consideration informs the development of tools to assess recovery-oriented care will become clear as we proceed.

A second, and related, assumption is that for a mental health practitioner to respect and honor the rights of adults with serious mental illness, his or her work will need to be characterized more by its *responsiveness* to each individual's strengths and goals than by its degree of *regimentation* or fidelity to a predetermined manual of structured interventions. While recovery-oriented practitioners need to be highly skilled and well trained in a range of manualized approaches (e.g., from cognitive-behavioral interventions to asset mapping), it is essential that they be perceived by their clients to be more responsive than regimented. The care they provide will be guided by each client's own strengths, interests, and self-chosen goals and thus will look somewhat different in each and every case.

This leads to our third assumption, pertaining to issues of diversity. If recovery-oriented practice assumes the self-determination of adults with serious mental illness and is oriented accordingly to the pursuit of the client's own unique and self-chosen goals, then recovery-oriented practice must also place a primary emphasis on human diversity. For choice to be free and substantive, it must be legitimate for people to choose different values, different things, and different roles and activities for themselves. Several recovery leaders have framed this issue by emphasizing that each person's recovery is a uniquely personal journey (Deegan, 1988). While we agree with this statement, we also feel a need to ground this assertion within its social and political contexts—contexts which psychiatry has not always been very good at acknowledging or appreciating.

What does it mean, we ask, to assert that recovery is a uniquely personal journey for each individual, such that no two people's paths will be the same? It means that choice generates diversity necessarily and fundamentally, rather than merely as a secondary or surface consideration. It is the very nature of human beings for there to be variability and difference as much as for people to be defined by vague commonalities. Were this not the case, then choice would not really be free and would refer only to insignificant changes in the quantity of some abstract, and largely irrelevant, universal. This point has been made pointedly by the Nobel laureate political economist Amartya Sen, who explains why theories of human nature are what he calls "inescapably pluralist." As he writes, "To insist on the mechanical comfort of having just one homogeneous 'good thing' would be to deny our humanity. . . . It is like seeking to make the life of the chef easier by finding something which—and which alone— we all like (such as smoked salmon, or perhaps even french fries)" (1999, p. 77).

While smoked salmon and french fries are, in fact, both foods, to say that a person who prefers smoked salmon to french fries has no real preference because they are both foods is to miss the point of having preferences to begin with. It is to gloss over the issue of choice, but this is precisely where our primary interest lies. Sen concludes, therefore, that "Investigations . . . that proceed with the assumption of antecedent uniformity . . . thus miss out on a major aspect of the problem. Human diversity is no secondary complication (to be ignored, or to be introduced 'later on'); it is a fundamental aspect of our interest" (1992, p. xi).

We suggest that this is an issue with which psychiatry has yet to grapple successfully, as it is a field whose history is replete with examples of lifestyles or other choices that it considered pathological (e.g., "runaway slaves," homosexuals) and which it now concedes are legitimate. Sen's point is reflected, in contrast, in D. W. Winnicott's unusual assertion that "with human beings there is an infinite variety in normality or health" (1986, p. 45). Were this principle to be accepted as foundational for our practice, we would reject any universal or predetermined notion of "normality" and would no longer make people wait to rejoin community life until they first regained it. This is because we have no way to know ahead of time what "normal" will look like for any given individual, and he or she will only be able to determine this over time through pursuit of those activities that he or she values. There is no other way, other than trial and error, to figure out what "normal" will look like for me, and this is as true of people with serious mental illness as it is for anyone, and everyone, else.

This is not to suggest that there will be no objective criteria by which to assess how recovery-oriented and/or how effective the care being provided is. It is to suggest, however, that these criteria will only secondarily refer to technical proficiency or fidelity and will refer primarily to how responsive and effective they are in furthering the person's pursuit of his or her own goals. Note that we are not suggesting that they must be effective in enabling the person to *achieve* his or her goals, as there are many factors involved in the achievement of goals over which the practitioner has little to no influence, including the success or failure of the person's own efforts. It therefore is only reasonable to focus on the degree to which the person is supported in *pursuing* his or her own goals, not the degree to which he or she is successful in achieving them. This, we believe, was the stumbling block that undermined the success of earlier, promising efforts to evaluate mental health care based on its effectiveness in addressing clients' own goals, such as "goal attainment scaling." What appears to be essential to recovery is that people are actively engaged in pursuing their goals, not what those goals are or whether the goals are ever achieved—in which case they will surely be replaced by yet other goals, as people continue to be goal-directed beings until their eventual demise (Davidson & Shahar, in press).

To begin to capture the different criteria by which a practitioner may assess his or her own recovery-orientation and competence, we suggest a series of questions, beginning with the one initially suggested by Carling (1995). Paraphrasing Carling, we suggest asking:

Does this person gain power, purpose (valued roles), competence
  (skills), and/or connections (to others), as a result of my

interventions, or have these interventions instead interfered with the person's acquisition of power, purpose, competence, or connections to others?

Other ways to frame this question include:

Is what I am doing currently assisting this particular person in initiating, furthering, or enhancing his or her own unique recovery journey, or is it perhaps getting in his or her way?

Am I assisting this person to identify his or her own strengths and to develop and pursue his or her own goals, interests, and meaningful life in the community, or am I encouraging him or her to rely on or comply with the wishes or desires of others (whether they be family members, residential support staff, or anyone else)?

Am I viewing and treating this person (according him or her the same rights and responsibilities) as a citizen (i.e., a "normal" individual) who is doing his or her best to deal with a particular set of challenges (e.g., like "battling" cancer)?

And finally, at the risk of falling into a tried but still true cliché:

Am I treating this person in the same ways I would want to be treated were I in his or her situation?

In sum, we are suggesting that reflecting upon the interactions that we have with persons in recovery, the treatment we provide, and the supports we offer, and adjusting them accordingly, based not solely on a particular set of rules or guidelines but also squarely on what is most helpful to this individual at this time—as in "responsive, not regimented"—are among the most important things we can do as recovery-oriented practitioners. With this in mind, we now turn to the measures we have developed to facilitate this work.

Three Measures of Recovery-Oriented Care

As one step in the process of operationalizing recovery, we have developed two initial scales based on the components described in Chapter 2 and the principles articulated in Chapter 4. These measures are (1) the Recovery Self-Assessment (RSA; O'Connell, Tondora, Evans, Croog, & Davidson, 2005), a tool used to gauge the degree to which recovery-oriented practices are implemented in a particular program; and (2) the Recovery Knowledge Inventory (RKI; Bedregal, O'Connell, & Davidson, 2006), a tool used to assess the knowledge and attitudes of mental health professionals about principles of recovery. These measures are described and provided below.

Assessing the Quality of Care in Programs and Systems: The Recovery Self-Assessment

Based on literature reviews, focus groups, and the model described in Chapter 2, the Recovery Self-Assessment (RSA) was created to assess the degree to which persons in recovery, practitioners, family members, significant others, advocates, and agency directors believe their respective agencies engage in a variety of recovery-oriented practices. The RSA contains 36 items and is available in four different versions for multiple stakeholders to assess an individual agency or program.

The items in the RSA were generated from an initial pool of 80 items that reflect objective practices associated with the nine conceptual domains of being in recovery presented earlier. For example, indicators such as the involvement of service users in management meetings and staff education, activities geared toward expanding social networks and social roles, degree of service user choice and self-determination, and staff attitudes and philosophy toward recovery were included in the measure.

All items consisted of a brief statement with a 6-category Likert response format from 1 (strongly disagree) to 5 (strongly agree) or N/A (not applicable). Persons in recovery, providers of mental health and addiction services, family members, and researchers with expertise in measurement development and clinical and community psychology reviewed all items for content and comprehension. Items were then edited, balanced with regard to conceptual domain, and eliminated until 36 items remained. The items on the RSA were then adapted for completion by providers/directors, persons in recovery, and family/significant others/advocates by changing the point of reference on each item (i.e., "staff at this agency focus on helping me" versus "staff at this agency focus on helping persons in recovery").

Based on an initial sample of 974 individuals (see O'Connell et al., 2005, for an overview of the study), we identified five primary factors within the RSA, which accounted for 53.8% of the total variance in the sample. Table A.1 contains the items and item loadings for each of the five factors. Factor scores are computed based on the mean of each group of items. Higher factor scores reflect greater agreement with the items in that factor. An RSA summary score is derived by computing the mean of all 36 items. Thus, scores can be used individually, as collectively in reflecting one of five factors, or in the aggregate to reflect the degree to which a service system or organization embodies principles of recovery-oriented care.

A first factor, *Life Goals*, contains 11 items that reflect perceptions of the extent to which staff help with the development and pursuit of individually defined life goals such as employment and education. This factor accounted for 13.7% of the total variance in the sample. The internal consistency estimate for this factor was 0.90.

A second factor, *Involvement*, contains eight items reflecting perceptions of the extent to which persons in recovery are involved in the development and provision of programs/services, staff training, and advisory board/management meetings. This factor accounted for 13.3% of the total variance in the sample. The internal consistency estimate for this factor was 0.87.

A third factor, *Diversity of Options*, contains six items that indicate perceptions of the extent to which an agency provides linkages to peer mentors and support, a variety of treatment options, and assistance with becoming involved in non–mental health activities. This factor accounted for 9.8% of the total variance in the sample. The internal consistency estimate for this factor was 0.83.

A fourth factor, *Choice*, contains six items measuring perceptions of the extent to which service users have access to their treatment records, staff refrain from using coercive measures to influence choice, and the choices of service users are respected by staff. This factor accounted for 8.9% of the total variance in the sample. The internal consistency estimate for this factor was 0.76.

The final factor, *Individually Tailored Services*, contains five items that reflect perceptions of the extent to which services are tailored to individual needs, cultures, and interests and focus on building community connections. This factor accounted for 8% of the total variance and had an internal consistency estimate of 0.76.

In addition to individual item, factor, and system-level scores, the RSA scores can be used to generate individual agency *Recovery Profiles* in which one agency's RSA scores can be compared to the average scores of other participating agencies, as demonstrated in

Table A.1 RSA Items and Factor Loadings (Practitioner Version)

Item#	Item	Loading
Factor 1: Life Goals		
25	Staff actively assist people in recovery with the development of career and life goals that go beyond symptom management and stabilization.	.73
29	Staff routinely assist individuals in the pursuit of educational and/or employment goals.	.66
33	The role of agency staff is to assist a person with fulfilling his or her individually defined goals and aspirations.	.61
26	Agency staff are diverse in terms of culture, ethnicity, lifestyle, and interests.	.59
24	Procedures are in place to facilitate referrals to other programs and services if the agency cannot meet a person's needs.	.58
23	Staff play a primary role in helping people in recovery become involved in non–mental health/addiction-related activities, such as church groups, interest groups, and adult education.	.53
22	Staff use a language of recovery (e.g., hope, high expectations, respect) in everyday conversations.	.45
36	Agency staff believe that people can recover and make their own treatment and life choices.	.43
20	The achievement of goals by people in recovery and staff is formally acknowledged and celebrated by the agency.	.41
14	Staff and agency participants are encouraged to take risks and try new things.	.38
16	Staff are knowledgeable about special interest groups and activities in the community.	.36

Factor 2: Involvement

30	People in recovery work alongside agency staff on the development and provision of new programs and services.	.75
27	People in recovery are regular members of agency advisory boards and management meetings.	.74
15	Persons in recovery are involved with facilitating staff trainings and education programs.	.71
12	This agency provides structured educational activities to the community about mental illness and addictions.	.61
21	People in recovery are routinely involved in the evaluation of the agency's programs, services, and service providers.	.58
31	Agency staff actively help people become involved with activities that give back to their communities (e.g., volunteering, community services, neighborhood watch/cleanup).	.55
32	This agency provides formal opportunities for people in recovery, family members, service providers, and administrators to learn about recovery.	.51
35	The development of a person's leisure interests and hobbies is a primary focus of services.	.38

Factor 3: Diversity of Options

18	This agency actively attempts to link people in recovery with other persons in recovery who can serve as role models or mentors by making referrals to self-help, peer support, or consumer advocacy groups or programs.	.54
34	Criteria for exiting or completing the agency are clearly defined and discussed with participants upon entry.	.53
8	People in recovery are given the opportunity to discuss their sexual and spiritual needs and interests.	.52

Continued

Table A.1 RSA Items and Factor Loadings (Practitioner Version) (*Continued*)

Item#	Item	Loading
19	This agency provides a variety of treatment options (e.g., individual, group, and peer support; medical care; holistic healing) from which agency participants may choose.	.51
17	Groups, meetings, and other activities can be scheduled in the evenings or on weekends.	.50
28	At this agency, participants who are doing well get as much attention as those who are having difficulties.	.43
Factor 4: Choice		
3	People in recovery have access to all their treatment records.	.62
13	Agency staff do not use threats, bribes, or other forms of coercion to influence a person's behavior or choices.	.59
10	Staff at this agency listen to and follow the choices and preferences of participants.	.56
6	People in recovery can choose and change, if desired, the service provider with whom they work.	.54
11	Progress made toward goals (as defined by the person in recovery) is monitored on a regular basis.	.49
7	Most services are provided in a person's natural environment (e.g., home, community, workplace).	.47

Factor 5: Individually Tailored Services

2	This agency offers specific services and programs for persons with different cultures, life experiences, interests, and needs.	.65
9	All staff at this agency regularly attend trainings on cultural competency.	.58
1	Helping people build connections with their neighborhoods and communities is one of the primary activities in which staff at this agency are involved.	.55
4	This agency provides education to community employers about employing people with mental illness and/or addictions.	.53
5	Every effort is made to involve significant others (spouses, friends, family members) and other natural supports (e.g., clergy, neighbors, landlords) in the planning of a person's services, if so desired.	.43

the histograms in Figure A.1. These histograms can then be used, if desired, to form a confidential Recovery Profile for each agency interested in using such a report in its own transformation efforts. Each Recovery Profile can also contain a brief description of the agency's sample and a description of its relative strengths (factors and items more than 1 standard deviation above the system average) and areas for improvement (factors and items more than 1 standard deviation below the system average). Finally, each Recovery Profile can offer an individual item analysis of the five highest-rated recovery-oriented practices at the agency and the five lowest-rated items (based on the average scores of all respondents). All of these options are illustrated in Figure A.1.

As part of an ongoing consultation and technical assistance initiative, the RSA and Recovery Profiles can help agencies build upon their existing strengths and focus on areas in need of improvement as they strive to offer recovery-oriented care to the people they serve. It should be noted that the ideal administration of the RSA is one that (a) is administered consistently across sites, program participants, and staff; (b) maintains anonymity of respondents; and (c) assesses the majority of the program participants/staff. This would help to minimize self-selection bias as well as allow for the most accurate description of perceptions of recovery-oriented practices at each agency.

Since the first administration of the RSA in Connecticut in 2002, we have adapted and tailored the instrument for use in several other systems across the country, and have also developed new questions for 24-hour residential settings and other specialty services of interest to different stakeholders. As one example of the evolving nature of recovery-oriented tools and the importance of these tools' being responsive to local systems, environments, and cultures, we expect that additional versions of the RSA will continue to be developed in the future as it gains more credibility as a useful tool for carrying out self-assessments.

The Recovery Knowledge Inventory: A Measure of Attitudes and Beliefs about Recovery

The Recovery Knowledge Inventory (RKI) was developed as part of a statewide training initiative in Connecticut to prepare the mental

MENTAL HEALTH CENTER

Agency Recovery Profile

Mental health center respondents:
- One Director/CEO
- Five Providers/direct care staff
- Five Persons in recovery
- Five Family/significant other/advocate

Comparisons to other state agencies

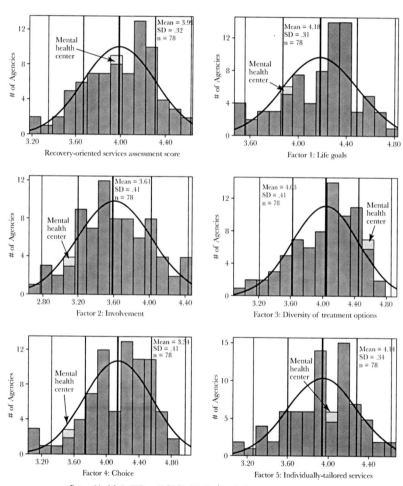

Prepared by Maria O'Connell, Ph.D., Yale Program for Recovery and Community Health

Figure A.1 Sample mental health center recovery profile (*cont'd*).

MENTAL HEALTH CENTER

Agency Recovery Profile

Strengths and Areas for Improvement

Strengths

Five highest-rated items by respondents at your agency
- Staff do not use threats, bribes, or coercion
- Natural supports are involved in the planning of services
- Sexual and spiritual needs are discussed
- Progress in goals is monitored regularly
- Procedures are in place to facilitate outside referrals

Other strengths (in comparison to other agencies)
Providing a diversity of treatment options
- Linking people to peers
- Having clearly defined exit criteria
- Flexibility in scheduling
- People doing well get as much attention as others

Areas for Improvement

Five lowest-rated items by respondents at your agency
- People in recovery help with the development and provision of services
- People in recovery can choose their service providers
- Education is provided to community employers
- People in recovery are regular members of advisory boards and management meetings
- Staff help people become involved in activities to give back to their communities

Other areas for improvement (based on camparisons to other agencies
Involvement in the provision of programs and services
Ways to improve in this area:
- Hire practitioners in recovery
- Have people in recovery sit on advisory boards and management meetings
- Have persons in recovery co-facilitate staff trainings
- Use consumer expertise as part of educational programs
- Persons in recovery should be included in all program/staff evaluation procedures
- Formally celebrate/acknowledge achievement of goals by staff and persons in recovery

Other suggestions
- Provide education to community employers about mental illness and recovery
- Allow people to choose their service providers
- Do more to focus on career and life goals, including, employment and education

For more information, please contact Maria O'Connell, Ph.D., at the Yale Program for
Recovery and Community Health, (203) 772-2086, x 102, maria.oconnell@yale.edu

Figure A.1 *Continued*

health workforce to deliver recovery-oriented care. As part of this training initiative, we used the model described above to identify those issues that were most integral to the provision of clinical and rehabilitative services and developed them into survey items for practitioners to complete. The resulting tool has various uses, from conducting training and education needs assessments to providing a process measure for the effectiveness of training and an outcome measure for pre–post tests of practitioner knowledge and beliefs.

The RKI is a 20-item instrument that assesses mental health practitioners' knowledge of and attitudes toward such issues as consumer directedness, the individual nature of recovery, cultural competence, self-determination, strengths-based care, choice and risk-taking, illness and symptom management, incorporation of illness, involvement in meaningful activities, overcoming stigma, redefining self, hope, and the nonlinear nature of the recovery process. Items on the RKI also follow a Likert-style response format ranging from 1 (*strongly disagree*) to 5 (*strongly agree*). In an effort to minimize the effects of social desirability, we tried to avoid framing questions in such a way as to enhance their face validity. In addition, responses to items did not follow the same direction: positive responses for half of the items reflected a stronger recovery orientation, while for the other half positive responses reflected less of a recovery orientation.

Based on an initial sample of 149 staff who participated in recovery training, four factors were identified (see Bedregal, O'Connell, & Davidson, 2006, for details of the study): (1) *Roles and Responsibilities in Recovery*, (2) *Nonlinearity of the Recovery Process*, (3) *The Roles of Self-Definition and Peers in Recovery*, and (4) *Expectations regarding Recovery*. The variance accounted for by these four components was 51%.

The first component, *Roles and Responsibilities*, included seven items regarding risk taking, decision making, and the various and respective roles and responsibilities of people in recovery and behavioral health practitioners (e.g., people with mental illness should not be burdened with the responsibilities of everyday life). This component explained 17% of the variance. The estimate of internal consistency for this factor was 0.82.

The second component, *Nonlinearity of the Recovery Process*, contained six items regarding the role of illness and symptom management and the nonlinear nature of recovery (e.g., recovery is characterized by a person making gradual steps forward without major steps back). This component explained 14% of the variance. The estimate of internal consistency for this factor was 0.72.

The third component, *The Roles of Self-Definition and Peers*, was composed of five items regarding the person's activities in defining an identity for himself or herself, and a life, that goes beyond that of "mental patient," including the valuable roles that peers can play in this process (e.g., the pursuit of hobbies and leisure activities are important for recovery). This component accounted for 12% of the variance. The estimate of internal consistency for this factor was 0.63.

The last component, *Expectations regarding Recovery*, included two items regarding expectations (e.g., not everyone is capable of actively participating in the recovery process). This component explained 8% of the variance. The estimate of internal consistency for this factor was 0.47.

Table A.2 contains the final 20-item Recovery Knowledge Inventory and the theoretical domains from which items were derived.

Initial results in Connecticut demonstrated that staff obtained the highest mean (SD) score of 4.29 (0.46) on component three, *Roles of Self-Definition and Peers*, indicating that providers appreciated the need for the person in recovery to develop a positive identity beyond that of "mental patient" and the importance of having the assistance of peers in this process. The next to highest mean score of 3.96 (0.76) was on component one, *Roles and Responsibilities*, which indicated that staff also showed good understanding of the importance of differentiating the roles and responsibilities of each party (i.e., practitioner and client) in the treatment and rehabilitation process. Staff's third-highest mean score of 3.13 (1.08) was on component four, *Expectations regarding Recovery*, suggesting that staff have less knowledge of how to develop realistic yet hopeful expectations of their clients with respect to their participation in their own recovery and in their lives in general. Staff's lowest mean score of 2.91 (0.82) rested on component two, *Nonlinearity of the Recovery Process*, indicating that staff had least knowledge about the nature of the recovery process, including of its nonlinear nature, or the idea that illness and symptom management are a part of, rather than precede, recovery, and the various ways in which people can, and need to, pursue recovery outside of formal treatment and rehabilitation settings.

These results have important implications for training and for identifying those aspects of recovery and recovery-oriented care that are least familiar or clear to practitioners at any given time. In its first administration in Connecticut, and since in several other systems as well, staff seemed comfortable with the idea that people in recovery need to rediscover or recreate a new life and new identity

Table A.2 Recovery Knowledge Inventory

Item#	Loadings
Factor 1: Roles and Responsibilities	
10. Only people who are clinically stable should be involved in making decisions about their care.	.79
7. Recovery from serious mental illness is achieved by following a prescribed set of procedures.	.69
9. It is the responsibility of professionals to protect their clients against possible failures and disappointments.	.67
18. The idea of recovery is most relevant for those people who have completed, or are close to completing, active treatment.	.64
6. People with mental illness/substance abuse should not be burdened with the responsibilities of everyday life.	.63
2. People receiving psychiatric/substance abuse treatment are unlikely to be able to decide their own treatment and rehabilitation goals.	.62
11. Recovery is not as relevant for those who are actively psychotic or abusing substances.	.50
Factor 2: Nonlinearity of the Recovery Process	
15. Recovery is characterized by a person's making gradual steps forward without major steps back.	.66
17. Expectations and hope for recovery should be adjusted according to the severity of a person's illness.	.66
19. The more a person complies with treatment, the more likely he or she is to recover.	.63
16. Symptom reduction is an essential component of recovery.	.57
14. There is little that professionals can do to help a person recover if he or she is not ready to accept his or her illness/condition or need for treatment.	.56
4. Symptom management is the first step toward recovery from mental illness/substance abuse.	.52

Continued

Table A.2 Recovery Knowledge Inventory

Item#	Loadings
Factor 3: The Roles of Self-Definition and Peers	
8. The pursuit of hobbies and leisure activities is important for recovery.	.76
20. Other people who have a serious mental illness can be as instrumental to a person's recovery as mental health providers.	.68
1. The concept of recovery is equally relevant to all phases of treatment.	.60
12. Defining who one is, apart from his or her illness/condition, is an essential component of recovery.	.60
3. All professionals should encourage clients to take risks in the pursuit of recovery.	.44
Factor 4: Expectations Regarding Recovery	
5. Not everyone is capable of actively participating in the recovery process.	.66
13. It is often harmful to have expectations for clients that are too high.	.60

beyond that of mental patient, and they were aware that their clients bear some of the responsibilities, and therefore should have choices, regarding how this will occur. Staff also seemed cognizant of the importance of their own roles and responsibilities in relation to treatment and rehabilitation and understood that most people were oriented toward regaining not only their health but their citizenship as well. What appeared to be less familiar was what expectations providers should have for their clients regarding what their clients might be capable of at different points in the process of recovery; the complex, nonlinear, and multidimensional nature of that process; and the fact that people can lead better and more gratifying lives even while they remain bothered by symptoms or disabled by their illness.

This evaluation of staff responses on the RKI allowed us to assess their knowledge of and attitudes toward recovery and how they currently operationalize recovery in practice. As a result of this analysis, these topics became natural focal points for the education and training of staff in providing recovery-oriented care, offering another example of technology transfer in action. As the RKI also has begun to be used by other systems outside of Connecticut, we can anticipate that different results will be generated over time, with different implications for the training needs of staff as they continue to evolve through the transformation process. As with the RSA, we offer this form of the RKI as a preliminary attempt, and we expect that it will be improved and refined over time as we learn more about processes of recovery and ways to promote and facilitate them.

The tools provided in this Appendix are geared toward assessing implementation of a particular model of care that is consistent with what we know thus far about the recovery process. However, we are early in the process of articulating and applying this model and are cognizant that the current model may not apply precisely to all situations, all environments, and all people. Thus, we highly recommend "fiddling" with the model and the measures to ensure that we remain responsive to the needs of the individuals with whom we work, rather than remaining faithful to a particular model (we thank Martha Long, from the Village Integrated Services Agency in Long Beach, California, for introducing us to the concept of "fiddling" with a model in place of requiring "fidelity" to a model).

Thus, we encourage systems to adapt and tailor these measures to suit the needs of particular environments and people, and to do so in an inclusive, collaborative way involving multiple stakeholders with different areas of expertise related to recovery. In doing so, we also encourage systems to share the three core assumptions we have described above: honoring the rights of adults with serious mental illness to make their own choices, making care responsive to these choices rather than remaining regimented within predetermined structures, and appreciating that diversity and variability are essential to what makes us all human beings, irrespective of *whether or not a person has a mental illness.*

Recovery Self-Assessment: Practitioner Version

Please indicate the degree to which you feel the following items reflect the activities, values, and practices of your agency.

1	2	3	4	5
Strongly Disagree			**Strongly Agree**	

1. Helping people build connections with their neighborhoods and communities is one of the primary activities in which staff at this agency are involved.　　1　2　3　4　5　N/A

2. This agency offers specific services and programs for individuals with different cultures, life experiences, interests, and needs.　　1　2　3　4　5　N/A

3. People in recovery have access to all their treatment records.　　1　2　3　4　5　N/A

4. This agency provides education to community employers about employing people with mental illness and/or addictions.　　1　2　3　4　5　N/A

5. Every effort is made to involve significant others (spouses, friends, family members) and other natural supports (e.g., clergy, neighbors, landlords) in the planning of a person's services, if so desired.　　1　2　3　4　5　N/A

6. People in recovery can choose and change, if desired, the therapist, psychiatrist, or other service provider with whom they work.　　1　2　3　4　5　N/A

7. Most services are provided in a person's natural environment (e.g., home, community, workplace).   1 2 3 4 5 N/A

8. People in recovery are given the opportunity to discuss their sexual and spiritual needs and interests.   1 2 3 4 5 N/A

9. All staff at this agency regularly attend trainings on cultural competency.   1 2 3 4 5 N/A

10. Staff at this agency listen to and follow the choices and preferences of participants.   1 2 3 4 5 N/A

11. Progress made toward goals (as defined by the person in recovery) is monitored on a regular basis.   1 2 3 4 5 N/A

12. This agency provides structured educational activities to the community about mental illness and addictions.   1 2 3 4 5 N/A

13. Agency staff do not use threats, bribes, or other forms of coercion to influence a person's behavior or choices.   1 2 3 4 5 N/A

14. Staff and agency participants are encouraged to take risks and try new things.   1 2 3 4 5 N/A

15. Persons in recovery are involved with facilitating staff trainings and education programs at this agency.   1 2 3 4 5 N/A

16. Staff are knowledgeable about special interest groups and activities in the community.   1 2 3 4 5 N/A

17. Groups, meetings, and other activities can be scheduled in the evenings or on weekends so as not to conflict with other recovery-oriented activities such as employment or school.   1 2 3 4 5 N/A

18. This agency actively attempts to link people in recovery with other persons in recovery who can serve as role models or mentors by making referrals to self-help, peer support, or consumer advocacy groups or programs.   1 2 3 4 5 N/A

Continued

19. This agency provides a variety of treatment options (e.g., individual/group/ peer support, holistic healing, alternative treatments, medical) from which agency participants may choose.   1   2   3   4   5   N/A

20. The achievement of goals by people in recovery and staff is formally acknowledged and celebrated by the agency.   1   2   3   4   5   N/A

21. People in recovery are routinely involved in the evaluation of the agency's programs, services, and service providers.   1   2   3   4   5   N/A

22. Staff use a language of recovery (e.g., hope, high expectations, respect) in everyday conversations.   1   2   3   4   5   N/A

23. Staff play a primary role in helping people in recovery become involved in non–mental health/addiction-related activities, such as church groups, special interest groups, and adult education.   1   2   3   4   5   N/A

24. Procedures are in place to facilitate referrals to other programs and services if the agency cannot meet a person's needs.   1   2   3   4   5   N/A

25. Staff actively assist people in recovery with the development of career and life goals that go beyond symptom management and stabilization.   1   2   3   4   5   N/A

26. Agency staff are diverse in terms of culture, ethnicity, lifestyle, and interests.   1   2   3   4   5   N/A

27. People in recovery are regular members of agency advisory boards and management meetings.   1   2   3   4   5   N/A

28. At this agency, participants who are doing well get as much attention as those who are having difficulties.   1   2   3   4   5   N/A

29. Staff routinely assist individuals in the pursuit of educational and/or employment goals.   1   2   3   4   5   N/A

30. People in recovery work alongside agency staff on the development and provision of new programs and services.   1   2   3   4   5   N/A

31. Agency staff actively help people become involved with activities that give back to their communities (e.g., volunteering, community services, neighborhood watch/cleanup).   1   2   3   4   5   N/A

32. This agency provides formal opportunities for people in recovery, family members, service providers, and administrators to learn about recovery.   1   2   3   4   5   N/A

33. The role of agency staff is to assist a person with fulfilling his or her individually defined goals and aspirations.   1   2   3   4   5   N/A

34. Criteria for exiting or completing the agency are clearly defined and discussed with participants upon entry.   1   2   3   4   5   N/A

35. The development of a person's leisure interests and hobbies is a primary focus of services.   1   2   3   4   5   N/A

36. Agency staff believe that people can recover and make their own treatment and life choices.   1   2   3   4   5   N/A

Recovery Knowledge Inventory

Please rate the following items on a scale of 1 to 5:

	1	2	3	4	5

Strongly Disagree					**Strongly Agree**

1. The concept of recovery is equally relevant to all phases of treatment.　　1　2　3　4　5

2. People receiving psychiatric/substance abuse treatment are unlikely to be able to decide their own treatment and rehabilitation goals.　　1　2　3　4　5

3. All professionals should encourage clients to take risks in the pursuit of recovery.　　1　2　3　4　5

4. Symptom management is the first step toward recovery from mental illness/ substance abuse.　　1　2　3　4　5

5. Not everyone is capable of actively participating in the recovery process.　　1　2　3　4　5

6. People with mental illness/substance abuse should not be burdened with the responsibilities of everyday life.　　1　2　3　4　5

7. Being in recovery with serious mental illness/substance abuse is achieved by following a prescribed set of procedures.　　1　2　3　4　5

8. The pursuit of hobbies and leisure activities is important for recovery.　　1　2　3　4　5

9. It is the responsibility of professionals to protect their clients against possible failures and disappointments.　　1　2　3　4　5

10. Only people who are clinically stable should be involved in making decisions about their care.　　1　2　3　4　5

11. Recovery is not as relevant for those who are actively psychotic or abusing substances.　　1　2　3　4　5

12. Defining who one is, apart from his or her illness or condition, is an essential component of recovery.　　1　2　3　4　5

13. It is often harmful to have expectations for clients that are too high.　　1　2　3　4　5

14. There is little that professionals can do to help a person recover if he or she is not ready to accept his or her illness/condition or need for treatment.   1   2   3   4   5

15. Recovery is characterized by a person's making gradual steps forward without major steps back.   1   2   3   4   5

16. Symptom reduction is an essential component of recovery.   1   2   3   4   5

17. Expectations and hope for recovery should be adjusted according to the severity of a person's illness/condition.   1   2   3   4   5

18. The idea of recovery is most relevant for those people who have completed, or are close to completing, active treatment.   1   2   3   4   5

19. The more a person complies with treatment, the more likely he or she is to recover.   1   2   3   4   5

20. Other people who have a serious mental illness or are recovering from substance abuse can be as instrumental to a person's recovery as mental health professionals.   1   2   3   4   5

REFERENCES

Adams, N., & Grieder, D. (2005). *Treatment planning for person-centered care: The road to mental health and addiction recovery*. San Diego, CA: Elsevier Academic Press.

American Psychiatric Association. (1980). *Diagnostic and statistical manual of mental disorders* (3rd ed.). Washington, DC: American Psychiatric Association.

Andreasen, N. C., Carpenter, W. T., Kane, J. M., Lasser, R. A., Marder, S. R., & Weinberger, D. R. (2005). Remission in schizophrenia: Proposed criteria and rationale for consensus. *American Journal of Psychiatry, 162,* 441–449.

Andres-Hyman, R. C., Strauss, J. S., & Davidson, L. (2007). Beyond parallel play: Science befriending the art of Method acting to advance healing relationships. *Psychotherapy: Theory, Research, Practice, Training, 44,* 78–89.

Anthony, W. A. (1993). Recovery from mental illness: The guiding vision of the mental health service system in the 1990s. *Psychosocial Rehabilitation Journal, 16,* 11–23.

Anthony, W. A. (1994). Characteristics of people with psychiatric disabilities that are predictive of entry into the rehabilitation process and successful employment. *Psychosocial Rehabilitation Journal, 17,* 3–13.

Anthony, W. A. (2000). A recovery-oriented service system: Setting some system level standards. *Psychiatric Rehabilitation Journal, 24,* 159–168.

Bassman, R. (1997). The mental health system: Experiences from both sides of the locked doors. *Professional Psychology: Research and Practice, 28,* 238–242.

Baxter, E. A., & Diehl, S. (1998). Emotional stages: Consumers and family members recovering from the trauma of mental illness. *Psychiatric Rehabilitation Journal, 21,* 349–355.

Becerra, R., Karno, M., & Escobar, J. (Eds.) (1982). *Mental health and Hispanic Americans: Clinical perspectives*. New York: Grune & Stratton.

Becker, D. R., & Drake, R. E. (1994). Individual placement and support: A community mental health center approach to vocational rehabilitation. *Community Mental Health Journal, 30,* 193–206.

Bedregal, L. E., O'Connell, M., & Davidson, L. (2006). The Recovery Knowledge Inventory: Assessment of mental health staff knowledge and attitudes about recovery. *Psychiatric Rehabilitation Journal, 30,* 96–103.

Bernstein, R. (2001). *Disintegrating systems: The state of states' public mental health systems.* Washington, DC: Bazelon Center for Mental Health Law.

Bero, L., Grilli, R., Grimshaw, J., Harvey, E., Oxman, A., & Thomson, M. A. (1998). Closing the gap between research and practice: An overview of systematic reviews of interventions to promote the implementation of research findings. *British Medical Journal, 317,* 465–468.

Biegel, D. E., & Tracy, E. M. (1994). Strengthening social networks. *Health & Social Work, 19,* 206–217.

Blessing, C., Tierney, M., Osher, D., Allegretti-Freeman, J., & Abrey, B. (2005). *Learning from other communities.* Washington, DC: Substance Abuse and Mental Health Services Administration.

Bleuler, M. (1978). The schizophrenic disorders: Long-term patient and family studies (Clemens, S. M., Trans.). New Haven, CT: Yale University Press.

Bond, G. R. (1991). Variations in an assertive outreach model. In N. L. Cohen (Ed)., *Psychiatric outreach to the mentally ill. New directions for mental health services, No. 52: The Jossey-Bass social and behavioral sciences series* (pp. 65–80). San Francisco: Jossey-Bass.

Borg, M., & Topor, A. (2002, October). Recovery from "chronicity": Some life experiences. *WAPR Bulletin.* Retrieved January 15, 2002, from http://www.wapr.net/v0114n03.htm

Breakey, W., & Fischer, P. (1995). Mental illness and the continuum of residential stability. *Social Psychiatry and Psychiatric Epidemiology, 30,* 147–151.

Brickner, P. W. (1992). Medical concerns of homeless persons. In H. R. Lamb, L. L. Bachrach, & F. I. Kass (Eds.), *Treating the homeless mentally ill: A report of the Task Force on the Homeless Mentally Ill* (pp. 249–261). Washington, DC: American Psychiatric Association.

Brown, B. S., & Flynn, P. M. (2002). The federal role in drug abuse technology transfer: A history and perspective. *Journal of Substance Abuse Treatment, 22,* 245–257.

Butler, J. P. (1992). Of kindred minds: The ties that bind. In M. A. Orlandi (Ed.), *Cultural competence for evaluators* (pp. 23–54). Rockville, MD: Office of Substance Abuse Prevention.

Butterworth, J., Hagner, H., Heikkinen, B., Faris, S., DeMello, S., & McDonough, K. (1993). *Whole life planning: A guide for organizers and facilitators.* Boston: Training and Research Institute for People with Disabilities.

Campbell-Orde, T., Chamberlin, J. Carpenter, J., & Leff, H. S. (Eds.). (2005). *Measuring the promise of recovery: A compendium of recovery measures.* Cambridge, MA: The Evaluation Center@HSRI.

Carey, K. (1998). Treatment boundaries in the case management relationship: A behavioral perspective. *Community Mental Health Journal, 34,* 313–317.

Carling, P. J. (1990). Major mental illness, housing, and supports: The promise of community integration. *American Psychologist, 45,* 969–975.

Carling, P. J. (1995). *Return to community: Building support systems for people with psychiatric disabilities.* New York: The Guilford Press.

Carpenter, W. T., & Kirkpatrick, B. (1988). The heterogeneity of the long-term course of schizophrenia. *Schizophrenia Bulletin, 14,* 645–652.

Casas, J. M., & Pytluk, S. D. (1995). Hispanic identity development: Implications for research and practice. In J. G. Ponterotto, J. M. Casas, L. A. Suzuki., & C. M. Alexander (Eds.), *Handbook of multicultural counseling* (pp. 155–180). Thousand Oaks, CA: Sage.

Chadwick, P., Birchwood, M., & Trower, P. (1996). *Cognitive therapy for hallucinations, delusions, and paranoia.* Chichester, UK: John Wiley & Sons.

Chamberlin, J. (1978). *On our own: Patient-controlled alternatives to the mental health system.* New York: Hawthorn Books.

Chamberlin, J. (1984). Speaking for ourselves: An overview of the Ex-Psychiatric Inmates' Movement. *Psychosocial Rehabilitation Journal, 2,* 56–63.

Chinman, M., Allende, M., Bailey, P., Maust, J., & Davidson, L. (1999). Therapeutic agents of assertive community treatment. *Psychiatric Quarterly, 70,* 137–162.

Chinman, M. J., Weingarten, R., Stayner, D., & Davidson, L. (2001). Chronicity reconsidered: Improving person–environment fit through a consumer-run service. *Community Mental Health Journal, 37,* 215–229.

Chirikos, T. N. (1999). Will the costs of accommodating workers with disabilities remain low? *Behavioral Sciences & the Law, 17,* 93–106.

Ciompi, L. (1980). The natural history of schizophrenia in the long term. *British Journal of Psychiatry, 136,* 413–420.

Cohen, P., & Cohen, J. (1984). The clinician's illusion. *Archives of General Psychiatry, 41,* 1178–1182.

Connolly, P., Marrone, J., Kiernan, W. E., & Butterworth, J. (1996). *Think tank on disability definitions and entry into the disability system: Results and recommendations.* Boston: Children's Hospital, Institute for Community Inclusion.

Cooke, A. M. (1997). The long journey back. *Psychiatric Rehabilitation Skills, 2*(1), 33–36.

Copeland, M. E. (1997). *Wellness recovery action plan.* West Dummerston, VT: Peach Press.

Corrigan, P. W., & Penn, D. L. (1998). Disease and discrimination: Two paradigms that describe severe mental illness. *Journal of Mental Health (UK), 6,* 355–366.

Coyne, J. C. (1976). Towards an interactional description of depression. *Psychiatry: Interpersonal and Biological Processes, 39,* 28–40.

Curtis, L., & Hodge, M. (1993). *Boundaries and ethics in community support services.* Unpublished training materials. Burlington, VT: Trinity College, Center for Community Change through Housing and Support.

Curtis, L., & Hodge, M. (1994). Old standards, new dilemmas: Ethics and boundaries in community support services. *Psychosocial Rehabilitation Journal, 18,* 13–33.

Dailey, W. F., Chinman, M. J., Davidson, L., Garner, L., Vavrousek-Jakuba, E., Essock, S., et al. (2000). How are we doing? A statewide survey of community adjustment among people with serious mental illness receiving intensive outpatient services. *Community Mental Health Journal, 36,* 363–382.

Davidson, L. (2003). Living outside mental illness: Qualitative studies of recovery in schizophrenia. New York: New York University Press.

Davidson, L. (1997). Vulnérabilité et destin dans la schizophrénie: Prêter l'oreille á la voix de la personne. [Vulnerability and destiny in schizophrenia: Hearkening to the voice of the person]. *L' Evolution psychiatrique, 62,* 263–284.

Davidson, L., Flanagan, E., Roe, D., & Styron, T. (2006). Leading a horse to water: An action perspective on mental health policy. *Journal of Clinical Psychology, 62,* 1141–1155.

Davidson, L., Haglund, K. E., Stayner, D. A., Rakfeldt, J., Chinman, M. J., & Tebes, J. (2001). "It was just realizing . . . that life isn't one big horror": A qualitative study of supported socialization. *Psychiatric Rehabilitation Journal, 24,* 275–292.

Davidson, L., Harding, C. M., & Spaniol, L. (2005). *Recovery from severe mental illnesses: Research evidence and implications for practice* (Vol. 1). Boston: Center for Psychiatric Rehabilitation of Boston University.

Davidson, L., Harding, C. M., & Spaniol, L. (2006). *Recovery from severe mental illnesses: Research evidence and implications for practice* (Vol. 2). Boston: Center for Psychiatric Rehabilitation of Boston University.

Davidson, L., Hoge, M. A., Godleski, L., Rakfeldt, J., & Griffith, E. E. H. (1996). Hospital or community living? Examining consumer perspectives on deinstitutionalization. *Psychiatric Rehabilitation Journal, 19*(3), 49–58.

Davidson, L., Hoge, M. A., Merrill, M., Rakfeldt, J., & Griffith, E. E. H. (1995). The experiences of long-stay inpatients returning to the community. *Psychiatry: Interpersonal and Biological Processes, 58,* 122–132.

Davidson, L., Kirk, T., Rockholz, P., Tondora, J., O'Connell, M. J., & Evans, A. C. (2007). Creating a recovery-oriented system of behavioral health care: Moving from concept to reality. *Psychiatric Rehabilitation Journal, 31*(1), 23–31.

Davidson, L., & McGlashan, T. (1997). The varied outcomes of schizophrenia. *Canadian Journal of Psychiatry, 42,* 34–43.

Davidson, L., Nickou, C., Lynch, P., Moscariello, S., Sinha, R., Steiner, J., et al. (2001). Beyond Babel: Establishing system-wide principles of collaborative care for adults with serious and persistent mental illness. *The Organizational Response to Social Problems, 8,* 17–41.

Davidson, L., O'Connell, M., Tondora, J., Staeheli, M. R., & Evans, A. C. (2005). Recovery in serious mental illness: A new wine or just a new bottle? *Professional Psychology: Research and Practice, 36*(5), 480–487.

Davidson, L., O'Connell, M. J., Tondora, J., Styron, T., & Kangas, K. (2006). The top ten concerns about recovery encountered in mental health system transformation. *Psychiatric Services, 57*(5), 640–645.

Davidson, L., & Shahar, G. (in press). From deficit to desire: A philosophical reconsideration of action models of psychopathology. *Philosophy, Psychiatry and Psychology.*

Davidson, L., Shahar, G., Stayner, D. A., Chinman, M. J., Rakfeldt, J., & Tebes, J. K. (2004). Supported socialization for people with psychiatric disabilities: Lessons from a randomized controlled trial. *Journal of Community Psychology, 32,* 453–477.

Davidson, L., Staeheli, M., Stayner, D., & Sells, D. (2004). Language, suffering, and the question of immanence: Toward a respectful phenomenological psychopathology. *Journal of Phenomenological Psychology, 35,* 197–232.

Davidson, L., Stayner, D. A., & Haglund, K. E. (1998). Phenomenological perspectives on the social functioning of people with schizophrenia. In K. T. Mueser & N. Tarrier (Eds.), *Handbook of social functioning in schizophrenia* (pp. 97–120). Needham Heights, MA: Allyn & Bacon Publishers.

Davidson, L., Stayner, D. A., Lambert, S., Smith, P., & Sledge, W. H. (1997). Phenomenological and participatory research on schizophrenia: Recovering the person in theory and practice. *Journal of Social Issues, 53,* 767–784.

Davidson, L., Stayner, D. A., Nickou, C., Styron, T. H., Rowe, M., & Chinman, M. L. (2001). "Simply to be let in": Inclusion as a basis for recovery. *Psychiatric Rehabilitation Journal, 24,* 375–388.

Davidson, L., & Strauss, J. S. (1992). Sense of self in recovery from severe mental illness. *British Journal of Medical Psychology, 65,* 131–145.

Davidson, L., & Strauss, J. S. (1995). Beyond the biopsychosocial model: Integrating disorder, health, and recovery. *Psychiatry: Interpersonal and Biological Processes, 58,* 44–55.

Davidson, L., Tondora, J., Staeheli, M., O'Connell, M., Frey, J., & Chinman, M. J. (2006). Recovery guides: An emerging model of community-based care for adults with psychiatric disabilities. In A. Lightburn & P. Sessions (Eds.), *Handbook of community-based clinical practice* (pp. 476–501). London: Oxford University Press.

Deegan, P. E. (1988). Recovery: The lived experience of rehabilitation. *Psychosocial Rehabilitation Journal, 11,* 11–19.

Deegan, P. E. (1992). The independent living movement and people with psychiatric disabilities: Taking back control over our own lives. *Psychosocial Rehabilitation Journal, 15,* 3–19.

Deegan, P. E. (1993). Recovering our sense of value after being labeled mentally ill. *Journal of Psychosocial Nursing, 31*(4), 7–11.

Deegan, P. E. (1996a). Recovery as a journey of the heart. *Psychiatric Rehabilitation Journal, 19,* 91–97.

Deegan, P. E. (1996b, September). *Recovery and the conspiracy of hope.* Paper presented at the Sixth Annual Mental Health Services Conference of Australia and New Zealand, Brisbane, Australia. Retrieved March 1, 2002, from http://www.intentionalcare.org/articles/articles_hope.pdf

Deegan, P. E. (2001). Recovery as a self-directed process of healing and transformation. In C. Brown (Ed.), *Recovery and wellness: Models of hope and empowerment for people with mental illness* (pp. 5–21). New York: Haworth Press.

Deitchman, W. S. (1980). How many case managers does it take to screw in a light bulb? *Hospital & Community Psychiatry, 31,* 788–789.

DeJong, P., & Miller, S. D. (1995). How to interview for client strengths. *Social Work, 40*(6), 729–736.

Dennis, D. L., Buckner, J. C., Lipton, F. R., & Levine, I. S. (1991). A decade of research and services for homeless mentally ill persons: Where do we stand? *American Psychologist, 46,* 1129–1138.

Department of Health and Human Services. (1999). *Mental health: A report of the Surgeon General.* Rockville, MD: U.S. Department of Health and Human Services, Public Health Service, Office of the Surgeon General.

Department of Health and Human Services (2000). *Healthy People 2010.* Rockville, MD: U.S. Department of Health and Human Services.

Department of Health and Human Services (2001a). *Mental health: Culture, race, and ethnicity—A supplement to Mental health: A report of the Surgeon General.* Rockville, MD: U.S. Department of Health and Human Services, Public Health Service, Office of the Surgeon General, Substance Abuse and Mental Health Services Administration.

Department of Health and Human Services (2001b). *Executive summary. Mental health: Culture, race, and ethnicity. A supplement to Mental health: A report of the Surgeon General.* Rockville, MD: Center for Mental Health Services.

Department of Health and Human Services, Office of Minority Health (2001). *A practical guide for implementing the recommended national standards for culturally and linguistically appropriate services in healthcare.* Retrieved March 20, 2002, from http://www.omhrc.gov/clas/guide3a.asp

Department of Health and Human Services (2003a). *Achieving the promise: Transforming mental health care in America.* President's New Freedom Commission on Mental Health. Final Report (DHHS Pub. No. SMA-03–3832.). Rockville, MD: U.S. Department of Health and Human Services.

Department of Health and Human Services (2003b). *Achieving the promise: Transforming mental health care in America.* Rockville, MD: Substance Abuse and Mental Health Services Administration.

Department of Health and Human Services (2005). *Transforming mental health care in America. Federal action agenda: First steps.* Rockville, MD: Substance Abuse and Mental Health Services Administration.

Drake, R. E., Becker, D. R., Biesanz, J. C., Torrey, W. C., McHugo, G. J., & Wyzik, P. F. (1994). Rehabilitative day treatment vs. supported employment: I. Vocational outcomes. *Community Mental Health Journal, 30,* 519–532.

Drake, R. E., Becker, D. R., Clark, R. E., & Mueser, K. T. (1999). Research on the individual placement and support model of supported employment. *Psychiatric Quarterly, 70,* 289–301.

Drake, R. E., Goldman, H. H., Leff, H. S., Lehman, A. F., Dixon, L., & Mueser, K. T. (2001). Implementing evidence-based practices in routine mental health service settings. *Psychiatric Services, 52,* 179–182.

Estroff, S. E. (1989). Self, identity, and subjective experiences of schizophrenia: In search of the subject. *Schizophrenia Bulletin, 15,* 189–196.

Estroff, S. E. (1995). Whose story is it anyway? Authority, voice, and responsibility in narratives of chronic illness. In S. K. Toombs, D. Barnard, & R. A. Carson (Eds.), *Chronic illness: From experience to policy. Medical ethics series* (pp. 77–102). Bloomington, IN: Indiana University Press.

Estroff, S. E., Zinuner, C., Lachiotte, W. S., Benoit, J., & Patrick, D. (1997). No other way to go: Pathways to income application among persons with severe mental illness. In R. Bonnie & J. Monahan (Eds.), *Mental disorder, work disability, and the law* (pp. 55–104). Chicago: University of Chicago Press.

Everett, B., & Nelson, A. (1992). We're not cases and you're not managers. *Psychosocial Rehabilitation Journal, 15,* 49–60.

Fabian, E. (1999). Rethinking work: The example of consumers with serious mental health disorders. *Rehabilitation Counseling Bulletin, 42,* 302–316.

Federal Task Force on Homelessness and Severe Mental Illness. (1992). *Outcasts on Main Street: Report of the Federal Task Force on Homelessness and Severe Mental Illness.* Washington, DC: Interagency Council on the Homeless.

Fein, R. (1958). *Economics of mental illness.* New York: Basic Books.

Fischer, W. F. (1970). *Theories of anxiety.* New York: Harper & Row.

Fisher, D. (n.d.) *Elements of managed care needed to promote recovery of mental health consumers.* Unpublished manuscript.

Fisher, D. (1994). Health care reform based on an empowerment model of recovery by people with psychiatric disabilities. *Hospital & Community Psychiatry, 45,* 913–915.

Flanagan, E., Davidson, L., & Strauss, J. S. (2007). Incorporating patients' subjective experiences into the *DSM-V. American Journal of Psychiatry, 164*(3), 391–392.

Fowler, D., Garety, P., & Kuipers, E. (1998). Understanding the inexplicable: An individually formulated cognitive approach to delusional beliefs. In C. Perris & P. D. McGorry (Eds.), *Cognitive psychotherapy of psychotic and personality disorders: Handbook of theory and practice* (pp. 129–146). New York: Wiley.

Frese, F. J. III, Stanley, J., Kress, K., & Vogel-Scibilia, S. (2001). Integrating evidence-based practices and the recovery model. *Psychiatric Services, 52,* 1462–1468.

Gerteis, M., Edgman-Levitan, L., Daley, J., & Delbanco, T. L. (1993). Medicine and health from the patient's perspective. In M. Gerteis, S. Edgman-Levitan, J. Daley, & T. L. Delbanco (Eds.), *Through the patient's eyes* (pp. 1–15). San Francisco: Jossey-Bass.

Gilmartin, R. M. (1997). Personal narrative and the social reconstruction of the lives of former psychiatric patients. *Journal of Sociology and Social Welfare, 24*(2), 77–102.

Green, M. F. (1999). *Schizophrenia from a neurocognitive perspective: Probing the impenetrable darkness.* Boston: Allyn & Bacon.

Grier, W., & Cobbs, P. (1968). *Black rage.* New York: Basic Books.

Grills, C. N., Bass, K., Brown, D. L., & Akers, A. (1996). Empowerment evaluation: Building upon a tradition of activism in the African-American community. In D. M. Fetterman, S. J. Kaftarian, & A. Wandersman (Eds.), *Empowerment evaluation: Knowledge and tools for self-assessment and accountability* (pp. 123–140). Thousand Oaks, CA: Sage.

Gutierrez, L., Ortega, R. M., & Suarez, Z. E. (1990). Self-help and the Latino community. In T. J. Powell (Ed.), *Working with self-help.* Silver Spring, MD: National Association of Social Workers Press.

Harding, C. M., Brooks, G. W., Ashikaga, T., Strauss, J., & Breier, A. (1987a). The Vermont longitudinal study of persons with severe mental illness, I: Methodology, study sample, and overall status 32 years later. *American Journal of Psychiatry, 144,* 718–726.

Harding, C. M., Brooks, G. W., Ashikaga, T., Strauss, J., & Breier, A. (1987b). The Vermont longitudinal study of persons with severe mental illness, II: Long-term outcome of subjects who retrospectively met DSM-III criteria for schizophrenia. *American Journal of Psychiatry, 144,* 727–735.

Harding, C. M., Zubin, J., & Strauss, J. S. (1987). Chronicity in schizophrenia: Fact, partial fact, or artifact? *Hospital & Community Psychiatry, 38,* 477–486.

Harry, B., Kalyanpur, M., & Day, M. (1999). *Building cultural reciprocity with families.* Baltimore, MD: Paul Brooks.

Hatfield, A. B. (1994). Recovery from mental illness. *The Journal of the California Alliance for the Mentally Ill, 5*(3), 6–7.

Hernandez, B. (2000). Employer attitudes toward workers with psychiatric disabilities and their ADA employment rights: A literature review. *Journal of Rehabilitation, 66*(4), 4–17.

Hoagwood, K., Burns, B., Kiser, L., Ringeisen, H., & Schoenwald, S. (2001). Evidence-based practice in child and adolescent mental health services. *Psychiatric Services, 52,* 1179–1188.

Hoge, M., Davidson, L., Griffith, E., & Jacobs, S. (1998). The crisis of managed care in the public sector. *International Journal of Mental Health, 27*(2), 52–71.

Hoge, M. A., Davidson, L., Griffith, E. E. H., Sledge, W. H., & Howenstine, R. A. (1994). Defining managed care in public-sector psychiatry. *Hospital & Community Psychiatry, 45,* 1085–1089.

Holburn, S. (2001). Compatibility of person-centered planning and applied behavior analysis. *Behavior Analyst, 24,* 271–281.

Holburn, S., & Vietze, P. M. (2002). *Person-centered planning: Research, practice, and future directions.* Baltimore, MD: Paul H. Brookes Publishing.

Institute of Medicine. (2001). *Crossing the quality chasm: A new health system for the 21ˢᵗ century.* Washington, DC: National Academies Press.

Jacobson, N., & Curtis, L. (2000). Recovery as policy in mental health services: Strategies emerging from the states. *Psychiatric Rehabilitation Journal, 23,* 333–341.

Jacobson, N., & Greenley, D. (2001). What is recovery? A conceptual model and explication. *Psychiatric Services, 52,* 482–485.

Joas, H. (1996). *The creativity of action.* Chicago: University of Chicago Press.

Johnson, A. B. (1990). *Out of bedlam: The truth about deinstitutionalization.* New York: Basic Books.

Joint Commission on Mental Illness and Health. (1961). *Action for Mental Health.* New York: Basic Books.

Jonikas, J., Cook, J., Fudge, C., Hiebechuk, F., & Fricks, L. (2005). *Charting a meaningful life: Planning ownership in person/family-centered planning.* Washington, DC: Substance Abuse and Mental Health Services Administration.

Kazdin, A. E. (2005). Treatment outcomes, common factors, and continued neglect of mechanisms of change. *Clinical Psychology: Science and Practice, 12*(2), 184–188.

Katz, E., & Danet, B. (Eds.). (1973). *Bureaucracy and the public: A reader in official-client relations.* New York: Basic Books.

Kingdon, D. G., & Turkington, D. (1994). *Cognitive-behavioral therapy of schizophrenia.* Nottinghamshire, UK: Bassetlaw Hospital.

Kirsh, B. (1996). Influences on the process of work integration: The consumer perspective. *Canadian Journal of Community Mental Health, 15*(1), 21–37.

Koegel, P. (1992). Through a different lens: An anthropological perspective on the homeless mentally ill. *Culture, Medicine and Psychiatry, 16,* 1–22.

Kosciulek, J. F. (1999). The consumer-directed theory of empowerment. *Rehabilitation Counseling Bulletin, 42,* 196–213.

Kretzmann, J., & McKnight, J. L. (1996). Assets-based community development. *National Civic Review, 85*(4), 23–30.

Kretzmann, J. P., & McKnight, J. L. (1993). *Building communities from the inside out.* Chicago: ACTA Publications.

Laine, C., & Davidoff, F. (1996). Patient-centered medicine: A professional evolution. *Journal of the American Medical Association, 275,* 152–156.

Lamb, H. R., & Weinberger, L. E. (1998). Persons with severe mental illness in jails and prisons: A review. *Psychiatric Services, 49,* 483–492.

Lehman, A. F., & Steinwachs, D. M. (1998). Translating research into practice: The Schizophrenia Patients Outcomes Research Team (PORT) treatment recommendations. *Schizophrenia Bulletin, 24,* 3–10.

Leete, E. (1994). Stressor, symptom, or sequelae? Remission, recovery, or cure? *The Journal of the California Alliance for the Mentally Ill, 5*(3), 16–17.

Lehman, A. F. (2000). Putting recovery into practice: A commentary on "What recovery means to us." *Community Mental Health Journal, 36*(3), 329–331.

Liberman, R. P., Kopelowicz, A., Ventura, J., & Gutkind, D. (2002). Operational criteria and factors related to recovery from schizophrenia. *International Review of Psychiatry, 14,* 256–272.

Lieberman, J. A., Stroup, T. S., McEvoy, J. P., Swartz, M. S., Rosenheck, R. A., Perkins, D. O., et al. (2005). Effectiveness of antipsychotic drugs in patients with chronic schizophrenia. *New England Journal of Medicine, 353,* 1209–1223.

Lin, K. M., & Kleinman, A. M. (1988). Psychopathology and clinical course of schizophrenia: A cross-cultural perspective. *Schizophrenia Bulletin, 14,* 555–567.

Lovejoy, M. (1982). Expectations and the recovery process. *Schizophrenia Bulletin, 8,* 605–609.

Lunt, A. (2000). Recovery: Moving from concept toward a theory. *Psychiatric Rehabilitation Journal, 23,* 401–405.

Manderscheid, R. W., & Henderson, M. J. (Eds.). (2001). *Mental Health, United States, 2000.* DHHS Pub. No. (SMA) 01–3537. Rockville, MD: U.S. Department of Health and Human Services, Substance Abuse and Mental Health Services Administration, Center for Mental Health Services.

Mark, T. L., Coffey, R. M., Vandivort-Warren, R., Harwood, I. I. J., King, E. C., & the MHSA Spending Estimates Team. (2005). U.S. spending trends for mental health and substance abuse treatment, 1991–2001. *Health Affairs, Web Exclusive,* pp. W5–135, W5–142. Retrieved March 29, 2005, from http://www.ncbi.nlm.nih.gov/pubmed/15797947?dopt=Abstract

Marrone, J., Gandolfo, C., Gold, M., & Hoff, D. (1998). Just doing it: Helping people with mental illness get good jobs. *Journal of Applied Rehabilitation Counseling, 29*(1), 37–48.

Marrone, J., Hoff, D., & Helm, D. T. (1997). Person-centered planning for the millennium: We're old enough to remember when PCP was just a drug. *Journal of Vocational Rehabilitation, 8,* 285–297.

McAlpine, D. D., & Warner, L. (2002). *Barriers to employment among persons with mental illness: A review of the literature.* New Brunswick, NJ: Center for Research on the Organization and Financing of Care for the Severely Mentally Ill, Institute for Health, Health Care Policy and Aging Research, Rutgers University.

McClellan, T. (2002). Technology transfer and the treatment of addiction: What can research offer practice? *Journal of Substance Abuse Treatment, 22,* 169–170.

McGlashan, T. H. (1988). A selective review of recent North American long-term follow-up studies of schizophrenia. *Schizophrenia Bulletin, 14,* 515–542.

McKnight, J. L. (1992). Redefining community. *Social Policy, 23*(2), 56–62.

Mead, S., & Copeland, M. E. (2000). What recovery means to us: Consumers' perspectives. *Community Mental Health Journal, 36,* 315–328.

Mezzina, R., Davidson, L., Borg, M., Marin, I., Topor, A., & Sells, D. (2006). The social nature of recovery: Discussion and implications for practice. *American Journal of Psychiatric Rehabilitation, 9*(1), 63–80.

Mischoulon, D. (1999). An approach to the patient seeking psychiatric disability benefits. *Academic Psychiatry, 23*(3), 128–136.

Monahan, J. (1992). "A terror to their neighbors": Beliefs about mental disorder and violence in historical and cultural perspective. *Bulletin of the American Academy of Psychiatry and the Law, 20*(2), 191–195.

Monahan, J., & Arnold, J. (1996). Violence by people with mental illness: A consensus statement by advocates and researchers. *Psychiatric Rehabilitation Journal, 19*(4), 67–70.

Morse, G. A., Calsyn, R. J., Miller, J., Rosenberg, P., West, L., & Gilliland, J. (1996). Outreach to homeless mentally ill people: Conceptual and clinical considerations. *Community Mental Health Journal, 32,* 261–274.

Mount, B., & Zwernik, K. (1988). *It's never too early: It's never too late: A booklet about personal futures planning.* St. Paul, MN: Metropolitan Council.

Mowbray, C. T., Moxley, D. P., Jasper, C. A., & Howell, L. L. (Eds.). (1997). *Consumers as providers in psychiatric rehabilitation.* Columbia, MD: International Association for Psychosocial Rehabilitation Services.

Mueser, K. T., Bond, G. R., Drake, R. E., & Resnick, S. G. (1998). Models of community care for severe mental illness: A review of research on case management. *Schizophrenia Bulletin, 24,* 37–74.

Mulvey, E. P. (1994). Assessing the evidence of a link between mental illness and violence. *Hospital & Community Psychiatry, 45,* 663–668.

Munetz, M. R., & Frese, F. J. (2001). Getting ready for recovery: Reconciling mandatory treatment with the recovery vision. *Psychiatric Rehabilitation Journal, 25*(1), 35–42.

Murray, C. J. L., & Lopez, A. D. (1996). *The global burden of disease: Summary.* Geneva, Switzerland: The World Health Organization.

National Council on Disability. (2000). *From privileges to rights: People labeled with psychiatric disabilities speak for themselves.* Retrieved August 20, 2003, from http://www.ncd.gov/newsroom/publications/privileges.html

National Council on Disability. (2002). The well being of our nation: An inter-generational vision of effective mental health services and supports. Retrieved September 17, 2002, from http://www.ncd.gov/newsroom/publications/2002/mentalhealth.htm

Neighbors, H., Elliott, K., & Gant, L. (1990). Self-help and black Americans: A strategy for empowerment. In T. J. Powell (Ed.), *Working with self-help.* Silver Spring, MD: National Association of Social Workers Press.

Nelson, G., Ochocka, J., Griffin, K., & Lord, J. (1998). "Nothing about me, without me": Participatory action research with self-help/mutual aid organizations for psychiatric consumers/survivors. *American Journal of Community Psychology, 26,* 881–912.

Noordsy, D. L., Torrey, W. C., Mead, S., Brunette, M., Potenza, D., & Copeland, M. E. (2000). Recovery-oriented psychopharmacology: Redefining the goals of antipsychotic treatment. *Journal of Clinical Psychiatry, 61*(Suppl 3), 22–29.

North, C. (1987). *Welcome, silence.* New York: Simon & Schuster.

O'Brien, J. (1987). A guide to life-style planning: Using the activities catalog to integrate services and natural support systems. In B. Wilcox & G. T. Bellamy (Eds.), *A comprehensive guide to the activities catalog.* Baltimore, MD: Paul Brookes.

O'Brien, C., & O'Brien, J. (2000). *The origins of person-centered planning: A community of practice perspective.* Syracuse, NY: Responsive Systems Associates, Inc.

O'Brien, J., & O'Brien, C. (1998). Person-centered planning and the quest for community membership. *Impact, 11,* 8–9.

O'Brien, J., & Lovett, H. (1992). *Finding a way toward everyday lives: The contribution of person-centered planning.* Harrisburg, PA: Pennsylvania Office of Mental Retardation.

O'Connell, M., Tondora, J., Croog, G., Evans, A., & Davidson, L. (2005). From rhetoric to routine: Assessing perceptions of recovery-oriented practices in a state mental health and addiction system. *Psychiatric Rehabilitation Journal, 28,* 378–386.

Onken, S. J., Craig, C. M., Ridgway, P., Ralph, R. O., & Cook, J. A. (2007). An analysis of the definitions and elements of recovery: A review of the literature. *Psychiatric Rehabilitation Journal, 31*(1), 9–22.

Osher, D., Dwyer, K., & Jackson, S. (2004). *Safe, supportive, and successful schools step by step.* Longmont, CO: Sopris West.

Parrish, J. (1989). The long journey home: Accomplishing the mission of the community support movement. *Psychosocial Rehabilitation Journal, 12,* 107–124.

Pearpoint, J., & Forest, M. (1998). Person centered planning: MAPS and PATH. *Impact, 11*(2), 6–7.

Pearpoint, J., Forest, M., & Snow, J. (1993). *The inclusion papers.* Toronto: Inclusion Press.

Perlick, D. A. (2001). Special section on stigma as a barrier to recovery: Introduction. *Psychiatric Services, 52*(12), 1613–1614.

Pope-Davis, D., Liu, W., Ledesma-Jones, S., & Nevitt, J. (2000). African American acculturation and black racial identity: A preliminary investigation. *Journal of Multicultural Counseling and Development, 28,* 98–113.

Ragins, M. (1994). Recovery: Changing from a medical model to a psychosocial rehabilitation model. *The Journal, 5*(3), 8–10.

Rapp, C. A. (1993). Theory, principles, and methods of the strengths model of case management. In M. Harris & H. C. Bergman (Eds.), *Case management for mentally ill patients: Theory and practice* (pp. 143–164). Langhorne, PA: Harwood Academic Publishers/Gordon & Breach Science Publishers.

Rapp, C. A. (1998a). The active ingredients of effective case management: A research synthesis. *Community Mental Health Journal, 34,* 363–380.

Rapp, C. A. (1998b). *The strengths model: Case management with people suffering from severe and persistent mental illness.* New York: Oxford University Press.

Rapp, C. A., & Wintersteen, R. (1989). The strengths model of case management: Results from twelve demonstrations. *Psychosocial Rehabilitation Journal, 13,* 23–32.

Rappaport, J. (1995). Empowerment meets narrative: Listening to stories and creating settings. *American Journal of Community Psychology, 23,* 795–807.

Reidy, D. (1992). Shattering illusions of difference. *Resources, 4*(2), 3–6.

Ridgway, P. A. (2001). Re-storying psychiatric disability: Learning from first-person narrative accounts of recovery. *Psychiatric Rehabilitation Journal, 24*, 335–343.

Ridgway, P., & Zipple, A. M. (1990). Challenges and strategies for implementing supported housing. *Psychosocial Rehabilitation Journal, 13*, 115–120.

Riessman, F. (1990). Restructuring help: A human services paradigm for the 1990s. *American Journal of Community Psychology, 18*, 221–230.

Rogers, E. M. (1995). *Diffusion of innovations* (4th ed.). New York: The Free Press.

Rosen, A. (April, 1994). Case management: The cornerstone of comprehensive local mental health services. *Australian Hospital Association, Management Issues Paper No. 4*, 47–63.

Rosen, A., Diamond, R., Miller, V., & Stein, L. (1993). *Becoming real: How to go from model program to enduring service.* Baltimore, MD: Hospital and Community Psychiatry Institute.

Rouse, L. W., Toprac, M. G., & MacCabe, N. A. (1998). The development of a statewide continuous evaluation system for the Texas Children's Mental Health Plan: A total quality management approach. *Journal of Behavioral Health Services & Research, 25*, 194–207.

Rowe, M. (1999). *Crossing the border: Encounters between homeless people and outreach workers.* Berkeley, CA: University of California Press.

Rowe, M., Kloos, B., Chinman, M. J., Davidson, L., & Cross, A. B. (2001). Homelessness, mental illness, and citizenship. *Social Policy and Administration, 35*, 14–31.

Saleeby, D. (2001). The diagnostics strengths manual. *Social Work, 46*(2), 183–187.

Sayce, L., & Perkins, R. (2000). Recovery: Beyond mere survival. *Psychiatric Bulletin, 24*, 74.

Scott, J., & Dixon, L. (1995). Psychological interventions for schizophrenia. *Schizophrenia Bulletin, 21*, 621–630.

Segal, S. P., Baumohl, J., & Johnson, E. (1977). Falling through the cracks: Mental disorder and social margin in a young vagrant population. *Social Problems, 23*(3), 387–400.

Sells, D. J., Rowe, M., Fisk, D., & Davidson, L. (2003). Violent victimization of persons with co-occurring psychiatric and substance use disorders. *Psychiatric Services, 54*, 1253–1257.

Sen, A. (1992). *Inequality reexamined.* Oxford: Oxford University Press.

Sen, A. (1999). *Development as freedom.* New York: Anchor Books.

Shumway, D. (1999). Freedom, support, authority, and responsibility: The Robert Wood Johnson Foundation national program on self-determination. *Focus on Autism and Other Developmental Disabilities, 14*, 28–36.

Sledge, W. H., Astrachan, B., Thompson, K., Rakfeldt, J., & Leaf, P. (1995). Case management in psychiatry: An analysis of tasks. *American Journal of Psychiatry, 152*, 1259–1265.

Smith, M. K. (2000). Recovery from a severe psychiatric disability: Findings of a qualitative study. *Psychiatric Rehabilitation Journal, 24*, 149–159.

Stein, L. I. (1989). The community as the primary locus of care for persons with serious long-term mental illness. In C. M. Bonjean, M. T. Coleman, & I. Iscoe (Eds.), *Community care of the chronically mentally ill: Proceedings of the sixth Robert Lee Sutherland Seminar in Mental Health* (pp. 11–29). Austin, TX: University of Texas Hogg Foundation for Mental Health.

Stein, L. I., & Test, M. A. (1980). Alternative to mental hospital treatment. I. Conceptual model: Treatment program and clinical evaluation. *Archives of General Psychiatry, 37*, 392–397.

Strauss, J. S. (1969). Hallucinations and delusions as points on continua function: Rating scale evidence. *Archives of General Psychiatry, 21*, 581–586.

Strauss, J. S., & Carpenter, W. T. (1972). The prediction of outcome in schizophrenia. I. Characteristics of outcome. *Archives of General Psychiatry, 27*(6), 739–746.

Strauss, J. S., & Carpenter, W. T. (1974). The prediction of outcome in schizophrenia: II. Relationships between predictor and outcome variables: A report from the WHO International Pilot Study of Schizophrenia. *Archives of General Psychiatry, 31*, 37–42.

Strauss, J. S., & Carpenter, W. T. (1977). Prediction of outcome in schizophrenia: III. Five-year outcome and its predictors. *Archives of General Psychiatry, 34*, 159–163.

Strauss, J. S., & Davidson, L. (1997). Mental disorder, work, and choice. In R. Bonnie & J. Monahan (Eds.), *Mental disorder, work disability, and the law* (pp. 105–130). Chicago: University of Chicago Press.

Strauss, J. S., Hafez, H., Lieberman, P., & Harding, C. M. (1985). The course of psychiatric disorders: III. Longitudinal principles. *British Journal of Psychiatry, 155*, 128–132.

Sullivan, W. P. (1994). A long and winding road: The process of recovery from severe mental illness. *Innovations and Research, 3*, 19–27.

Susser, E., Goldfinger, S. M., & White, A. (1990). Some clinical approaches to the homeless mentally ill. *Community Mental Health Journal, 25*, 463–480.

Swayze, F. V. (1992). Clinical case management with the homeless mentally ill. In R. H. Lamb, L. L. Bachrach, & F. I. Kass (Eds.), *Treating the homeless mentally ill: A report of the Task Force on the Homeless Mentally Ill* (pp. 203–219). Washington, DC: American Psychiatric Association.

Telles, C., Karno, M., Mintz, J., Paz, G., Arias, M., Tucker, D., et al. (1995). Immigrant families coping with schizophrenia: Behavioral family intervention vs. case management with a low-income Spanish-speaking population. *British Journal of Psychiatry, 167*, 473–479.

Tomes, H. (1999). Ignoring serious mental illness. *APA Monitor, 30*(10).

Tondora, J., Pocklington, S., Gorges, A., Osher, D., & Davidson, L. (2005). *Implementation of person-centered care and planning: From policy to practice to evaluation.* Washington, DC: Substance Abuse and Mental Health Services Administration.

Torrey, W., Drake, R., Dixon, L., Burns, B., Flynn, L., & Rush, A. (2001). Implementing evidence-based practices for persons with severe mental illnesses. *Psychiatric Services, 52,* 45–50.

Tsemberis, S. (1999). From streets to homes: An innovative approach to supported housing for homeless adults with psychiatric disabilities. *Journal of Community Psychology, 27,* 225–241.

Turner, J. C., & TenHoor, W. J. (1978). The NIMH community support program: Pilot approach to a needed social reform. *Schizophrenia Bulletin, 4,* 319–349.

Turner, J. E., & Shifren, I. (1979). Community support systems: How comprehensive? *New Directions for Mental Health Services, 2,* 1–23.

Vandercook, T., York, J., & Forest, M. (1989). The McGill Action Planning System (MAPS): A strategy for building the vision. *Journal of the Association for Persons with Severe Handicaps, 14,* 205–215.

Vandiver, B. (2001). Psychological nigrescence revisited: Introduction and overview. *Journal of Multicultural Counseling and Development, 29,* 165–174.

Walsh, D. (1996). A journey toward recovery: From the inside out. *Psychiatric Rehabilitation Journal, 20,* 85–90.

Wehman, P. (1986). Supported competitive employment for persons with severe disabilities. *Journal of Applied Rehabilitation Counseling, 17*(4), 24–29.

White, W. (2001). The new recovery advocacy movement: A call to service. *Counselor, 2*(6), 64–67.

White, W., Boyle, M., & Loveland, D. (2003). A model to transcend the limitations of addiction treatment. *Behavioral Health Management, 23,* 38–44.

White, W. L., & Godley, M. D. (2003). The history and future of "aftercare." *Counselor Magazine, 4*(1), 19–21.

World Health Organization. (1973). *The international pilot study of schizophrenia.* Geneva, Switzerland: World Health Organization.

World Health Organization. (2001). *The world health report 2001. Mental health: New understanding, new hope.* Geneva, Switzerland: World Health Organization.

Winnicott, D. W. (1986). *Home is where we start from.* New York: W. W. Norton & Company.

Wylonis, L. (1999). Psychiatric disability, employment, and the Americans with Disabilities Act. *Psychiatric Clinics of North America, 22,* 147–158.

Young, S. L., & Ensing, D. S. (1999). Exploring recovery from the perspective of people with psychiatric disabilities. *Psychiatric Rehabilitation Journal, 22,* 219–231.

INDEX